For Bob and Betty

Best Wishes

Arthur

Sept. 2003

THE GLASS CAGE

An Autobiography

Arthur E. McCann

© Copyright 2002 Arthur E. McCann
All Rights Reserved

ISBN: 0-938041-94-0

No part of this book may be reproduced or transmitted in any form or by any means, electronic or mechanical, including photocopying, recording or by any informational storage or retrieval system except by a reviewer who may quote brief passages in a review to be printed in a magazine or newspaper, without permission in writing from the publisher or author.

ARC Press of Cane Hill
13581 Tyree Mountain Road
Lincoln, Arkansas 72744
479-824-3821

Printed in the United States of America

Dedication

This book is dedicated to my loving wife, Laura, who has made it possible for me to continue to face and overcome obstacles placed in my way. She has shown me the true meaning of love, which I never had or could not have known before I found her.

Acknowledgements

I have typed this over a period of ten years and three drafts on an old manual typewriter, the kind I used in high school. I never learned to use the computer although when this is complete, I plan to learn. I have been too busy updating the three homes we have had to be able to concentrate on the computer. The text for the following story was no problem. The words flowed easily one after another. It was what Laura did along the way that brought the desired ending. She has retyped it in its entirety on her computer adding all punctuation marks that I had omitted because of time and making story placement suggestions. She has spent long hours at her computer and has shown unusual patience in deciphering some of my longhand scrawl. In addition, she spent a great deal of time on the phone with the publisher, making arrangements and deciding the best way to proceed. I could not have completed this project without her encouragement and help.

I further want to thank the following for their help in locating long-lost photos.

Gretchen Kelley, the daughter of Norma Morrison Beinlich, and Alma Lee Morrison Verkamp, Norma's sister, sent a picture of Norma. She was my first teacher after arriving back on the farm in 1932 after I lost my hearing. Norma and her daughter live in Erie, Pennsylvania. Alma Lee lives near St. James, Missouri.

Kenneth Morrison, a nephew of Ruth Morrison Muench, for a picture of Ruth. She was my first teacher at Benton Creek School in 1927. She was also my last teacher there in 1934-35. She lives in Benton, Illinois. Kenneth lives in St. James, Missouri.

Meredith Morrison, cousin of Kenneth, for her help

in locating Kenneth. She lives in St. James, Missouri.

Sophie Cardetti Bodine, the sister of Anna Cardetti Donati, for sending a beautiful photo of Louis and Anna Donati. Sophie lives in St. James, Missouri.

Roy Kirgan, Jr., "Bud," for the picture of his father, Roy Kirgan, Sr. Bud and Davene reside in Jefferson City, Missouri.

Nola Jean Lay Coleman, of Beaufort, Missouri, sent a picture taken at Benton Creek School in 1935.

My sister, Wilma Roller, sent photos of her and her husband Jim and the only remaining picture of our sister, Frieda, who died in 1929 at the age of four. They live in Clovis, New Mexico.

My brother, Raymond McCann, for pictures of our grandparents and himself. He lives in Jefferson City, Missouri.

Eleanor Schmieg, the widow of my oldest brother Wayne, Dorene McCann, the widow of my brother Earl, and her daughter, Connie, and Lois Wade, the daughter of my brother Leonard, for pictures of my brothers Wayne, Earl and Leonard respectively. They all live in the St. Louis area.

Kathy McCann, the widow of my brother Howard, for pictures of Howard. She lives in Steelville, Missouri.

Other photos came from the Central Institute for the Deaf for which I am grateful. The photo of Heather Whitestone, Miss America 1995, and myself was taken by photographer Patti Gabriel.

I also want to thank my many friends throughout the years of struggle in an alien world, where at times all that was needed was a warm encouraging word. Many were instrumental in offering help or a smile whenever needed. Many of them have long since gone, but their memory lives on in my heart. There were times when I did not know or realize that they were a component which was helping to make life easier and more full, and was not aware of that either at the time of physical association. It has been in later years that my mind has gone back in time and in my silent world, I was and am able to relive the times I had with them and can reminisce and mentally talk with them. This affords a release from the loneliness engulfing me at times and gives me renewed hope for a brighter future. It is times like this that God becomes a member of those who have helped to pave the way and I'm thankful to Him for being there with and for me.

I have ears but I cannot hear. I also have eyes but there are, as well, things that I cannot see. It is the times that I stumble and fall that I have been fortunate to have these special friends who have caught me and shown me the way. One or the other has always been there when needed. I can feel their compassionate care when they are near and I especially thank them for that. They are:

Granvil and Ara Bates
Everett and Rachel Davies
Louis Donati
Uncle Bill and Aunt Thelma Kampman
Roy L. Kirgan, Sr.
Raymond McCann
Elmer and Ruth Meyer
Dr. Alfred Morioka
Kimio Obata
Frank and Carolyn Petelik
Charles Potter
Wilma and Jim Roller
Dr. Richard Silverman
Herbert and Fanya Worth

Foreword

Detroit, 1929 –

It seemed strange to see sun streaming through the windows, flowers blooming in the yard, leaves fluttering gently on the trees with birds flitting through the branches. Having gone to sleep while blackened patches of snow could still be seen in places, and with a cold, late winter drizzle falling steadily, my first thoughts were that I was still dreaming.

I wondered why they kept the windows closed. I couldn't hear the rustling of the wind in the trees, or the singing of the birds, but I thought perhaps it was still chilly out and when it warmed up, the windows would be opened. Then I noticed they were open and a warm breeze was floating in.

I suddenly realized that I hadn't had breakfast, and I thought I would get up and dress; but then I began to wonder about my surroundings-- never before had I seen a room like this. Looking around I saw other kids in the room -- a boy about nine, my own age, and two girls -- one black and much younger. She was sitting up in bed with a tray on her lap. The bright red ribbons adorning her braids were a happy contrast to the white throughout the room. Upon trying to rise, I found I was unable to move. My arms and legs were leaden, I could only move my head from side to side.

Suddenly the door opened and a lady in white came in, placing a tray on the table beside my bed. I thought it contained breakfast but two men, also in white, had followed her in and then I saw the tray held a small glass tube with a handle on one end and a long needle on the other. Never having seen anything like it before, I harbored no thought as to its significance. One of the men assisted the lady in rolling me over onto my stomach and held me while the other man proceeded to insert the needle into the base of my spine. The pain was excruciating. I could not understand why they would be doing that and moving their lips, but making no sounds. This went on every day for two weeks.

Having been born and raised on a small Missouri farm in the Ozark foothills, and never having seen a doctor or nurse, much less a hospital room, I had no inkling of what was happening, or why. Months passed before I was to fully realize that I had been in a coma for several weeks, and was recovering from an attack of cerebro-spinal meningitis, leaving me totally deaf.

Besides leaving me stone deaf, I have scar tissue on the cover of my brain, partially affecting my memory, especially in recalling names. My equilibrium has been ninety percent destroyed to the extent that I cannot walk a straight line, and cannot walk in total darkness without help. I was left sterile and cannot have children and my nervous system was affected.

In many instances throughout this book will be found transgressions by my parents, as well as others. I have tried to overlook them and each time one surfaced, I have hoped that there wouldn't be others. I continued to love them and have tried to understand that their actions were outgrowths of a total ignorance of how to accept something which has come into their lives, a deaf child, and their inability to adjust to it. Their lack of knowledge has prompted this book, in the hope that others will learn from what I have been forced to live.

On the following pages I have attempted to give an autobiography of my life after the total loss of hearing at the age of nine. This all came about in the twenties when deafness was still looked upon as something to be snickered at. Little knowledge was available to pass on to those who possessed it and a lot of them were pushed aside and tolerated as well as being considered stupid and dumb and in some instances, insane. My parents were guilty of the above and never allowed me to forget that I was different, and made no allowance or offer of help outside of what the rest of the siblings received in their normal world.

I was able to finish grade school in a one-room country school where I had gone when I could hear and was fortunate in having succeeding teachers who showed understanding and help and, yes, compassion. My three older brothers had gone to the local high school, but when it came my turn, the board refused my admission. It was only after the intervention of the principal, when he threatened to leave if I weren't allowed to attend, that the board relented. I was fortunate to have the same five teachers all through the four years of high school and each was helpful and offered encouragement to the extent that the principal presented me with the medal for scholarship upon graduation. I had only a couple of friends in high school other than one or two who helped me in study hall. I received a few greetings of "Hi. How are you?" in the hallways but no invitations to parties on weekends although I knew they were going on. I realized in later years that they had been afraid of the unknown and as time passed, they came forward and offered their friendship.

Following high school came years of struggle and learning, which have both been beneficial in their own ways. All the way to the present, I have constantly been reminded that I am deaf but with help from an understanding hearing wife, the road has become less bumpy. I remain in the glass cage where I can see out but nothing reaches me. My wife has made the prison more livable and, with each passing year, it has become more bearable.

Although I have overcome, I still live in the past when I was forced to fight and cry for things that are given to so-called normal people as their birthright. I do not speak only of myself but also for handicapped individuals everywhere who are hidden from view but who must struggle each day for recognition. They – we – are like the Bard's "infant crying in the night, an infant crying for the light, but with no sound except a cry."

Arthur E. McCann

The Author

(Courtesy of Kenneth Nicolai)

Table of Contents

Acknowledgements	i
Foreword	iv
Early Childhood on a Missouri Farm	1
Moving to Detroit, Michigan	31
Contracting Meningitis	43
Detroit Day School for the Deaf	51
Return to the Farm in Missouri	59
Benton Creek School	62
St. James High School	79
The Campbell Home	89
Rehabbing the Farm House	102
Trip to California	104
My First Job	109
Building a New Barn on the Farm	111
Central Institute for the Deaf	114
S. Richard Silverman, Ph.D.	131
Dr. Hallowell Davis – Research	140
Dr. Max Goldstein, Founder of CID	143
Curtiss Wright Aircraft Company	150
Granvil Bates	154

McCann and Company	165
Mrs. Spencer Tracy	167
U.S. Marshal Roy L. Kirgan, Sr.	179
Sister M. Lillian McCormack, S.S.N.D.	183
Arcy Manufacturing Company	193
McDonnell Douglas Aircraft Corporation	197
Some Deaf People I Have Admired	207
James S. McDonnell	222
Return to CID as Building Engineer	225
Donald R. Calvert, Ph.D.	229
Life with Laura	249
My Last Years at CID	269
Reflections	284
Miscellaneous	290
My Family	303

The author's parents' wedding Christmas Day 1912

Early Childhood on a Missouri Farm

My father, Charles Edward McCann, was born on a farm near Oak Hill, Missouri, in 1886, in a community called Brush Creek, which lies between Cuba and Oak Hill. His parents, Edward and Anna, were born and grew up in the same area. They spent their lives there until their children were grown and had left the home. Then they moved into Owensville. Dad was the oldest of six boys and four girls. The family ancestors were from Pennsylvania Dutch country and had come west in earlier generations and had mostly been farmers. Somewhere along the line a great-"something" grandfather had married a Cherokee Indian woman and certain ancestral traits have persisted and are evident in many of us, most especially so in square jaw lines.

Dad and his brothers and sisters attended a one-room school nearby called Three Mile School. The name originated from the distance to Cuba, Missouri. The building is still there. Upon reaching adulthood he went into Illinois and worked in the cornfields near Decatur, Illinois. His brother James followed, and after a few years, they both returned to Missouri and worked as streetcar conductors in St. Louis.

My mother, Mamie Friederica Campman, was born in St. Louis in 1890 and received her early education in a school on Hampton Avenue. Her father, Henry Campman, worked for the Anheuser Busch Brewing Company as a six-horse hitch wagon driver delivering full beer barrels. On a hot day in mid-July, he lost consciousness and collapsed in front of the city hall. He was taken to the St. Louis City Hospital where he passed away within hours in a tub surrounded by ice. It was never established whether he died of heat stroke or a heart attack. He was thirty-seven and my mother was about seven. Her brother William was a few years younger.

A few years after the death of her father, her mother, Ida Campman, married a family friend, Gustave Riefenstahl. They had one son, Harry, who lived to be 93. They were married for more than sixty years. Gus was the only grandpa we knew on our mother's side so we called him Grandpa Gus. He was one of the woodsmen helping to clear land in Forest Park in preparation for the 1904 World's Fair. While he was working in the park, he and Grandma also had a restaurant on the northwest corner of Tamm and Clayton Avenues in the area of St. Louis that is currently known as "Dogtown." Mom would talk about how she helped her mother prepare lunches for the workers to take along to eat in the park at noon.

Grandpa Gus was an affable fellow who loved to imbibe and often had more than he could handle. During the months of the Fair, he drove a city owned "bus" which was actually a colorful sled shaped wagon pulled by two horses and with four bench seats for fair goers. At the end of the day he would take up the bottle under his seat and usually took too much, and as I have been told, he would pass out on the floor and the horses knew the way home. He never became violent or things like that, but would just get plain old-fashioned drunk. That stopped in later years and he would take us kids fishing and hunting. He lived to be ninety.

After the World's Fair, when Mom was about fourteen, her family left St. Louis and bought a farm about ninety miles west of St. Louis in a community known as Three Mile, near Oak Hill, Missouri, which is where Dad's family lived. Mom and her brother, William, completed the final years of their schooling at Three Mile School. This is where she and Dad met.

Mom returned to St. Louis after finishing school and worked for a while in what was called "service work" doing housework in the homes of well-to-do families. Dad had returned to Illinois and resumed his work with corn growers. After a number of years, they renewed their relationship, returned to Three Mile and were married in Grandma's home on Christmas Day 1912. After their marriage they lived in Illinois for a short time while Dad completed his work in the cornfields. Mom's brother William had joined the navy.

Mom and Dad returned to Missouri and moved to St. Louis where Dad returned to his former work as a conductor on the streetcars. An incident happened one day that they would talk about for many years. They lived on Hodiamont Avenue, the same street that Dad's streetcar took him over each day. When his shift was over for the day, and after the car had been turned in to the car sheds, he would hop on another car going past his house. He would ask the motorman to stop for him in front of his house, but the operator refused to do so and continued on to the next stop at the end of the block. Although he refused to stop, he would slow down so that Dad could jump off the moving car and cross the street to his house. This worked well until one day Dad's open topcoat caught on the open car door and he was dragged for quite a distance before the motorman became aware of what had happened and stopped. Dad was unconscious when he was finally found and was carried into their house. He carried a scar on his temple for the rest of his life and told the story often.

Wayne and Earl were born in St. Louis and Leonard

was born at Grandma's house at Three Mile. I was born on a farm on the outskirts of Bourbon, Missouri, in 1920. Always striving for something better in their lives, the folks purchased a 236-acre farm on the Meramec River near Steelville, Missouri, when I was three years old. They paid three thousand five hundred dollars for the acreage that became the family homestead. Our address was Cook Station, Missouri. The loan on the farm was from the Federal Land Bank in St. Louis at two percent for twenty years, although it was paid off sooner.

Perhaps half of the land was tillable and the rest timber and pasture land. The farm was bounded on two sides by the Meramec River. Most of the time, the river was tranquil, meandering, clear water, which was ideal for swimming, fishing or pleasant family picnics on the banks or gravel bars. However, they learned that after heavy torrential rains, the river could turn into a raging, swirling sea of debris, fallen trees, and an occasional dead cow or some other animal, and often reached a width of a half-mile in places and a depth of fifteen feet. In time they learned that the river was a friend or a thing to be feared, depending upon the season involved. The farm had one-half mile of river frontage, but miraculously, when the river was at its highest, only about one acre in the bottoms flooded. The rest of the farm was protected by bluffs and high land.

The house had seen much better days. It had originally been a two room, two story log house. Subsequent owners had added a total of five rooms including a kitchen and long front porch. There was a breezeway in back connecting it to a smokehouse, which doubled as a storage and chicken feed area when not being used for smoking meat. There was no electricity or water in the house and no heat except for a large heating stove in the dining room, which together with the huge range in the kitchen provided all the heat in winter. There was a cistern with a hand pump outside the back door, however, the water had come off the roof and was not drinkable.

In further exploration, it was found that a half dozen or so one-room log shanties with dirt floors were spread about in the hills south and west of the house. They were no longer in use but had been used by families of woodcutters. The numerous springs on the farm gave them access to drinking water. No one ever knew whether they had permission to build them. In a few years, all except two had disappeared. These two were used as sheep sheds and are probably still there.

The outbuildings consisted of two chicken houses, a large barn across the road from the house, a silo and a machine shed, which served as a garage for the Model T Ford which they had bought two years earlier. There was a large orchard and garden area. Set back from the side of the house was a large rounded roof concrete storm cellar, which also served as a storage area for canned goods since the thick walls made it cool in summer and warm in winter. There was an ever-present smell of freshly dug potatoes and fruits in season. Eggs were also stored there before taking them to market. There were four springs on the property. The nearest spring furnished water for drinking and cooking. Any other needed water was hauled from the river about a quarter mile away.

The reason for buying this farm was probably based on the fact that Grandma and Grandpa Gus had bought the farm two miles away on Benton Creek after returning from Enid, Oklahoma, where Grandpa Gus had been working in the oil fields. Their farm wasn't as large as ours but it was in a more convenient location. The fields were in sight of the house. There was only a barn and small chicken house and concrete cellar. The house was of two levels with the kitchen and dining area and one bedroom on the upper level. I have memories of Leonard and I taking naps on the floor of the living room while the family visited on Sundays and, hearing the mantle clock strike. The clock was given to Mom on her mother's death and she in turn gave it to me. It still strikes but for me there is no sound. In a few years, they had built a beautiful two-story house. Mom had always wanted a new house but it never came about. Many years later I did a total rehab of the house, adding siding, electricity and plumbing including a bathroom and new kitchen.

      The move from Bourbon to the farm, about 12 miles south of Steelville, was made in two buckboards, one was ours and the other grandma's. Uncle Harry was nineteen at that time and told of how he had driven one of the wagons, a trip that took two days. I was three at the time and don't remember much about the beginning of life on the farm but succeeding years found plenty of things to do. The first spring was a busy time with planting a large garden and plowing for the field crops. We had found a sixteen-foot boat that had been washed up by a flood. There had been plenty of time to get to know the neighbors on surrounding farms, and several parties had been held. We were fortunate to have good neighbors: the Bill Bells, the Frank Howalds, the Bill Earneys, Judge Henry Morrison, the Fred Morrisons, the John Joneses, "Uncle Jimmy" Edgars, Giles Williams, the Fletcher Beezleys, and of course Grandma and Grandpa Gus.

      The first year on the farm was spent in a lot of exploration. A stream which we called a "branch" came down past below the house. This stream was fed by two springs and it afforded untold opportunity to play in it. Another spring on the Bell's property, just past the property line at the bottom of the hill across the creek, had a two-inch round pipe extending from the hill and had a steady fairly forceful flow of water, which was very cold. We used this spring for drinking when we wanted really cold drinking water until several years later when a refrigerator came into being. The distance to this spring was about as far as one long city block. After losing my hearing, I was often asked to go to the spring in darkness with two three-gallon pails. There was no path so the way was through high undergrowth and over a wire fence. I never knew if a snake might be in my way. The stress was merciless. I was around 12 at the time. Still another spring was at the bottom of the hill past the road. Eventually this spring was dug out to four feet deep and three feet across and lined with stone. Later a spring house of stone was built over it and an electric pump was installed for house and chicken use. In the springtime wildflowers were abundant and I know, now that I am much older, that the folks took pride in watching the plants come through in the garden and fields.

The folks had only a small amount of farm machinery and it was necessary to purchase more in order to get the spring crops in. After buying the needed machines, all horse drawn, Dad proceeded to construct an addition to the barn to store them. The first year brought in a satisfying harvest of corn and hay. The mow of the barn was filled to capacity with perhaps fifty tons of hay. The corncribs were bulging with yellow corn. The last loads of hay had been put in just before dark and there was an aura of satisfaction that the hay work was finished for the season and that there was a good supply of livestock feed for the winter months. Wayne and Earl were in the barn milking the cows and Leonard and I were holding lanterns for them and playing in the walkway between the mangers. Dad had finished his work with the horses and came in to warn us to be careful with the lanterns so as not to set the barn on fire, then went on into the house across the road. Having finished the milking, we all went to the house where Mom was preparing supper. After what amounted to half an hour, as Wayne was setting the table, he remarked that the front yard was lit up with a bright light and that he thought a car was coming down the road. Dad got up from where he had been reading the paper to see who it might be and froze in horror when he saw the barn engulfed in flames. The last few loads of hay had not been completely cured in the field and spontaneous combustion, which had probably been smoldering for quite a while suddenly erupted. Dad leaped over the railing on the porch and ran to the barn where he released the livestock and then tried desperately to save the new machinery. An axle of the corn planter was wedged against a stud in the shed and with all the rest of the implements behind it, he was forced to let the entire contents burn after losing about half of his hair to the flames. The flames from the hay were shooting two hundred feet into the chilly night air and were seen for miles around which brought most of the neighbors to give what help they could. Since the house was just across the road and embers were falling on the roof, as much of the furnishings as was possible were removed and taken to a safe place farther up the road. One of the neighbors, Nonie Morrison, a brother of the school teacher, climbed to the top of the silo with an axe and was able to hack the iron rods holding the cypress boards together. After getting a long rope around the silo, several of the men were able to pull it down, saving the lumber, which was later used to build a needed chicken house. The Ford was pulled out of the shed and pushed down the hill where it came to rest against a stump, bending an axle. The hay smoldered for more than a month. Two of the horses that had been released were found several days later about twenty miles away. The tragedy came one year to the day after they had moved to the farm, and the loss was not covered by insurance. They apparently were able to accept their misfortune in stride and start over. Since it was near the onset of winter, a temporary barn was hastily built near the site of the burned one. It was sixteen years later that a beautiful barn rose on the same spot where the original one had burned.

There were three brooders, a box-like closed compartment with twenty-inch high legs with a copper tube full of water around the top of the inside. The water was kept heated by a kerosene lamp on the side made for that purpose and each box had two slide-out trays with perhaps four dozen eggs each. They bought fertilized eggs from a supplier who had the necessary rooster. The trays were taken out daily and put on a table and each egg was rolled over. All three of the brooders were kept in the bedrooms and I can still smell the pungent odor from the lamps, which was sort of relaxing. At the end of perhaps three weeks, we anxiously awaited the cracked eggs bringing forth their cute chicks.

A year and a half after moving to the farm, a daughter, Frieda, was born. A girl, after so many boys was a welcome addition to the family. It was two years later that another boy, Raymond, joined the family, and it was to be shortly afterwards that the relatively happy and easy-going life to which we had become accustomed was to come to an end with the upcoming ill-fated move to Detroit, Michigan. I remember asking that they name the new girl Norma Morrison McCann after my favorite neighbor. Norma was the oldest daughter of the Fred Morrison family.

The days of early childhood on the farm while I was still in the hearing world were happy times for me. Although money was in short supply, it was hardly missed since most of our needs were raised on the farm. The huge garden and orchard kept us in fruits and vegetables all season long and the surplus was canned and stored for winter months. Pigs were butchered and the meat was either preserved or smoked and salted also for use in winter months. There were social gatherings where rugs would be rolled up and local talent would be utilized to play their musical instruments, usually fiddles, guitars and banjos, for square dancing. There was the usual "Swing your partner in a half-way whirl. Promenade the corner girl." to the tune of *Turkey in the Straw.* Six-foot-six Glennon Fahey did the calling and jigging while dancing and would reach over their heads to put errant dancers in the proper place. Food would be brought in by everyone and dancing would go on until past midnight on weekends. During the summer months there would be spontaneous picnics at the Meramec River, which was only a quarter mile down the hill from our house. The crossing was traditionally known as Cedar Ford, named for the many cedar trees in the clearing which had become a favorite place for campers out from St. Louis who would stay for a week or two and buy their supplies of milk and vegetables from the neighbors. We would hurriedly finish the evening chores and eat our supper so we could walk down to hear stories of the city which never failed to leave us with dreams of one day traveling to the places they so vividly described.

Wesco, the closest town, with a population of perhaps a hundred or so, was four miles away and consisted of two general stores. The largest, known as the Wesco Mercantile Company, owned by Warren Perkins and Edgar Shoemate, carried a variety of merchandise and smelled of harness leather, shoes, tobacco, motor oil, denim overalls, candy in open glass cases and just about everything the surrounding farmers needed. There was a post office and a blacksmith shop where you could find the smithy shoeing horses any time you walked in. Another man would be at the bellows cranking up a white-hot fire to make shoes for the horses or perhaps a new iron tire for a wagon wheel. There was also a small hotel of sorts and a restaurant for the Frisco Railroad travelers who would stay overnight waiting for family members to pick them up. There was also a school high up on a hill. The train was a never-ending source of excitement. It was a rather short line which went from Salem to Cuba, a distance of perhaps forty miles. We could not see the train as it went past our farm since the tracks were over the hill in a valley. But we could hear the long drawn-out whistle twice a day, once about ten in the morning and again on it's return trip about three in the afternoon. The whistle and the rumblings of the heavy locomotive were a thrill, which I can still hear in my mind each time I think of it. It takes me back to the time when I could hear and the world I lost.

The town also boasted a barber shop which we never got to use since Dad always cut our hair. The shop was located in the same building that housed the feed mill and was owned by Sant Housewright. The mill had one of the few water wheels in the state, which furnished power from the Meramec River to grind grain for the farmers. A gasoline service station consisted of one gravity-flow pump which had to be pumped by hand to fill a glass bottle at the top, which held only ten gallons and when empty had to be pumped up again. Most of the trips to Wesco were made in the Model T Ford since it was such a short distance, and occasionally, we would go in the evenings on weekends to see a vaudeville show which consisted mostly of local amateurs. One night Grandma and Grandpa Gus took Wayne, Earl, Leonard and me to the show. I was six at the time. They picked us up at home in their Dodge and before leaving, Grandma said, "One for the money, two for the show, three to get ready and four to go." I told Grandma I couldn't go because I was the fourth one and I wasn't ready. The stage was a raised platform across the tracks near the river and bed sheets hung on wires served as curtains. I remember one time when one of the actors came out on the stage with cotton twisted in his nose hanging down a half inch and said that he had caught a cold the night before. Most of the skits were spontaneous and unrehearsed. This gave it an air of home-spun comedy which today would be described as corny.

General household staples and work clothing including shoes and denim overalls were generally found at the Wesco stores. Livestock feed and farm supplies, including fencing, were found at St. James, eighteen miles away. The trip to St. James was made once a week in the high wheel buckboard behind a team of mares, one roan colored named Doll and the other, solid white, named Flora. The mares were retired to pasture when the mules came into being. The 36-mile round trip usually started at about four in the morning and ended back at home around dark. We would often stop on the way home at Grandma Verkamp's farm on the Dry Fork River. I believe we bought some of the hatching eggs from her. She always had something good for us to eat – pie, cake or fresh baked bread and butter. I remember coming home with dad from town in darkness and trying to count the stars as they became visible. Dad was in his thirties and still a young man at heart and happy with the large acreage he and Mom controlled. It was that night coming home from town in the buckboard, and looking at the stars that he taught me the tune:

> Twinkle, twinkle, little star.
> How I wonder what you are.
> Up above the world so high,
> Like a diamond in the sky.
> When the blazing sun is set
> and the grass with dew is wet,
> Then you shine your little light,
> Twinkle, twinkle all the night.

After arriving in town, the horses were unhitched and tied to the back of the wagon, which had hay and corn for them. After a few hours, most farmers would come out with a bucket of water for their teams. There were several wagons and teams in the lot reserved for them across the street from the Farmers Exchange. The farmer would go about town taking care of business, buying things that were then put on hold and later the wagon would be brought around to pick them up. Once when I was about six, I was walking around town with Dad and when we got to Wegers Hardware Store, Mr. Weger leaned over the counter and said, "How are you, little boy? What can I do for you?" I asked him for an ice cream cone! Once we were putting some new windows in a part of the house, Dad bought two full size windows at the Verkamp Lumber Company and went to pick them up first, covering them with loose hay. The next stop was at the Farmers Exchange where several hundred-pound bags of feed were waiting for him on the dock. Before he could get down from the high spring seat on the wagon, one of the workmen tossed some of the bags into the loose hay covering the windows. I never did know what settlement was made for the broken windows. Later, a truck bought while living in Detroit brought on the demise of the trips to town in the wagon, which I believe were really enjoyed by the farmers, who would sometimes go to sleep, knowing the horses knew the way home.

Walter S. Miller was the manager of the Farmers Exchange. One ice-covered night the building burned to the ground. Mr. Miller naturally denounced the city for not having a fire department "prepared for something like this." The fire department consisted of a 1920's era Ford Model T fire truck. Later a beautiful modern building, much larger, rose in its place.

Practically every farm homestead possessed a versatile utensil known as a wash boiler among other names. It was made of copper and about two feet long, twelve inches wide and sixteen or so inches deep with round ends. It is sought after today in antique shops for holding magazines. It was used to boil clothes in during the winter on two open burners of the kitchen stove. In warm weather the task was often done outside, a distance from the house in a large round black cast iron pot supported on a three legged stand about 8 inches from the ground so as to leave room for the wood fire. The boiler was also used for making apple butter. Once the apples were peeled, cored and cut up, they were put in about half full with the right amount of water and cooked past applesauce consistency until the concoction emerged as smooth apple butter. Sometimes, depending on the family's taste, cinnamon sticks were dropped in to cook with it. For stirring, one inch holes were bored into a one inch thick oak board about twenty inches long and five inches wide with a six foot pole through a hole at the top. Stirring had to be kept up almost continuously to prevent burning on the bottom. Once burned, the whole batch usually had to be destroyed or given to the pigs. And once burned, it was pretty sure that it would not be allowed to happen again to future batches. Sometimes neighbors or friends would drop by on a wintry evening and were served a delicacy consisting of fresh baked bread (often a dozen loaves at a time), occasionally fresh churned butter and apple butter or grape jelly, sometimes grouped around the large kitchen stove. Dad's brother, our Uncle Tom, and his family were frequent visitors in winter months. They lived in Union, Missouri, and owned a dry cleaning business. They would stay the weekend.

    A couple of our cats were always in the barn at milking time to receive a squirt of milk aimed at their face. Milking was a chore that I never had to do. Earl and Leonard usually took care of five or six cows morning and evening. Earl would sometimes tie a rock to the cow's tail in fly season to keep the switching out of his face and incidentally, the milk bucket. It fell to Earl to do the separating of milk and cream. The huge DeLaval separator had a large bowl on top where the fresh milk was poured. After several continuous fast turns of the crank, a steady stream of milk would come out of the higher spout and cream would flow more slowly from the lower one, or maybe it was the other way around. After finishing, the flask holding the separating discs had to be taken apart, washed and sterilized, mostly by putting them in scalding hot water. Earl hated the job and often spoke of it until the day he died. The cream was put in a heavy metal cream can in the cellar and taken to town once a week and sold to the Charles Henry Egg and Cream Company in St. James. In summer months we kids would go to the pasture and lay under a cow and get the milk from the "faucet." The cream had to be sold for economic reasons and only a small amount was used. Instead of churning the cream into butter, margarine would be bought in pound brick sizes along with a plastic bubble of orange powder to mix with it to make it look like butter.

  Chicken feed was put into hundred-pound cotton bags, which had all sorts of different patterns and floral designs printed on them. Farm women used them for skirts, aprons, bed sheets and even underwear for kids. Dad would buy about six to ten bags a week and Mom would tell him what patterns to get. She would wash them, rip them open, iron them and sell them to farm women who couldn't buy many themselves. She got a quarter apiece for them. Enough of a similar pattern would make nice window curtains. This went on for several years after we returned from Detroit.

  One day Dad and my brother were doing some repair work on a chicken house. Someone had left a 2x4 with a rusty number 16 nail sticking up about two inches. I was about five or six and barefooted running around in there. I wasn't watching where I was going and stepped on it. It went completely through the soft part of the foot at the arch. I started screaming and Dad put his foot on the 2x4 and pulled me off. They washed it and went to the cow barn with a shovel, waiting for a cow to do her thing. The manure was fresh and they put it on my foot and wrapped it in an old pillow case. The next morning it was hard and when they pulled it off, a half-inch long round white piece of poison came with it. They then washed it with turpentine and put cloverine salve on it and bound it. It healed quickly and never posed any problems. I have told doctor friends this and they say it is the chlorophyll in the grass the cows eat that makes it a good cure, but none of them would use it.

Besides its "medicinal" value, the stuff had other uses for farm boys. After it has been hardened in the sun for some time, it forms twelve-inch frisbees that the boys used to play with. They collected large piles of them along with basketfuls of dried horse biscuits, which were used for summer snowball fights. When our parents weren't around, we would also smoke wild grapevines, which were harmless but would "draw" freely and it made us feel important until Mom caught us. Another adventure we had was when Leonard was about nine and I was six. We came across a plug of our dad's *Horseshoe* brand chewing tobacco. We took it upstairs on a rainy day and tried chewing a bite of it. Mom called to us and we hurriedly swallowed it. Needless to say, we never tried it again. Once when I was three, Leonard and I were on the wood lot above the house. He was six and pretending to cut wood with a double bit axe. It flew out of his hands and hit me in the head at the bridge of my nose. I still have the scar. He couldn't sit down for a month after our dad got through with him.

Each fall would bring the family together along with near-by neighbors for what had long been a sort of ritual. Molasses making was looked forward to and as soon as the cane was ready, we would go into the fields to strip the leaves from the stalks and cut off the tassel at the top. Then the stalks would be cut and laid in piles along the rows. After all was ready, a horse drawn wagon would come to pick them up for hauling to the mill. In later years a truck would replace the wagon. The mill consisted of a set of vertical rollers, which were powered by a horse at the end of a long pole. The horse was tied in such a way as to continue in a circle. The operator would sit on a bench near the ground feeding the stalks into the rollers, and would have to duck each time the pole came around. The extracted juice was funneled into a tub, which when full was transferred into a barrel and kept for the next cooking which was done in a pan about seven feet long and three feet wide and ten inches deep. The pan was made of timbers and had a metal bottom which was bent to cover the sides so that it would not burn. A pit was dug about a foot and a half deep and lined around the sides with stones which acted as a support for the pan. The front end of the pit was open so logs could be pushed in for the fire. After coming to a boil, the juice would give off a greenish substance, which was skimmed continuously with metal pie pans attached to a long pole after holes had been punched into the bottom. The boiling and skimming went on long into the night until the molasses turned a golden brown color and which, after tasting was declared finished. After cooling, the molasses and pouring into jugs, the pan was cleaned for another batch the following morning. Hot dogs would be roasted over the flames coming from the front of the pit and sandwiches and coffee were plentiful. It was a time of the season when the neighbors looked forward to coming and brought their own cane. Ours was the only mill for many miles around. Wherever a mill could be found, you could be sure that similar activities were going on.

    Besides molasses making and apple butter, fall brought in other things in season. Turnips had to be pulled and stored in the round-roof concrete cellar outside and beans had to be taken in and processed. I am not sure what kind of beans they were, but they were white and Mom pulled the low bushes out by the roots and put them in a large wash tub, squishing them down with her foot until the tub was full. She would let them dry more for a few weeks on the long front porch and having long since removed the bushes, would mix them about in the tub, and wait for a strong windy day. She would hold a pot full as high as she could and pour them out. The chaff would blow away and the beans would fall into the tub. Sometimes she would repeat it until she had very clean white beans. Each fall also brought out the kraut cutting board. Perhaps two dozen cabbage heads were brought up from the garden and the loose outside leaves were discarded and the heads cut in half. The halves were rubbed back and forth over the board which had a sharp knife imbedded crossways halfway down the length of the board at a forty-five degree angle. The cuttings dropped into a washtub, which sat on a bench. These cuttings were stored in a twenty-gallon covered stone jar and stored in the outside cellar. It was usually cooked with spare ribs, but one of us could often be seen dipping into the jar for a handful to eat raw. Another fall favorite was persimmons. We couldn't seem to get enough of the plump pink fruit. And, of course, there were the beautiful Ozark trees with full color foliage. It seemed strange that we never really saw and appreciated this until we moved away to the city.

  Late fall or early winter brought on butchering time. The large 30-gallon round black pot was filled with water and brought to a boil. Dad would back a pig or shoat as pigs of that size were called, into a corner and straddle it. Holding it by one ear, he would bring a twenty-pound sledgehammer down between its eyes. Before the hammer hit, the pig's squeal, which was more of a frightened scream, was ear piercing. Years later after I lost my hearing, I thought I must have been in a better position than others since I was not able to hear that any more. The screams slowly subsided into weak grunting death knells. Lastly a long sharp knife was plunged into its heart to bleed it or perhaps it was the jugular vein. By this time, the large black pot was boiling violently and the pig was put up on a raised platform about two feet high with a fifty-five gallon metal drum leaning at an angle against it. The drum was filled about halfway with the hot water and the pig was put in, first headfirst, then turned around and sloshed up and down in the drum. Dad would put ashes in the water to help soften the hair. After they thought it was ready, they pulled it onto the platform and scraped the hair off with sharp butcher knives. When it was clean, a large stick about twenty inches long was sharpened on both ends and put through the tendons of the hind legs. It was then hoisted to a hook on a tree limb and gutted into a tub. Dad left the carcass hanging on the limb overnight to freeze. The next day he would take it to the back porch and saw it into parts. Later on came sausage making.

      Our Christmases on the farm while I was still in the hearing world, were perhaps identical to others although I never knew. A month before Christmas we would all group around the dining table with the kerosene lamp and the Sears Roebuck catalog. The only one I can remember is the time we all got very nice heavy colorful sweaters. It usually took two weeks for the order to come back from Chicago. When the date neared, we would always wait for the postman in his covered one-horse buggy. We always had a tree. Cedars were abundant in the area but we always had a pine, no doubt because of the dropping needles of the cedars. My very first memories were of candles in small candleholders, which were lit Christmas night. The danger of fire probably wasn't considered since there were only a few and closely watched. The colorful shiny pages of the Sears Roebuck catalog were taken out and cut into narrow strips and pasted together to make chain links. Some chains were up to ten feet long and after putting them on the tree, more chains of popcorn were added, along with decorative baubles, some going back several years. Laura and I have several of them which we use each year. One of them is a celluloid Mrs. Santa about four inches high that Uncle Bill gave to Frieda in 1928. Raymond has the matching Mr. Santa. There was always the roast chicken or two for dinner – we didn't have turkeys – and everything that went into a Christmas dinner. It was always topped by the mince meat pies and fruit cake which had been made at Thanksgiving and sprinkled with rum and wrapped in cloth and stored in a tin container. There were always bowls of nuts and oranges and candy and of course Dad always had a cigar. The day after Christmas we always went to Grandma's house two miles away over the hill and through the woods, (It actually was!) in the buckboard with plenty of hay in the bottom and heavy quilts to cover with. On the last New Year's Day before moving to Detroit, we all went to Owensville fifty miles away in the Ford with many heavy quilts to cover with to see Dad's family, Grandma and Grandpa Edward McCan, to say good bye before being gone for three years. The entire family except Uncle Henry and Aunt Ruth Crider who lived in Sullivan were there. They were all married. There was Aunt Alice Branson, Aunt Maude Depperman, Aunt Ella Walls, Uncle Tom, Uncle Walter and Uncle Jim. Uncle Walter was the only one who had served in the Army overseas. Uncle Willie had died a number of years before. He had worked as a streetcar conductor in St. Louis with his brothers Uncle Jim and Dad.

Easters as I remember them as a small child were happy times. Mom always made cookies with three holes filled with sweetened egg whites baked in. We would save Quaker oats boxes and cut them in half and wrap them in colorful tissue paper. Then we went to the barn and got small bits of hay and put them in the boxes. All of us kids went to bed early hoping to see the Easter Bunny in the morning. On Easter morning, we each found four colorful eggs, some with our name on them and candy and cookies in our homemade Easter baskets. Out on the porch and down the steps, we found lots of drops of color paint that we were sure the Easter Bunny had dripped on his way out. Another reason for looking forward to Easter was because we could always start going barefooted on that day. These were happy days in the hearing world before the ill-fated move to Detroit, and the following depression years.

There was a lot of excitement when an airplane would fly over. Sometimes they were so low that we could read the numbers on the sides. It was a day especially looked forward to in Steelville when it was announced that a man would jump from a plane. All of us except Mom went to town to see it and afterwards Dad and I were in the feed mill and saw a man with a cast on his leg. Dad jokingly asked him if he had jumped from the plane and the man said yes and laughed. Of course, being only five years old, I thought he had and I couldn't wait to tell Mom all about it. It was a few years later that the county was buzzing with excitement after the flight to Paris by Charles Lindbergh. All the boys had to have aviator type headgear with goggles in front, which were usually on the top over the eyes. It was the beginning of the airplane era and hobbies usually consisted of making toy planes.

In the beginning, the mares did all the fieldwork and supplied transportation around the neighborhood and to town. As they grew older, they were retired to pasture and replaced with two huge mules, which were named Beck and Mag. Beck was from Doll and Mag had been bought as a match to Beck. At an early age, Mag slipped and fell on the ice and broke a hind leg. The custom was to destroy an animal if it had a broken leg, but it was decided to put splints on the leg and it healed very well although she walked with a limp the rest of her life. As she became older she slowed down in the fields which no doubt tried Dad's patience and he was often observed mistreating her at day's end in a way, which caused pain and she reacted violently. Generally Dad was proud of the mules which were the largest in the area and he boasted that they were seventeen hands high. I had never been able to understand what a hand was in relation to the height of a mule. Both mules lived and worked to a very old age. Beck was given to a neighbor for the children to ride, but Mag's health had deteriorated to the point where she had difficulty breathing. One weekend years later while I was visiting the farm, a neighbor came to the house carrying a high powered rifle. After many years, I can still see Dad and the neighbor climbing the hill behind the field. Dad was leading Mag, who was walking slowly with difficulty. I watched as the trio disappeared around a bend in the hill. Shortly afterwards, Dad and the neighbor returned. Dad was carrying Mag's bridle. After having worked with Mag for so many years while living on the farm, watching her demise remains as a sad memory.

The county fair at Cuba was an affair looked

forward to eagerly each summer. Mom often had a quilt or some other thing she had made, usually a hooked rug, for display and came home with one if not two blue ribbons. Dad would sometimes put in a calf or hog for display and instead of taking them home, someone would usually buy them for butchering. They had a crafts display and one year Wayne worked for a couple months making a really nice birdhouse which won first prize and was bought by the town doctor for an unheard of sum of eight dollars. There were the ferris wheels, merry-go-rounds and sideshows, which usually didn't take more than a dime to enjoy. It was a time for the "Old Timers" to meet and sit on benches talking and enjoying cigars.

    I remember one time Grandma and Grandpa Gus had just arrived at the fair and were getting out of their Dodge touring car when some nice looking girl asked plaintively "Where's Harry?" At that time Harry was perhaps twenty and was in Ohio working for the Davey Tree Expert Company. It was that year that the Meramec was slightly flooded, but was going down. There was no bridge of any kind at that time and cars simply drove into where they were used to where the bottom was graveled and smooth. The trough bridge didn't come until we were in Detroit, about 1931. Back to the river though. Dad must have gone in too fast, since half way through the Ford T stopped. We were all dressed for the fair and Dad crawled over the fake door on his side and over the fender, and with a foot in the spokes of each front wheel and holding on to the radiator cap, started cranking and yelling to Mom to "choke" it. The choke was a wire that went from the bottom of the radiator to the steering column. There was a ring on the front for the one doing the cranking to pull back and forth but with one hand on the crank and one on the radiator cap, Dad couldn't pull his end so Mom did the pulling. Finally the motor started and Dad came back in over the fender. I believe that a few cuss words had something to do with it starting. These things were accepted and taken in stride. Dad never owned a jack for flat tires, which were common. Instead, he had a block of wood. One of us kids would crawl under the car while Dad put his back to the car and pulled on the wood spokes in the wheel, lifting it enough for the block of wood to fit under the axle.

Although the Model T Ford suffered a bent front axle when the barn burned, it was repaired and it served well for several years. There were many steep hills in the area and it was necessary to back up them because the gas tank was under the front seat and the gas flowed by gravity. In 1928 Ford put the tank under the windshield and that worked well for two years or so until the tank was put in the back with a fuel pump. Lacking a tractor, the Ford could do many things, including sawing wood. The tire would be taken off the rim and the wheel jacked up. A leather belt was then run from the rim to a 30-inch saw blade and it worked very well. Of note – the Model T could run on kerosene in an emergency, although with plenty of backfiring.

The Benton Creek schoolhouse was a hub for community activities and served as a church on Sundays. The school always had a Christmas program with a potluck supper following. The teacher was paid one hundred fifty dollars a month. The school board consisted of three members, a president, a secretary and a treasurer. Dad served as president several times, and since the County furnished little more than the teacher's salary, it was up to the board to raise money as best it could for general operation supplies and books. A favorite way of raising money was through what was called "pie suppers", which were held usually around Halloween and Christmas. A pie supper got its name from when the ladies brought a pie in a box beautifully decorated but with no identification as to who had brought it. Often a girl's brother would tell whoever had eyes for the girl which pie was hers, and he would try to outbid competition for the pie, which he would then eat with the girl. The auctioneer would try for as much as he could get before saying "sold" and naming the lucky fellow who got it. Prices very seldom went as high as two dollars and when one did, it brought gleeful applause. Elsworth Grubb, in his early twenties, usually outbid everyone for the teacher's pie. Often, if lucky enough, the fellow was able to talk the girl into letting him take her home, and indeed many marriages started out this way. I was never able to participate in this endeavor in later years. An addendum about the school: It was in my second year that an announcement was made at the start of school. The board had approved the purchase of a pencil sharpener, which was screwed to the teacher's desk. Before that, it was left to the older boys to sharpen pencils with their pocketknives for anyone who asked. Schools were rather primitive even at that date.

      Once at Halloween a dress-up program had been scheduled with a potluck supper following. Since money was in short supply, Dad, as board president, wanted to use the occasion to have a pie supper afterwards. It happened that at this particular time the teacher, Ruth Morrison, had decided that she was not in favor of going along with Dad's wishes, but she could give no valid reason for her decision. Dad was naturally easily irked and was adamant in pursuing the issue. A week before the time for the program, he saddled up Doll and with me behind him set out for the Morrison home where Ruth lived with her parents, County Judge and Mrs. Henry Morrison, about a mile and a half away. Approaching the front gate of the yard, he called out and Ruth came out to the porch of the beautiful Victorian home, which the Judge had built for the family of four boys and two girls. I do not recall the exact exchange between them but Dad's manner was angry and Ruth was trying to appease him. In the end I recall that Dad had given an ultimatum that if she would not go along with the pie supper which, incidentally, had the support of the other board members, that he would not allow his kids to participate in the program. Ruth plaintively said, "Oh, Mr. McCann, you wouldn't do that, would you?" to which Dad angrily replied, "I sure would," whereupon he spurred Doll to a gallop down the road. A few days later Ruth sent a note to him by one of us kids that she would go along with the board's wishes. In the end, the program and potluck supper with the pie supper following turned out to be a most enjoyable and profitable evening and lasted well past midnight.

More on Judge Morrison: One day while all the boys were still living at home, they were blasting stumps out of the pasture below the house with dynamite. Their dad told them to be careful where they were aiming the stumps. A short time later, a stump landed on top of the house, through the roof and wedged in an upstairs closet where it stayed until the house burned many years later.

In the summer several of the neighbors would meet at Cedar Ford at four in the morning with boots, flashlights, gigging poles as well as fishing poles and plenty of worms for bait. They would usually come home with about forty fish and all would return that evening for a fish fry and cornbread which was brought from home, along with odd amounts of pies and cakes.

Sometimes during the year, we would see the sheriff, Chris Enke from Steelville going by the house in his Ford Model T Roadster with the top down. He was too tall to keep the top up usually so he liked it better this way. He was like as not on his way to Grandpa Gus Riefenstahl's for some home brewed beer. Since Gus never sold any, it was legal during Prohibition, known as bootleg.

Once in late afternoon, we heard a rumbling coming up the hill beside the house. It came closer and we could see four horsemen driving what looked to be about a hundred and fifty cattle. As they came closer to the house, one of the horsemen came ahead and told us they were driving the cattle to St. James, about eighteen miles farther to the railroad for shipping to a packing house in St. Louis. Since it was becoming dark, he asked if they could corral the cows in our barnyard for the night since they wouldn't be able to handle them in darkness, and further asked if they could sleep in the hayloft. He said that this was the second night on the road, having started up around Keysville. The four men owned the cattle and at that time, it was difficult to find transportation for the herd. After the herd was taken care of, Mom told them she had supper for them and they could sleep in the house. Next morning, after breakfast, they left at daylight, each showing great appreciation for the kindness shown them.

The year before the last Christmas on the farm before the move to Detroit brought on a special program in which the entire student body had parts. A side window had been made into a fake fireplace at the end of the stage. Mom made suits for Santa and Mrs. Santa. Earl was the Santa and Marie Morrison, Mrs. Homen Marshall, was the

Mrs. Santa. She had dyed plain feed sacks red and fastened carded sheep's wool on Santa's suit and hat. Marie's mother was in the hospital having a baby, probably Alma Lee, the present Mrs. Bernard Verkamp. Earl was to put his Santa suit on over his regular clothes outside and on signal come through the window to the glee and happiness of all the younger ones not part of the school. I was seven and don't remember what part I had, except probably one of the singers.

At the beginning of the second year before the move to Detroit, the family decided to purchase an electric power plant, principally for use in the chicken houses. Finn Sanders, a large chicken operator near Wesco, had used electricity for many years and we thought it feasible to follow suit. The lights would go on at four in the morning, getting the chickens busy on additional egg production and it was found that a large electric bulb under the water supply would keep the water from freezing. The plant was a 32-volt Delco. I still have the automatic switch box that activated the lights.

It was at about this time in 1928 that news was going through farms in the country like wild fire. Henry Ford in Detroit had announced that he was paying five dollars a day in his plants and compared to the one dollar a day that was usually being paid on farms, many farmers were making plans to go to the motor city. Ford had made the last Model "T" in 1927. He had brought out a new model in 1928 called the "A," which had metal spoke wheels and a closed body. Closely following Ford's announcement came one that the sixteen year-old daughter of the Oscar Jones, one of the first to move to Detroit, had died from meningitis. At that time such news was of an isolated type and no significance was attached to it.

Perhaps it might have been a veiled omen because it wasn't much more than a year later that we had made the move, resulting in my own deafness from meningitis.

The Watkins man came around three or four times a year. His buggy was like a flat-roofed covered wagon with all sorts of drawers, compartments and shelves, with doors on back and both sides gaily painted. This wagon was pulled by two beautiful horses with very fancy harnesses. He had just about anything farm women would want or need, including candy, spices and thread, and an array of salves and even bolts of cloth. His average length of stop was an hour. The driver himself was always a happy, friendly fellow and would give the kids a piece of candy or two.

Although money was short, there was always enough to eat, mostly supplied from the huge garden and butchering. In those days field corn was not of a hybrid type, so it was common to see Dad come in from the field in season with a basket full of corn which was put into a huge pot and there was corn on the cob for everyone. That, with fried chicken, which we had almost every day, and new potatoes and gravy, topped off with apple, peach, cherry or blackberry cobbler made only as farm women knew how and topped with real cream.

McCann family on the farm in 1928 one year before moving to Detroit. Charles, Arthur, Earl, Wayne, Leonard, Mamie holding Raymond, and Frieda in front.

In Grandpa Gus Riefenstahl's farmyard on the way home from church in 1926, in a spring wagon pulled by Doll and Flora. Leonard, Wayne, Mamie, holding baby Frieda, Charles, Arthur, and Earl.

Moving to Detroit, Michigan

It was a cold, rainy morning in late September of 1928. We had looked forward to this day for many weeks and were filled with both pride and excitement at the turn events were taking. It was four o'clock in the morning and the car had arrived which was to take Dad on his journey to Detroit. In retrospect, now that I am older, I feel that the decision to move to Detroit was brought on in hopes of recovering the huge loss of the barn, which had not been covered by insurance.

Detroit was some six hundred miles away. To the members of a family that had never been farther away from home than Owensville, fifty miles to the north, the six hundred miles seemed to be a journey into Never-Never Land. That, literally, is what it eventually turned out to be for me. The trip was being made in a Ford Model T touring car. There were four men besides Dad who had decided to act as pioneers to the Motor City in quest of fortune. Their plans were to make this trip to seek employment and then send for their families when they were settled. A man who was about to leave a wife and six kids alone on a farm situated twelve miles from the nearest town, Steelville, with a log house, few outbuildings, no electricity or water, a phone which would call only the nearest neighbor, and no transportation except a team of mules and a Model T that wouldn't run, must have been either an optimist or a very stupid man.

After fighting hard to hold back the tears at parting and having Dad go so far away, we regained our composure and at breakfast were able to banter and guess at how far they would be on their way by nightfall. We lived in awe that they would be going through such cities as St.

Louis, Indianapolis and Toledo. In our world, these cities may as well have been Paris, London and Dublin.

It was with a great deal of excitement that we set out for school that morning. How important we felt. After all, not everyone's dad was on his way to Detroit to make his fortune. We thrilled at the thought that soon we would all be following to live in that mystical city where everyone lived in boarding houses and made cars and earned five dollars a day.

It was raining when we began the trek to school over the hill and through the woods that took us past Grandma's house. We stopped to see her and were all excited in telling her about the way the old Ford sagged at the back with the five men and with the luggage tied on the running boards. We surmised that they would have a broken axle or that a wheel would fall off, or the motor would explode, but deep down we knew we were only squealing in delight at the prospects of things to come and were sure the trip would be made without mishap. We ran the last few hundred yards just as the bell in the bell house atop the school began to peal the beginning of another day. But this day would be different. After all, we were pretty important kids now. Dad was on his way to Detroit.

At the end of the first week, the anxiously awaited letter came. They had arrived in Detroit after no more delays than the usual blowouts and a broken fan belt. The trip had taken four days and they found lodging, as we had thought, in a boarding house on Lillibridge Avenue. We heard that some men who had gone before were living on Lillibridge Avenue, so naturally that was the place to live. Dad found a job, not with Ford as he had hoped, but with Chrysler at the Briggs Bodies Plant. We talked of how rich he was getting, and of how he would be bringing back all sorts of presents and fine clothes for us when he came to take us back with him.

It was Friday evening in the middle of December. School was out at four, so it was past dark when we had walked the three miles home. Mom acted a little strange when we opened the kitchen door. There was a glow on her face that we hadn't seen in a long time. It was snowing and we were cold. We went into the living room to get near the large wood-heating stove, when suddenly Dad jumped out from the corner. He hugged us all and, after supper, began the stories of life in the big city. He hadn't gotten rich, or bought fancy clothes or any of the things we imagined would come of the trip, but he brought each of us a small gift. In order to make the return home a complete surprise, he walked the four miles from the depot in the hamlet of Wesco. We all sat around the table with its kerosene lamp late into the night while he told us tales of our future home. He told of an amusing incident on the way to Detroit. It was their second night out and they were lost in Indiana. Stopping at a farmhouse at one in the morning, Dad knocked on the door. A farmer came to the door with a shotgun and with his wife holding a lamp behind him. Dad said, "You don't have to shoot me. There are four more in the car and we are lost." The farmer asked where they were from and Dad said, "Missouri. We are on our way to Detroit to work in the auto plants." The farmer lowered his gun and laughed. He said several farmers from around there were doing the same thing. They were invited inside. The farmer's wife fixed a meal for them and gave them beds and they stayed all night. Next morning, she had a big breakfast for them and after talking a while, they thanked them and resumed their journey.

While Dad was in Detroit, things on the farm went

along pretty much as they had before he left. Wayne had taken on more responsibility in telling the rest of us what to do. He had graduated from Benton Creek the year before. Rebul Marcellus had been the teacher that year. That last year before moving to Detroit, we had a man teacher, Cage Malone, at Benton Creek School. He was popular with the boys but he had at times been a source of embarrassment for the girls. Cage was from a family who lived nearer to St. James and at one time during the year came close to being removed by the board. He had been encouraging the kids to filch pennies from home and at recess and noon we were matching them. Earl, Leonard and I had depleted the family coin bank and we were forced to tell Mom what was going on. When Dad arrived home from Detroit and discovered the situation at school, he called a school board meeting. Dad, as president of the board, met with Corbett Lay and Fred Morrison one Saturday at the Morrison home where Cage was staying, and they took him to task for his behavior. Instead of asking him to leave for misconduct, he was given a severe censure. The following Monday morning found a quiet and humble teacher who apologized to the school for any trouble he had caused us at home, and things then went on in a stricter manner. It was after Christmas in the middle of January that it was called to Cage's attention that someone had been stealing lunches while everyone was out on the playground at recess. After a few days the reports continued. The entire lunch wasn't being stolen. Most of the kids had lunch boxes with lids, which could be removed and a small part of the lunch taken. The one or ones taking the lunches were well known and from very poor families. One day Mr. Malone gave my brother Earl his pocket knife and told him to go up in the woods behind the school and cut a switch four feet long as big as Cage's thumb on one end and as big as his little finger on the other. When Earl brought it in, Cage put it on top of the map case on the wall and said if he ever heard any more about stolen lunches, he would use it. On our return from Detroit three years later, it was still there and had never been used.

Grandma and Grandpa Gus were moving along with us and had an auction sale a week before ours, and since neither of us had many pieces of furniture or appliances left, they spent a lot of time at our house. About a week before departing, Dad and Grandpa Gus had gone into St. James for some supplies in the Dodge touring car that Grandma and Grandpa Gus had bought new in 1922 while they lived in Enid, Oklahoma. My Uncle Bill, Mom's brother, who had been living with them along with their son Harry, had gone to Detroit with Grandpa Gus to buy the Dodge and they were driving it back to Oklahoma. As they told the story for many years, there were only dirt roads, and many times they found themselves at the end of a road and in a farmyard. The farmer would often cut a fence wire to let them through to another road farther on, and offer advice on the best way to go. It took a week and a half to make the trip from Detroit to Enid. Now, to get back to the story about the trip to St. James, they were on the way out of town after doing the necessary shopping. Grandpa Gus had been drinking, something that he was well known for, and he was driving erratically. Dad told us later that he had swerved at parked cars in front of the high school and laughed and said he was going to see how far he could knock them. Dad asked him to stop and let him drive, which he did after some sarcastic comments. Dad had never driven anything except his Model T Ford and he was finally able to get moving by shifting into the right gear which went well until they neared home and came to a steep hill. As the engine started to sputter, Dad yelled to Grandpa Gus and wanted to know how to shift it into a lower gear. Grandpa Gus told him to push the shift lever up, which Dad did, inadvertently putting the car into reverse. Lurching backwards down the hill, it left the road and crashed into a tree, badly damaging the rear of the car. Dad became angry and walked the remaining distance, but since Grandpa Gus was in no condition to go home, he disappeared for several days. I am not sure what transpired between him and Grandma when he finally arrived home, but I have been told that he never again took a drink as long as he lived.

Preparations for the auction were hectic. Mom cried when she realized that she would have to part with things she would rather keep but thought she could find better ones in the city. The auctioneer was Silas Roberts and we had gone to various auctions before and liked to watch how fast he talked and would drool from the corner of his mouth. He would give a short description of most articles and would joke about not being able to afford some of the pieces he was selling. I believe he was the father of Mrs. Bill Gravatt. The day of the auction brought a large crowd and as with all farm auctions, afforded a time of socializing. I believe the total for the auction was six hundred dollars, more than half of which went for the move.

Preparing for the move and leaving school behind was both an exciting and difficult time. With the auction sale, most of the furnishings in the house were gone and the rest had been packed, so we had to make do with what we could find. The truck had come and everything was loaded in preparation for the next morning's departure.

Grandma's things had been loaded the day before. There was no bridge across the Meramec at the crossing, and early spring rains had swollen the stream. It was with some apprehension that we watched the heavily laden "REO Speedwagon" ford the river. Dad and Wayne were riding along with the driver, and Mom and the rest of the family were to travel to St. Louis by train, then from there by Greyhound Bus to Detroit. The renter of the farm, Dee Tighe, loaded us into his low-wheeled farm wagon and we were off to the depot in Wesco where we met Grandma and Grandpa Gus.

Looking back at the farm for the last time as we rounded the bend in the road at the crest of the hill, little did we realize the things which lay in store for us and which would begin materializing within a few short weeks after our arrival in Detroit. The train ride from Wesco to Steelville was a short one and afforded a short visit with Harry who had been living in town while finishing high school. After the incident with the Dodge, a new Chevrolet touring car was purchased which Harry was to drive to Detroit later with a family friend, John Cain. We boarded another train for the final leg of the trip to St Louis, and after a few hours, were met at the Tower Grove station by Mom's cousin, Joe Weissenberg. It was dark and our first sight of the big city with its lights left us awe struck. We boarded a streetcar, which in itself was another thrill and after about a half hour got off at North Broadway. After a short walk we arrived at Joe's sister, Mom's cousin, Della La Baube's home. After walking up a long outside stairway, we came into an opening that afforded entrances into both Della's and Mom's Aunt Emma's apartments, as well as to the stairway to the third floor apartment of Joe and Della's parents, Mom's Uncle Joe and Aunt Annie.

The next morning Uncle Joe took us kids for a walk down around Gasconade Street past the City workhouse where he explained how the prisoners had to break up rock and other labor while they were in prison. The work area was about thirty feet deep and enclosed with twelve-foot wire fencing. Later we stopped at a doughnut shop and bought a large bag of doughnuts for breakfast. Later in the day Joe Junior took all of us to the Zoo, a place which fascinated us since we had never seen any thing except horses and mules, cows and pigs on the farm. The rest of the day was spent touring Forest Park and eating ice cream. We were exhilarated at our new found excitement in the city, but little did I know that what I was seeing then was to be close to the end of my participation in the hearing world as we normally know it. A change was to come into my life which would make Hell seem like a country club in comparison.

    The three-day trip by bus was rather uneventful except for a lengthy stop in Terre Haute, Indiana. There was no heat and the roads were rough, so it was with relief that we finally arrived and were met by Dad. He had found a place on Montclair Avenue, a nice little house with a large backyard, which a few weeks later was ablaze in tulips. Never having lived in anything except the farmhouse, we found everything exciting and set out to explore the neighborhood. After our three-mile trek to Benton Creek in Missouri, we were happy to find so many changes in our lives.

    The day after our arrival, we met the McKay family. There were three boys, all near our ages, and a girl. They lived three houses down the street. The family sort of took us under their wing and had us join their church where Mr. McKay was a pastor. His regular work was with

Chrysler where he was a foreman. They had a beautiful home and a new Plymouth. We often played in their backyard and had lunch there on Saturdays. Mrs. McKay would ask us if we had studied our lessons for the next day's Sunday school. They later took us to the Belle Isle Park in the Detroit River and spent the day.

Our first exploring trip was to the St. Clair School a half block up the street. We just walked around it and when we got back to the house, the McKay boys were waiting for us. A little later twin girls whom we only knew as Rosa and Liza came by. We were beginning to feel as though we belonged. Monday morning found us in school. My class, the second grade, was on the second floor and the room itself was larger than the entire Benton Creek School had been. My memories of the school are still there and there were some that stand out above the others.

Being in totally different surroundings I was naturally nervous and remember that the teacher put sealing tape on my mouth for talking too much in class. I couldn't get it off so I had to go home that way. Mom was angry and finally got it off. I believe she made a trip to talk to the principal since my face was red from the glue. I also recall one day after lunch I was running up the stairs when a teacher, not mine, called to an older boy to catch me and take me to the principal's office and confiscate the pocketful of marbles that had been rattling around in my pocket. I also remember the large art room with long goldfish tanks on the window ledges.

Before we had started to school, a play had been organized for each grade. I was too late to enter it but Leonard had a part in his class play. Earl went to Foch High School a few blocks away. I vividly recall the play given by my class. About twelve little girls were squatting on the floor of the stage with large green paper leaves covering them. Other members of the class in the background started to sing the theme song "Little yellow dandelion growing in the grass." I don't remember the rest, but as the song progressed, the girls rose and were costumed to look like dandelions. Then they started to dance. Those are memories that I cherish.

One afternoon we were playing with several of the school kids. The twins Rosa and Liza had a nice rubber ball that I was throwing against the schoolhouse. I threw it too hard and it went onto the roof and we couldn't get it down. I remember that the girls came to the house and told Mom. This must have been only a few days before I went to the hospital. When I returned from the hospital and was well enough to walk around, I looked everywhere for a beautiful five-inch rubber ball that Uncle Bill had given me one Christmas, but I couldn't find it. It was light yellow with animals and flowers embossed into the rubber. I never said anything about it, but I have been sure that Mom gave it to the twins to replace their ball that I had thrown onto the roof.

Our four-year-old sister Frieda had caught a cold on the bus from St. Louis, and while it was treated as an ordinary cold in the beginning, it gradually developed into pneumonia. Mom was not a believer in hospitals and was sure that Frieda would be able to overcome the terrible coughs, so continued to care for her at home. Within a week it became necessary to accept the advice of our newly made friends, the McKays, and have their doctor bring a specialist to the house. However, too much time had been lost. Plans were made to remove her to a hospital, but she died that evening. I remember hearing her call to Mom to come in and take her shoes and stockings off and lie down with her. Mom said she was getting supper and would lie down later. She died half an hour later. I know Mom never forgot this.

Mom and Dad accompanied her body back to Missouri for burial in the family cemetery at Owensville after Mr. McKay and some church members had conducted a service at the house. We kids stayed with Grandma in their home on Mack Avenue, three blocks from our home. It took a little while for the family to adjust, as Frieda had been the only sister in a family of five boys. Gradually, we became accustomed to the loss and life began to unfold again.

Dad had been unable to find work since we arrived and walked the streets looking for anything available. The motor plants were no longer hiring. It was an uneasy time that was to materialize into the Great Depression. Our oldest brother, Wayne, had gone to work for A & P and was able to bring home enough money for the family to get by, but the change in our living was evident. We had always been able to produce our own food and satisfy our needs on the farm.

Wayne would bring home perishables on weekends that his boss would give him. One Saturday evening he brought home a bag of dates. I had never tasted a date before, and wasn't sure I liked them, but ate enough to become ill. The following day, a Sunday afternoon in late April, we were playing on the school playground and jumping off the fire escape. The school guard warned us to quiet down or he would chase us out and lock the gates. Still sick to my stomach from the previous day's dates, I suddenly developed a headache that became more severe as I ran around. In a little while I asked Wayne to take me home. I had difficulty walking the half block.

I was put in Mom and Dad's bed to sleep off the headache. I immediately fell into unconsciousness and later remembered hearing someone ask Mom if I should be awakened for supper; she said no, to let me sleep. Later I heard Mom call to Wayne to watch me and if I woke up to give me some supper and put me in my own bed, as they were going to church and would return about ten. Then I heard the front door close. What was thought to be a headache and something I would sleep off turned out to be a coma from which I was to awaken three weeks later in a hospital to a strangely silent world. Several years passed before I was able to understand that my deafness had not been brought on by the newly found dates, but rather by an attack of cerebro-spinal meningitis, which brought a city-wide epidemic resulting in most stores, factories and schools closing for the duration.

Contracting Meningitis

Dorothy in the Land of Oz would have been an apt companion during my travels through the misty Comaland. I could hear voices raised while the family was making arrangements for the trip to the hospital. I could hear Grandpa trying to bring some order into the confusion, and I saw some men come into the bedroom to lift me onto a stretcher. I remember being taken out into the chilly night air and being placed in an ambulance. It was raining and I could hear dogs barking next door. I remember being jounced from side to side as the heavy vehicle lurched over the cobblestones speeding toward Detroit's Herman Kiefer Hospital. At that time, ambulances had solid rubber tires. In my dream I was being taken across the Detroit River into Windsor, Ontario, Canada. Many times we had talked about making the trek into what to us was a foreign land, and I knew that at last I was going to see the great city of lights across the river. I remember the ride in the elevator and wondered why I was being taken up so high. Leonard, an older brother, was with me and I called out to him in the elevator to hold on tightly so as not to fall into the shaft below. After we stopped and I was taken out, I never saw him again. I supposed that he had been taken to some other part of the city. I remember going back to our home on Montclair Avenue, but I was too late – I found that the entire family except Dad had died. He and I rode on the train with the bodies to Missouri and I watched as one by one they were buried in the cemetery at Owensville. After the trip back, in which I lost Dad somewhere on the train, I tried to reconcile myself that Dad and I would be returning to the farm in Missouri. I wondered why he never came to see me. I decided that I must have been mistaken about the trip to Missouri when the family members were buried and that he was also dead and that I was left alone. Gradually I became conscious of people around me. Strange figures in white that moved about silently, but I was not able to move or look directly at them or gain any recognition.

When finally I became fully conscious of my surroundings and woke to see the sun streaming into the room that May morning, I thought I was in an orphan's home in Canada. I hoped Grandma and Grandpa would come to get me and take me back to Missouri, but no one came. Some letters came and a lady would try to have me read them; but my eyes had become weakened and, coupled with the general mental confusion, I was unable to recognize who they were from. Some oranges were brought into the room with a tag on them saying, "From Grandma," but I wondered why she didn't come to see me and take me home. Darkness would fall and I could see the lights of the silent cars moving to and fro on the streets. I wondered at the weird things that were happening to me. The door was closed and the others in the room were asleep; I would lay and look at the crack of light under the door and watch as the lights from cars played on the ceiling and walls. From time to time, the door opened and the lady in white would come in and bend over me and put her finger to my eyes, closing them. (I was to learn much later that the ladies in white were nurses.) I did not know she was trying to get me to go to sleep. All I could do was wonder. I felt as though I had been placed in a glass cage, where I could look out and see movements, but no sound would reach me. Morning would come and with it a repeat of the two men in white with the needle. I became used to the pain and tried to tell them they didn't have to hold me and I would be quiet. But they continued to get me into a position where I was unable to move. I would close my eyes and clench my hands and wait for the needle to be inserted and withdrawn from my spinal cord.

I looked forward to breakfast that usually consisted of something I had never had on the farm. It was here that I had my first taste of fresh fruits such as grapefruit and orange juice. I was propped up in bed with the tray across my lap. I couldn't yet sit straight up, so had to do the best I could to feed myself. Lifting the spoon and glass became an ordeal, but the food was so good and I was so hungry that I forced myself to eat all that was on the plate. There were three others in the room, a boy about my age and two girls, one colored. The bright red ribbons adorning her braids were a happy contrast to the white in the room. Each day I would be bathed and dressed in clean pajamas. Sometimes I would be taken out into an open wing at the side of the building in a wheelchair. I could see people coming and going, and watched intently for someone I knew. I could not know that the ones coming and going were doctors and nurses and others who worked in the building. I could not know that I was in an isolation hospital and that no one could come to see me. Many days passed and I wondered why I wasn't able to move my legs. I also wondered why I was so weak that I was content to just lie in bed and watch others do things for me and the others in the room. Women in white would come to the side of my bed and look down at me and smile, then look at each other and move their lips and laugh; but, I had no idea what they were doing, or why. The days became warmer and the windows were opened to let the fresh air and breezes in. I would see men in the yard tending the flowers and grass. I was living in a world of deep confusion. There was nothing I could look forward to, and no one that

I felt I would ever see again that I would know.

One Sunday morning I was put into a wheelchair and taken into another room. On the bed lay some new clothes, including a pair of brown sandals. I had never had sandals and was happy to see that I was now to have a pair. I still couldn't move my legs, so it was with some difficulty that a lady in white was able to dress me in these clothes.

Later, dinner was brought in and although I had no idea why I had been dressed, I was excited at having clothes on after being in bed for so long. After dinner, I was placed, fully clothed, on the bed. Suddenly, I was surprised and overjoyed to see Dad come into the room. His hair, which had been dark when I last saw him, was now almost completely white. He ran to the side of the bed and tried to talk to me. There were tears in his eyes. A lady in white came and they talked for a few moments. She wrapped a blanket around me and Dad picked me up and carried me out of the room to an elevator. The lady accompanied us and kept smiling at me, and nodding to Dad. I felt that at last we would be going back home to Missouri, but I couldn't imagine how it would be with just the two of us. When the elevator reached the ground floor and the door opened, I was startled and frightened to see Mom sitting in the lobby waiting for us. I was overwhelmed at the turn events were taking. She was crying and came and hugged me, and tried to say something to me. However, all I could do was nod my head and wonder why everyone moved their lips and made no sound. I wondered why they didn't want me to hear them and why there were whispering. A cab was waiting at the door and the lady helped me onto Dad's lap. As we moved away from the hospital, I saw others being carried into waiting cars and wondered why they were like me.

Mom and Dad moved their lips excitedly and I wanted to ask them what they were saying, but wasn't able to talk. I was still weak and confused and had no idea where I was or where we were going.

When the cab came to a stop in front of the house on Montclair, I was taken into the house and put in a bed that had been moved into the front room. I was further mystified to see all my brothers. They filed into the room to see me. This was reminiscent of Dorothy's friends and family running in to see her. They tried to talk to me and touched me, but all I wanted to do was to go to sleep and wondered at what was happening. It was suppertime when I awoke. I was alone and was afraid to try to talk, as I was sure the things that had been happening that day were all part of another cruel dream. But then they all began coming back into the room, and I was becoming accustomed to the fact that I was really at home again and that something had happened to me but as yet I didn't know what. I gradually realized that the family was alive and not dead as I had thought for so many weeks. I reasoned that since they were all there that perhaps Frieda was still there, too, and that she had not died and had been a part of the dream as well. I was able to say her name and Mom left the room. I thought she was going to bring her in, but she was crying when she brought in a large colored picture instead. By then I was able to put part of it together and knew that Frieda was gone.

About two weeks after my arrival home, the family moved into a house on Fairview Avenue two blocks away. Since we didn't have a car, I was again wrapped in a blanket and Mom held me while we rode in the truck with the driver. This house was more spacious and the kitchen opened onto a long back porch where we sometimes moved the table and ate our meals. There was a large backyard with blooming hollyhocks around the fence. It was early summer. The warm weather and my weakened condition, together with my lack of understanding, left me in a state of wondering as to what was going to happen next. They would carry me onto the porch where I watched the neighborhood kids playing in the yard and alley. Some would come up and say something, probably out of curiosity, to which I wasn't able to reply, then run off to do something more constructive. A bed had been moved into the front room in the new house also, where it was easier to care for me. The changed surroundings had at first been a little frightening. I gradually became accustomed to being left alone at night. I would lay and watch the shadows from the lights in the street as they danced about the room. I wasn't yet able to understand why everything was so quiet and why everyone moved so silently and made no sound when they talked to me.

We had lived in the Fairview house about a week when one night, after everyone had gone to bed, I lay in the darkness watching the shadows from the lights on the street. A faint breeze was coming through the open windows, moving the curtains to and fro gently. I started to doze off, when suddenly I was wide awake. A beautiful familiar melody was drifting in. The music continued for several minutes. I listened in wonderment and thought someone was playing an instrument. Then I heard someone singing the words of the song. It was a familiar song that I knew from having sung it in church. Someone was singing "Bringing in the Sheaves." I became frightened and tried to get up but couldn't. I began to cry and when the music didn't go away, I became terrified. The family came running into the room and tried to comfort me, but since they couldn't understand what had happened, they gave me a drink and went back to bed after I had quieted down. The music persisted and I was finally able to accept it and go to sleep. That was the beginning of my experience with tinnitus, commonly known as head noises, which has continued in one way or another to the present time. Sometimes it's in the form of beautiful music that awakens me at night, and I can lie listening to it, or in the form of past conversations with people I once talked with, or just about any sound imaginable. I have become accustomed to them and can channel them into something constructive. Pseudo experts say these sounds are merely memories of past things. This might be partly true on occasion, however, I have heard music so beautiful that no instrument in this world could ever produce it. Certainly there was no way I could have heard it as a hearing child living in a log house situated in the foothills of the Missouri Ozarks.

After several weeks, I was gradually regaining the use of my legs. One afternoon, while sitting on the front porch, a car stopped in front of the house. I recognized the driver and a man with him as Uncle Harry who had driven into Detroit from Missouri and one of our farm neighbors, John Cain. I slowly walked to the car and climbed onto the running board. He was driving a new Chevrolet Touring Car, which had replaced the Dodge that had been wrecked. My uncle said something to me but I just nodded my head. Turning to his friend he said, "He can't hear anything." I was beginning to understand that something was very wrong. My ability to lipread was just beginning to develop.

The summer months passed quietly and swiftly. Dad was still walking the streets looking for work and I was gradually learning to walk again. Cerebro-spinal meningitis affects the equilibrium and coupled with my long stay in bed, it took some doing to be able to use my legs again. Even today, I cannot walk in total darkness without assistance. Most of my efforts were fruitful with the aid of a chair that I pushed ahead of me. Each time Mom or Dad left the house, I would ask where they were going. I hoped they would be going back to what I still thought was the orphans' home to get some of the toys that had been sent in while I was there. Of special importance were two small metal cars I played with in bed and to which I had become attached. I could see boys pulling similar cars on the street and I missed them. I asked for them many times and hoped someone would bring them to me, but since the hospital was of an isolation type, all the things left behind were destroyed.

The end of summer brought another move for the family, this time only two blocks up Fairview into a house being vacated by family friends. The friends had come to see me several times and tried to make me understand a few words, but I remember how they would shake their head and turn to talk to Mom and Dad. While these friends moved into a new home in a distant part of Detroit, Mom and Dad were anxious to take the house they were leaving since it was a larger two-story house. It was next door to the family of a friend I had known at the St. Clair School, Billy Steinmetz. They lived in a beautiful brick house and his Dad drove a new Buick. This house gave the folks a chance to take in some boarders, which afforded a small income and made the following winter months a bit easier.

Detroit Day School for the Deaf

September brought with it the decision for me to return to school. Mom and Grandma were taking me, and I couldn't understand why it was necessary for both of them to go along since the school was only a few blocks away over on Montclair. I was looking forward to returning to St. Clair School and found it difficult to sleep the night before the big day. That morning we set out and walked up Fairview to Canfield and over to Montclair. As we approached St. Clair, however, we continued on by. I tugged on Mom's hand reminding her that this was the school. She shook her head and we continued on a few blocks to the streetcar line. Upon boarding the car, I was confused and wondered where we were going. I had looked forward to seeing the kids I knew and thought of how important I would be back in school after being sick for so long, but now all this was changed and we were on our way to some place where I was to be among strangers. Following a long ride, we got off the streetcar near a large playground and walked around the block to what turned out to be the Detroit Day School for the Deaf on Stanton and McGuire Avenues.

Upon entering the building we were taken to the office of Miss Von Der Ahe, a prim, old-maidish principal who looked us up and down as if wondering what brought these country-looking people into her school. After answering questions and writing some things on a piece of paper, we were taken on a tour of the school, including what was to be my homeroom. A very friendly lady, Mrs. Keller, was to be my teacher and a colored girl was to be my seatmate. I wondered if she was the same girl I had seen in the hospital, but decided she couldn't be as she was older than I remembered the girl to be. Mom and Grandma stayed to become acquainted with the surroundings. Then we all went home together.

We had been introduced to a girl of perhaps twelve who lived on Lillibridge Avenue a few blocks from our house. Mary was to see that I got to and from school each day. It was necessary for someone to walk me to her house each morning and meet me each evening. I could sense that she did not relish this task. One day after my lipreading had improved I saw a man on the street car ask her if I was her brother. She replied with disdain that she was only taking me to school. I was beginning to realize that I was deaf, but I still did not know that she was, too, or that everyone else in the school was. And in fact, I didn't even realize what the word "deaf" at the school meant.

My first year with Mrs. Keller was rather uneventful. I remember reading in "My Weekly Reader" that Princess Elizabeth of England had a new baby sister who was to be named Margaret Rose. I remember reading in the same paper about the Lincoln Monument and how the Japanese had planted cherry trees in the far-off city of Washington, D.C. I also remember how Miss Keller had taken a prize string top away from me after I persisted in spinning it in the hall. I remember seeing it in the bottom of her desk drawer on the last day of school and asking her for it, but she refused to return it.

My second year in the Detroit Day School for the Deaf was much improved over the first one. I was moved into a higher class and found many new faces. The new teacher, Miss Ethel Chover, was a rather short, stout woman with graying black hair. We got along well except for the exasperation she would show in talking to me. There were times when we could communicate well since I was unconsciously picking up lipreading at home. Prior to losing my hearing, I had acquired a good vocabulary and was entirely familiar with everyday things and happenings. It was easy to understand what people were saying and what they meant. But in school I went into reverse and when Miss Chover read to the class, I wouldn't pay any attention to what she was saying. I would look out the window. I received a few sharp raps for my inattention. It was at about the beginning of the fourth quarter when she must have decided that something was amiss. One day she kept me in during play period and patiently explained that everyone else in the class was deaf as well as everyone in school, and that they watched her lips as she talked and read to them and were able to understand what she said. She explained that this was called lipreading. Up to that time, I had thought I was the only one in class who couldn't hear and as a result didn't pay any attention to anything said to me. After being briefed on the facts as they were, my report cards contained a nice black "one" instead of the usual red "five" in lipreading.

  The second year in school I was advanced into third grade and also made me eligible for shop class. The shop teacher, Paul Nutten, was very patient but demanding. He had us make simple drawings of projects and after having completed the drawings favorably to his satisfaction, we were required to make the project in the shop. The machines and tools in the shop fascinated me and their presence opened up a totally new scope of interests. We had the class for an hour only three times a week and I looked forward to it eagerly. I would collect scraps of wood from orange crates or anything I could find at home and make things in the basement. I remember sawing half way through the arm of one of Mom's rocking chairs which she kept down there, and which I was using for a sawhorse in the absence of anything else handy. The family bought me some tools for Christmas that consisted of a hammer, a saw, some chisels and a plane. I spent every spare moment creating crude articles. I made some lamps and wired them for electricity. It was then that I discovered how electric wires had to be kept separate and not twisted together, and that I should not put a penny in back of a blown fuse, an item that earned me a tanning with Dad's razor strap.

It was at about this time that Mom and Dad were trying anything and everything suggested to them in an effort that they hoped would restore my hearing. Among other things they would take me to faith healers. One of them, a very fat lady in Rochester, Michigan, appeared to have quite a following. Her home was sort of an estate and I remember a large apple orchard whose fruit everyone appeared to help themselves to while waiting their turn. She would put me in front of her on a stool and mumble something while holding my head in her hands and pressing firmly, very firmly, on my ears and looking toward the ceiling. This would go on for about ten minutes. After each of these sessions, Dad would assure me that she would make me stronger and that I would be able to hear again. We went to her once a week for two months at fifty cents a visit. We had no car, so a neighbor, George Bodenbach, a young man, would drive us the thirty-odd miles in the evening. In the meantime, I had lost interest in school. I was sure I would be able to hear again and could return to St. Clair School. When it became evident that it wasn't going to be as simple as was at first thought, they quit taking me to her and began taking me to an old Indian healer in downtown Detroit. He also mumbled while holding my head in his hands and calling to the Great Spirit. But apparently the Spirit wasn't to be moved at that time as nothing came of this quest either. Some time later, they were taking me to a chiropractor, Dr. Arthur C. Berry on East Grand Boulevard, who popped my neck and twisted my spine, apparently trying to change something that he hoped would do some good. I now realize that his fondest hope was probably to get the dollar for each visit which I don't think was ever paid up in full, nor should it have been, since I am sure he knew his efforts were hopeless. It was finally decided that I was hopelessly deaf and the family appeared to accept the fact. Life went on as best it could.

After our move into the city, Dad was never again able to regain full employment at the auto plant. He tried small jobs from time to time whenever something came up, but the remuneration was only enough for the barest necessities. By the beginning of the second winter, we had moved a total of three times, the last time into a nicer place in Highland Park. Our grandparents lived in the flat upstairs so the family was together once again. A truck was rented and a trip was made into northern Michigan to purchase a load of horseradish roots. All winter long every member of the family went into the basement to scrape the things clean as soon as we came home in the evening. Dad had found an oversized food grinder with which to grind the roots after we had cleaned and chopped them into small pieces. It was necessary to grind them on the back porch in bitterly cold weather since the smell was too pungent to work inside. They had purchased a fifty-gallon drum of white vinegar and several pounds of sugar and salt. After mixing and putting the concoction into jars and labeling them, Mom and Dad would put them into baskets and ply the streets going from door to door. In a short time they were able to build up a route of regular customers, and were able to increase the amount we could produce and branched out into the better parts of the city. They must have made quite a bit of money as they were able to pay off all outstanding debts and the following spring saw a one-year-old Chevrolet in the garage. A short time later, a Ford truck came into being. After two years of this sales venture, it was decided to return to the farm home in Missouri, a decision they lived to regret.

With the advent of the Chevrolet the second year, the family was able to do some traveling. In the summer of Thirty-One, a trip was made back to Missouri to visit the farm. It was different for me. I could no longer communicate as I did when I last saw our friends and relatives. I was subject to a good deal of staring and discussions. Gradually my deafness was accepted and as the novelty wore off, they found something else to talk about. I could never again feel the closeness with relatives and family friends as I once had. There was a consciousness that became a permanent barrier in the form of strained relations to which they were not able to adjust. A deaf member was something the family had never known and adjustment to the reality of accepting it was difficult. Shortly after we returned from Missouri, the family left for a two-week trip to the east and Niagara Falls. Stops were made to see friends on the way and the trip was an enjoyable one.

There are memories of my childhood in Detroit that stand out. One afternoon I had gone down to Fromms Hardware Co. to get a key for my clamp-on roller skates. I was barely ten and still living in the country as far as knowing my way around the city was concerned. The clerk brought out a key and told me it was five cents. I had four pennies in my hand and started to leave when a man standing beside me gave the clerk a nickel. I wanted to give him my pennies, but he laughed and patted my on the head and shook his head.

It was about dark and snowing on Christmas Eve of 1931. I had walked a block past our street on Woodward Avenue and was looking in the windows of the S.S. Kresge Company. One window had on display a beautiful toy truck about twenty inches long. I noticed a large black car had stopped in the street and a well-dressed gentleman got out and came up to me. He said something I couldn't understand, then he pointed at the truck. All I could do is nod my head, and he took me by the arm and into the store and bought the truck and gave it to me. All I could do is smile and he patted me on the arm and got back in his car. I had the truck for many years as well as the memories of the gentleman's kindness.

At Christmastime in Detroit, we would wait until midnight on Christmas Eve when Earl and Leonard would go to a tree lot and were given a leftover tree that they couldn't sell. We would decorate it before going to bed. On our last Christmas in Detroit, the family, our grandparents and Harry decided to spend the day with friends, the Bodenbachs, and since their dining table wasn't large enough for all of us, Mr. Bodenbach came over with his truck and took our table, which opened to twelve feet. I have fond memories of that day which didn't end until early the next morning. Mrs. Bodenbach was at the piano and the grown ups spent a lot of time singing. These are especially fond memories.

Dad bought Mom a new set of knives, forks and spoons with pearl handles. One year they bought me a marx caterpillar type tractor, and another year a plane and hammer and some chisels. I don't know what the rest of the family got. On the return to the farm, in 1932, money was practically nonexistent. Regardless, Mom always made anise cookies using a cookie board with impressions, which left designs on the cookies before baking. That year, my gift was a set of Jacks. Dad always had a cigar. I have a tree ornament, which Uncle Bill gave to Frieda in 1927. It is a celluloid figurine of Mrs. Santa. Raymond has the matching Santa. They have come out every Christmas.

  This year, the folks gave Wayne a gold watch for Christmas on his seventeenth birthday. Two years later Earl got one on his seventeenth birthday. Two more years brought another watch for Leonard on his seventeenth. It was three years later that I was seventeen and looked forward to the watch. I continued looking at my eighteenth and nineteenth when Wayne gave me his old one, a bit corroded but still good. It looked nice after I had cleaned it up. I gave it to one of his daughters many years later after his death. These watches had all been bought very cheaply in "hock shops" but were like new.

  In Detroit I would spend practically every Saturday afternoon in a movie theater on Grand Avenue. I remember Rin Tin Tin in "The Lightning Warrior" and Seth Parker in "Coming Home" and others. I quickly learned to decipher the mimes and understand what was going on.

  I had quit going to school the Thursday before we were to leave for the return to Missouri. I went down on Friday to see a show but they wouldn't let me in. I didn't know why but Dad went with me later and they said it was a school day. They let me in then when he explained the situation.

Return to the Farm in Missouri

    Preparations were made in anticipation of leaving the city. Friends of the family would come to see us and say good-bye. On my last day at school, I was a bit excited and I remember how Miss Chover had to leave the room for a while and asked one of the older girls, Yvonne Allen to report to her upon her return of any behavior problems. I didn't realize that I would be reported and did several things that earned me a mark on the board each time. Upon her return, the teacher saw the numerous marks and punished me by not letting me go to lunch. When school was dismissed, Mom and Uncle Harry came to get me. Miss Chover had not known it was my last day and appeared to be sorry that she had kept me from lunch. Mom explained that we were leaving the city the next day. Miss Chover hugged me and I believe there were tears in her eyes. The return to the farm in March of 1932 was uneventful. All household belongings were brought back in the Ford truck. My two older brothers, Wayne and Earl, drove ahead with the truck and the rest of the family followed in the car. There were no heaters in the vehicles, making the three-day trek a miserable one.

    I have never been able to fathom the reasons for the return to the farm at the bottom of the Great Depression. Our parents were making money in Detroit and life had become a bit more comfortable. Dad was a stubborn man with the dirt and sweat of farming in his blood. Mom was never happy on the farm. Before they first started farming, as stated before, Dad had been a conductor on the streetcars in St. Louis and she was happy there. Most of her family, her cousins, aunts and uncles, and many friends were in St. Louis. Farm life was a complete change for her. I remember finding her crying the day we arrived at the farm from Detroit. She was standing in the bedroom looking at a boarded-up window. It was this window that had been broken three years earlier and had not yet been repaired. Frieda had broken it some way, obviously by accident. Mom had felt compelled to spank her although she was only three and had cowered in a corner, pleading that she couldn't help it. These must have been bitter memories.

Many adjustments had to be made to compensate for the changes I found on the farm. The animals were all different than I had remembered them. The braying of the mules was gone. The cows, the pigs and the chickens were silent, although I could imagine from memory the sounds that each would make. I could see the birds flying from branch to branch and could remember the singing that greeted us each morning when we woke. The clanking of the high-wheeled iron-tired buckboard as it lumbered over the rock-strewn road was stilled. Everything was strange. The rain that I used to listen to as it fell on the iron roof of the house no longer beat the staccato that I had loved. The wind was strangely quiet as it lashed the trees during the spring storms. The rustling of the leaves, which lulled us to sleep at night, was no longer there. Especially missed was the chirping of the crickets in the creek below the house. Lying in bed in the stillness was terrifying in the sudden darkness after having been accustomed to the lights in the city. When I could no longer bear it and began crying, Mom and Dad would get up and after lighting a kerosene lamp, would do what they could to quiet me.

The days of early spring on the farm after the years in the city were filled with excitement. We could always find something new to do. It was fun to run barefoot in the furrows of the freshly turned earth that rolled off the plowshares in cool moist layers. We would look for Indian arrowheads that were abundant in that part of the country. The fields, bordered by the Meramec River, had at one time been camping grounds for Cherokee Indians. Tomahawks and stone arrowheads were there for the picking up after the plows had turned them to the light. It was good to watch the team of mules straining at the tugs as they pulled the plows, furrow after furrow.

Although it took several days to plow with mules the same amount of land then as could be turned with a tractor in a few hours today, the satisfaction and contentment that was available then is not there now. At that time a farmer was proud of the straight rows of corn which he was able to make with a crude check attachment of the planter. If he missed a few hills of corn, he would work back over the field just after the shoots came through and laboriously plant the missing hills by hand. As the years passed and each spring brought out the plows, I wanted to work in the fields along with Dad and my brothers, but Dad would never let me use a plow. He would sometimes let me use a disc harrow since it was a riding machine but even then he was afraid I wouldn't be able to handle the team of large black mules.

Benton Creek School

    Summer passed swiftly that year. In August it was time to return to school. There was talk that I would have to go to the Missouri School for the Deaf in Fulton. The more they talked about it, the less I thought of the idea. Mom wrote a letter to the school and one day a car pulled into the drive. A man we had never seen before got out and came into the yard. He introduced himself as a representative of the school in Fulton. When Mom told me who he was, I was filled with fear that he was going to take me back with him and I became resentful that she had sent for him. He came closer to me and I backed away. He said something to me but I wasn't trying to understand him and didn't want to. Finally, Mom told me he just wanted to talk to me. He asked me some questions and I answered them. He looked surprised and smiled. He came over and put his arm around my shoulders and said something to Mom, but I didn't know at the time what he said. He laughed and shook my hand and got into his car and drove away. I was very relieved. After he had gone, I asked Mom what he had said. She laughed and said that he had told her there was no reason for me to go to Fulton if I was able to understand and talk as well as I did to him. In fact, he doubted if I would be accepted for admission, as there were so many less fortunate children who needed the school more than I did. I was happy and felt a load lift. I knew I wouldn't have to leave home now. But at the same time I was dreading the start of school at the little one-room school I had gone to before I lost my hearing. Most of the same students would be there, but the nagging fear persisted that I would have trouble. The first day of school arrived. Dad drove me that day but after that, I would have to walk the three miles along with neighbors Arthur Howald and Russell and Bud Bell. They all had to walk another mile home. The oiled floor was the same as I had remembered it and the room smelled of new books and sharpened pencils. I had the feeling that perhaps I would have been better off if I had gone to Fulton as the other kids were in groups, whispering and looking at me. The teacher welcomed me and said something that made me feel better, but still not completely secure. Dad left and I was alone with the kids I once knew on an equal plane but of whom I was now afraid. I didn't know if they wanted to help me or if they were going to make fun of me. As it turned out it was neither. They didn't offer any help, and no one said anything to me. By recess, it was a little better. By the time assignments were passed out, I was beginning to feel as though I was going to fit in. Norma Morrison, the teacher, came over and sat with me and assured me that she was going to do all she could to make it easy for me to fit in and that all the kids were going to help me, too. I went home that evening feeling happier than I had been in a long time. Benton Creek School was still the same. Norma was the oldest daughter of the Fred Morrison family who lived about a half-mile from school across Benton Creek.

As the term progressed, I became more confident in my surroundings and began to feel more a part of the school instead of being an outsider. Some of the older kids would laugh outright at the way I pronounced certain words, but this was more of a help than hindrance. When I found them laughing, I knew I had done something wrong and would make it a point to correct myself. Sometimes when I wasn't sure of the right way to pronounce a word, I would purposely say it the way it looked in spelling knowing I would get a rise out of the rest. I was able to gain a lot this way since I knew when something wasn't right. One day, while reciting in agriculture class, I came across a word I couldn't say so I eliminated it. Instead of saying the soil "contained nitrate", I said it "had nitrate in it." Later the teacher came to my seat and sat down and explained many things which were beneficial. With only a high school education, Norma Morrison did an excellent job. She was able to handle all eight grades with aplomb and could hold her own against some of the older boys who tried to bully her. At the time, I thought she was pretty old although she couldn't have been much over twenty.

    At recess and noon we usually played ball. At first they were reluctant to take me on either side but after they found out I could hit a ball into the creek, which was a home run, I didn't have any more trouble getting into the game. The teacher would often play along with us. She would pull her skirt above the right knee to make it easier to run. This brought laughter when her skirt would also ride up her left knee. When it became too cold to play, the boys would go up into the hills above the school and sit under the overhanging cliffs while we ate our lunches. We would gather leaves and sticks and burn them to keep warm and always managed to keep our clothes from catching fire and would come back to school smelling of smoke. The teacher was good-natured about it and didn't mind so long as nothing happened, although she warned us to be careful.

    At Christmas time, a program would be prepared in which everyone had a recitation of some kind while the parents and community friends would beam in approval. I was usually given a small part that I could handle, but could never take part in the dialogue depicting a Christmas story, or in the group singing. Sometimes I was asked to stand in with them so I wouldn't be left out entirely.

Norma Morrison, my teacher at
Benton Creek School from 1932-1934

Ruth Morrison, my first grade teacher in 1927 and my eighth grade teacher 1934-35 at Benton Creek School

The second year found me in the sixth grade and with the same teacher. By this time I had found a niche and was accepted by everyone but was still the source of an occasional whispered comment. It was not necessary to give me any special favors although there were times when I had to ask for assistance. An incident involving lipreading came up one day. It was customary for the teacher to read out the words from the spelling book and we were to write them down as received. She would wait for me to look up before proceeding on to the next word. The spelling part was of no concern as I could spell any word that I had seen a few times. The difficulty came when she would give out the words and I couldn't understand what she said. After struggling through class sessions for the better part of a month, I found a way which I thought would make it easier for me to get the words and take the strain off the teacher. I would write an abbreviation of the words lightly on the top of the desk or inside my hand or any place I thought wouldn't be noticeable. I did not think this to be cheating since I could spell the words. It was getting them that was hard. For instance, for "automobile" I would write "car"; for "electricity" I would write "light." This worked out fine for some time. One day while in the process of correcting the papers, I saw the teacher looking at me from her desk in the front of the room with a half-quizzical and half-sympathetic look on her face. She was discovering what I had been doing. Instead of giving out the words in order as she usually did, I had not taken into account that she might mix the words and give them out at random. I had them written down in order. She came and asked me how I had done it and I told her. I showed her the writing on the desk and she realized there was no cheating involved. From then on, she would sit with me while she gave the words out and if I didn't get one, she would abbreviate it herself for me. She was wonderful and I loved her for the way she was helping me.

In the fall of the second year back on the farm, a new sister came into the family. Since the tragedy in Detroit, we had missed having a sister around, and now one had come to be with us. Wilma should have been spoiled as an only sister in a family of boys usually is. However, the unpleasant turn of events over the years had adversely affected our parents. The easy-going life we had known before going to the city was no longer there. The Depression had left its mark on everyone's lifestyle. Families were frantically trying to regain what they had lost. The struggle for survival had taken its toll. Regular farming activities could no longer serve as an economic bulwark. Something unrelated to field production of crops had to be undertaken in order to supplement what farmers could get at the marketplace for what they had produced. Like many of our contemporaries, it was decided to raise chickens. It was necessary to build new houses to hold them. We usually had about two thousand chickens in various stages of development during the year. I could remember the sounds of the chickens and would sometimes sit in the pens and watch them, trying to imagine how they would sound from the way their mouths were opened or closed. I could imagine the clucking, ruffling of feathers and the early morning call of the rooster as he signaled the beginning of a new day.

A new brooder house had been constructed below the house across the road. There were about three hundred chickens in this house that had progressed from being baby chicks to pullets. Just before they were due to start laying eggs, they had to be transported to another larger house back across the road on a hill above the house. They had to be moved in darkness so as not to excite them too much and that meant carrying them three in each hand by the legs. I hadn't yet regained full strength and with my erratic equilibrium, this was a disagreeable task. Before constructing the house, we had a dance on the concrete floor and Raymond would roller skate on it.

The farm machinery and electric power plant offered an abundance of incentives to learn the mechanics of their operation. I became adept at disassembling the gasoline engine which kept the large glass storage batteries of the low voltage electrical system charged; cleaning it, grinding the valves and whatever it took to keep it operating properly. This brings to mind an incident that came up involving my deafness. Besides us, our grandparents and the Fred Morrisons, Norma's parents, were the only ones in the area with electric power. Before the trip to Detroit, a thirty-two volt plant was purchased as mentioned. It was a General Motors product called a "Delco." One day Grandpa Gus came over and said that their power plant wouldn't start. He wanted Leonard to come fix it but Leonard wasn't home. I told him that I fixed ours and could do the same job Leonard could, but he insisted. At that point, Mom told him that there was no reason I couldn't do it. He finally agreed, and I went over to work on it. After about two hours, I had taken it apart and cleaned the valves and had it back together and running. He gave me fifty cents. I went in and told Grandma that he had given me only fifty cents and he always gave Leonard a dollar. She asked him why he hadn't given me a dollar and he said, "Aw, he's deaf." She made him give me a dollar. Once when Mom was alone on the farm, the plant wouldn't start and she tried to start it. She never knew how it happened but an electric arc hit her wedding ring and burned it in two, badly burning her finger. She wore her mother's ring that had been given to her when Grandma died. Many years later, Dad had the ring repaired for their fiftieth anniversary.

One Saturday in mid-March of 1934, my older brother Earl, who was graduating from St. James High School that year, wanted the car to go to town for the afternoon. Our dad said no, that he needed the car to go to Steelville for Benton Creek School business. He was the board president. Earl started cussing and Dad told him to shut up and go and hitch up the team to the manure spreader and clean out the stables. Leonard went to help and I was up in the manger laughing and making Earl madder and madder. I was saying, "Ha! Ha! Ha! You want to go to town to see your girl and Pop won't let you have the car. He's making you pitch horse shit." The stalls hadn't been cleaned all winter and straw was put in each evening. By now it was soggy and dripping. First thing I knew, he was throwing a pitchfork full directly at my face, and it hit squarely. I told him I was going to tell Pop and he said, "Go ahead and I'll give you another face full." I told Dad about a month before he died at the age of 93. He said, "I never knew about that." I said, "That's because we never told you."

One of our neighbors, the teacher's father, Fred Morrison, had a large flock of sheep. Occasionally, upon the birth of twins or even triplets, a ewe would disown one of the lambs. When this happened, the one left out would have to be bottle-fed by hand. Mr. Morrison once gave me a male lamb that I named "Buck" and looked forward to feeding each morning and upon returning from school in the evening. After a few weeks, he no longer needed the bottle and ate regular feed and grass. He was very gentle and I would wrestle with him and chase him around. As he grew to almost normal size, he became very beautiful with thick wool. I planned to shear him when the time came and sell the wool for some extra money.

One evening, after returning from school, I looked for him but couldn't find him. Upon asking Mom if she had seen him, she told me matter-of-factly that Dad had taken him into town and sold him for needed money. This was the first of a series of disappointments brought on by my parents in their ignorance of the needs of a deaf child, which I gradually came to accept. The shock of losing the one diversion in a lonely world was difficult to shake off and I cried for several nights.

During the winter months most of the ponds, which were numerous in the area, were frozen over and became popular gathering places for skaters. There was an especially large one across the river on land belonging to a neighbor, Fletcher Beezley, who allowed us to use the area any time we wanted to and often brought his skates down and joined us. To get to this pond we had to cross the hog trough type bridge over the Meramec. The bridge consisted of two half troughs tied together with not-so-secure planking and which ran across the river about two feet above the water. The entire contraption was made of hand-hewn logs. Pilings of more logs had been driven into the bottom of the river to bedrock. The water wasn't deep, perhaps three feet at the deepest under the bridge. The troughs were narrow, being just wide enough for an auto wheel. When the spring rains came with the resulting floods, the river would rise about fifteen feet and would invariably wash the bridge out. After the water had receded, the farmers would gather and put it back together, usually with troughs hewn from newly fallen logs to replace those lost in the flood. When going to the pond to skate at night, it was necessary to catwalk across the bridge. With my shaky equilibrium, I had to crawl the sixty-odd feet to the other side. This brought laughter and ridicule from the group, but I was becoming used to being laughed at and didn't mind. We had to walk the half-mile from the bridge to the pond through open fields since the road went in another direction. I had difficulty keeping my balance on skates. The skates were of a clamp-on type and kept falling off. I lashed them on with straps and was able to keep them on long enough to tire myself out. The walk home in the dark, including the crawl back over the bridge, left me exhausted. I had not yet regained my full strength since my bout with meningitis. We usually arrived home around midnight and had to go to school the next morning.

    Mornings during the winter months were filled with the usual chores that were made more complicated by the cold. We would be up at about four and one of the first orders of the day was a trip to the outhouse. At four in the morning with the mercury hovering around zero, this was an ordeal which, like other unpleasant things relating to early farm life, we accepted and became used to. Cows had to be milked, which fortunately was not one of my duties, and chickens had to be fed and watered. The droppings boards in the chicken houses had to be scraped, with the residue being collected into a metal tub for spreading on the garden. After most of the chores were completed, we would go in to a breakfast of ham or sausage and eggs, fried potatoes, hot biscuits and gravy. After that would come the trip to school.

    During the long winter evenings there would

usually be lengthy family discussions after the evening meal. Talking would be animated and everyone except myself would join in. I never knew what they talked about and no one took the time to tell me. On the few occasions when I would try to join in or ask an informative question, I would usually be cut short with an abbreviated answer or none at all. I gradually withdrew and gave up all attempts at participation and found whatever I could to read. There was very little reading material in the house. Although I had asked several times for a subscription to one of the St. Louis daily papers which were available in the area for only four dollars a year, I could never convince my parents how much it would have meant to have a daily paper to read each evening. The news coming over the radio was never repeated to me. I lived in a world of my own imaginings. I would learn what I could from bits and pieces of information I was able to pick up at off times. My younger brother Raymond would at times tell me of things he had heard discussed. I would become curious and ask Mom for more details. Sometimes she would tell me what I wanted to know but more often she would become angry and berate my informer for telling me things that she didn't think I should know or wouldn't understand. One diversion in winter was trapping. I had about six steel traps and would walk around them before school. They were down by the river and I would catch a variety of fur bearing animals. A lot of opossums, some muskrats, skunks and beaver. Dad would skin them for me. It wasn't unusual for several farm boys to come to school smelling of skunk. Henry Williams would ship my furs along with his to the Funsten Fouke Fur Company in St. Louis.

As I have mentioned previously, we had the 32-volt electric system put in just two years before we left for

Detroit. The renter of the farm didn't want to fool with it, so the large glass batteries went dead over three years and new ones had to be put in after we returned. That meant that Mom could have a clothes washer and refrigerator, a great help and relief from all the work she had to do. The batteries, ten glass jars a foot high, eight inches deep and four inches wide were available at that time only in Sears Warehouse in Kansas City, Missouri. This was 1933. They would have shipped them to us but Mom's Aunt Tillie Fesslabend lived in Kansas City and Mom hadn't seen her since before her marriage so we drove up in Wayne's panel truck, the forerunner of today's van. We stayed two days and the first night had a delicious beef steak supper. Beef was something we never had on the farm, so we really enjoyed it. When we were finished, Aunt Tillie motioned to me and I thought she said, "Do you want some more?" I said, "No, thank you." Everyone laughed because she had actually said, "Did you have enough?"

      Summer months were generally more bearable and less lonesome than those in winter. There were more diversions and more time in which to do them. We had the old Model T Ford that would no longer run. I proceeded to take it apart piece by piece. I used the chassis to make a cart that was powered by a blind mare, old Flora. I would use it to haul water from the river for the chickens during the months when the regular supply would diminish. In later years we had an electric water system. Hauling the two heavy water-filled fifty-five gallon drums up the long steep hill from the river must have been harder for the mare than I thought at the time, but she did not complain. Sometimes while driving up the middle of the narrow road leading from the river, a car would come up from behind and I never knew how long they had patiently waited before I would finally think to look around and pull over for them to pass. After a few instances of this nature, I would drive on the edge of the road so there would be room for a car to pass. A deaf kid driving a blind mare was probably a source of discussion and laughter in the area.

In the evenings we would go to the river to wash off the day's accumulation of sweat and grime from the fields and work with the chickens and gardens. We would gamble that no traffic would come by and would not bother with swimming suits. One night we were busily cleaning ourselves when a lone car came around the bend. We all ran for the underside of the bridge until it had passed, but before it was over, I had bumped into a wasps' nest in a corner of one of the cross members of the troughs and several of the wasps got mixed up in my wet hair. The result was a swollen scalp and a very severe headache for the rest of the night. After these trips to the river, we were glad to get back and into bed. There was no insulation in the house that had a sheet-iron roof, so the upstairs rooms were none too comfortable even with the windows open. We had become as used to the heat of summer as we had to the cold of winter so the seasons were accepted in stride.

Often on summer weekends the members of the community would gather in the clearing at the river crossing, which was shaded by huge cedar trees and enjoy a respite from the week's toil. Baskets of food would be brought and spread on boards supported by saw horses. Ice would be brought from town and several freezers would be put to work making ice cream. Later, we would go swimming along with the water moccasins. After a lazy afternoon, an appetite would have been worked up and everyone was ready to eat again. After the tables were cleared and things had quieted down later in the evening, songs were sung and there would be guitars and violins. I would sit and watch and wonder at how things would be if I had been able to continue the violin lessons I had started at St. Clair School in Detroit before everything had so suddenly and swiftly changed.

     One day in mid-summer when I was about fifteen, I had gone to the orchard below the house to pick blackberries. I had a large pail and was standing barefooted in waist-high grass and undergrowth. The large plump berries were a luscious deep purple. I was so absorbed in picking and eating almost as many as found their way into the pail that I lost all caution and moved forward from time to time to get at the more ripened berries. Suddenly my foot landed on something round and moving violently. Terrified, I looked down and saw to my horror that I had stepped on a copperhead. The undergrowth was too thick for the snake to coil and strike. It thrashed around while I got the hell out of there, paying no attention to the briars which were tearing my pants to shreds and lacerating my legs as I ran. An incident of like nature occurred a few years later. The electric water pumps were not operating so it was necessary to carry drinking water from the stone spring house at the foot of the hill. After dipping the two large pails into the spring and watching the water ripple for a few minutes, I turned to leave with the filled pails. I stopped petrified when I found the door blocked by a copperhead coiled in the middle of the doorway. It was spitting and flicking its tail menacingly. I backed into the far corner of the small building that had no windows and screamed for help. No one heard me from inside the thick walled stone building that was several hundred yards from the house. I hoped the snake would become tired and leave but after an hour it was still there. In desperation, I decided to do something to get out. Taking one of the pails, I edged closer to the snake, which was still coiled but in a more relaxed position. Throwing the filled bucket with all my strength on top of the snake, I jumped over it while it was writhing about and ran to the house. Dad went down and killed it with a pitchfork. As time passed, I found it more and more difficult to walk about the farm after dark to do the chores. Being unable to hear warning hisses, I never knew when a snake would be in my path, resulting in stress and depression.

My last year at Benton Creek School went well. We had the same teacher for the term that I had started first grade with before we left for the city. The teacher's name was also Morrison, a cousin of some sort of the former one and the transition was made after the first one had married. Dad was President of the School Board and he had some nutty idea that married women should not be teachers. He was afraid they would not be able to finish the term if they became pregnant. The year was a pleasant one and Ruth Morrison did everything she could to help me. I was fortunate in being able to ride the bus to school the last two years at Benton Creek. Wayne was the driver and the bus was an old Chevrolet. The bus went on to high school in town and I was dropped off on the way. I arrived an hour early. I would unlock the door, sweep the school and take out the ashes from the large stove in the center of the room. Afterwards I would carry in a supply of wood and start a fire and have the room warm before the teacher and the rest of the students arrived. At year's end the teacher showed her appreciation for my help by giving me five dollars. She was paid one hundred fifty dollars a month. She had been able to give me individual attention that year since I was the only one in the eighth grade. Instead of calling me to class in front of the room, she would sit with me in my wide double desk and we would go over the day's assignments. This arrangement removed the strain of reciting and I looked forward to the personal sessions. She taught me many things and was a very patient person. Toward the end of the term, we made the usual preparations for a program that was to be given on the last day of school. I had no class of my own to prepare for so I was asked to help the lower classes assemble the material they needed for their particular parts. Each member of one of the classes was to hold up a large rose on the back of which was a letter. At the conclusion of a short recitation, each was to turn the rose around. Ultimately the group was to spell the word "VACATION."

     I was asked to draw a large rose to use as a model. I selected a beautiful rose from a seed catalogue and proceeded to enlarge and copy it in detail. After several trial starts I produced what I thought was a perfect outline and was very pleased with what I had accomplished. The rose was about eight inches in diameter and had a long stem with several leaves. I took it home that evening and planned to draw in the petals and color it red with tiny white streaks like the one in the catalogue. I was very proud that I had been asked to do this. I knew that all the people coming to the last day's activities would be there to see it. I was doubly proud since it would be my Graduation Day. That night after supper, I immediately left the table and went to where I had put the rose and started working on it. Before I had gone far, Mom asked that I clear off the table and wash the dishes. I did not think it fair for her to ask me to do that since no one else seemed to be doing anything at the time and I was anxious to finish the rose. I told her I wanted the rose finished so the class could start making others the next morning. She became angry and insisted that I do as she asked. I continued working and was horrified when she grabbed the rose from me and tore it in half and, opening the top of the wood-burning heating stove, tossed it in. As she closed the stove, I could see from her changed expression that she was immediately sorry for what she had done. I was too numb to protest so I washed the dishes and went up to bed. The next morning I told Miss Morrison I had dropped the rose in the mud and ruined it and that I would make another one. That evening Mom helped me finish it. Nothing was said about the previous night.

Graduation Day came in March. School was out early in the rural areas so there would be help in the fields when planting time arrived. Completing the Eighth Grade was still considered an accomplishment. I was excited during the last few weeks preceding Graduation. J. H. Brand, the County Superintendent came to school and gave me an examination that was required over and above the final examination administered by the teacher. It was a rather long test that had kept me after the regular closing hour. When it was completed, the Superintendent smiled and nodded that everything had gone well and drove me home. On the last day of school there was the usual program depicting the year's events along with recitations and songs and, of course, the skit with the roses. Finally the teacher gave a short speech which I never knew the contents of and presented my diploma. I was proud when I walked to the front to receive it. Everything else was forgotten, including the cut-down suit that Mom had worked on for me. An uncle had left the suit at the farm.

In spite of the coat being too long and there being a patch on the seat, made from material taken from another part in the process of altering but which was effectively covered by the too-long coat, I was very proud of it. Besides being my Graduation suit, it was also the first suit I had ever owned and the last until I was given a new one for graduation from high school.

My eighth grade year at Benton Creek School, 1934-35
Back: Nola Jean Lay, Evelyn Morrison, me, Edna Michael, Pearl Talbert; *Middle:* Beryl Talbert, Robert Talbert, Betty Jean Morrison, Alma Lee Morrison, Carl Lay
Front: Raymond McCann, Junior Talbert, Harvey Everheart

St. James High School

The summer months that followed were hectic. There was the usual work on the farm and my mind was in turmoil with prospects of entering high school in the fall. Though I had done well in grade school, I felt my handicap would keep high school out of reach. I told the family I didn't want to go. I prayed over and over that my hearing would return before the day arrived. I harbored the hope that my hearing would be restored as mysteriously as it had left. As the time for school to open drew nearer, it was discovered that problems had arisen within the town's School Board. Although my brothers had gone to school there, the Board was reluctant to accept me as a member of the student body. This school was St. James High in St. James, Missouri,. It was here that I began to more fully realize that I was different. It was the Board's open display of rejection that instilled a growing feeling of inferiority that ultimately developed into a determination to succeed. In the end, it was Mr. Potter, the Principal, who came to my aid. Mr. Potter was also the coach. He had taken the St. James Tigers basketball team to two state championships and the board didn't want to lose him. He had said, "If that deaf McCann kid can't go to school here, I will be leaving." He had an invitation to become the principal and coach in St. Louis at Riverview Gardens High School. He told them of his confidence in my ability. In light of his intervention, the Board reluctantly agreed to allow my entrance. In view of the Board's skepticism, I secretly hoped I would not be accepted. I thought of the possibilities of going to a school for the deaf. The old fears that had haunted me before entering Benton Creek had come back to torment me. I dreaded the coming of the first day, but the inevitable hour arrived and we were on our way. Arriving at school, I went directly to Mr. Potter's office as I had been told to do and waited. I watched the clock on the wall as it crept closer and closer to the time for school to start. I dreaded going into class and having to look around the silent room full of totally strange students. I had never experienced anything like this before and continued to watch the clock as its hands moved silently to the time when classes would begin. Mr. Potter still hadn't arrived at his office and I became concerned that he hadn't been told I was waiting for him. I wondered what the consequences would be for being late to class on the first day. I wondered if I had been mistaken about being accepted for enrollment. Through the open door, I could see kids rushing through the hall and realized that it was time for classes to begin. I wondered if I should ask someone what I should do, but then I was afraid that if I left the office and the Principal came in and found me gone, he would be angry. My palms became sweaty and my throat was dry. I had never been in such a position before. I felt as though I had to go to the bathroom but was afraid to do that since I would have to leave the office. Suddenly he walked in. I had never been alone with him before and having read stories about high school principals, I had no inkling of what to expect. He came to where I was sitting and spoke to me.

      Mr. Potter was a kindly man, perhaps thirty-two, with blonde wavy hair. He was about six feet three and always had a broad grin on his face. I suddenly remembered that I should be standing and abruptly rose to my feet. He held out his hand and I was startled that the Principal would want to shake hands with me. He said he was sorry to be late but that he had been talking to assembly and wanted to introduce me to the classes I would be attending and that time had run out on him. I immediately felt more at ease and followed him into Mr. Hodge, the Superintendent's office. I had a feeling of awe at being in the presence of these two men. They talked among themselves for a moment, then turned to me and asked some questions which I answered. They asked how I had lost my hearing and where I had gone to school. After telling me the names of my new teachers and what they would be teaching me, they smiled and continued talking together for a few minutes. I realized later that they were giving me an opportunity to show how well I could communicate and apparently they were satisfied. I was taken by the Principal into each classroom and he in turn introduced me to the teacher and students. He explained my handicap and said that I would need some assistance and he hoped they would give me the help I needed. Most of the students smiled and appeared to be friendly, although there were a few who appeared skeptical as though wondering how a country kid who couldn't hear anything would be able to keep up in class. I was taken to the study hall and introduced to the study hall teacher whose job it was to keep order and help with assignments. He also taught Economics and Math. Mr. Cahill expressed a willingness to help me and later, after we became better acquainted, would fill me in on the usual gossip going around the school with notes punctuated with sage advice. By the end of the first week I had become well oriented with schedules and procedures and was accepted academically.

   I was friendly with a senior girl, Wanda Beezley, who would spend summers on her grandfather's farm near ours. She would often write out long notes about happenings at school and bring them to me and sit in a vacant seat across from mine. One day while I was reading an especially long one, Mr. Cahill came back and asked me to give him the note. After looking it over, he handed it back and looked embarrassed. Wanda laughed and said, "You see what comes of being nosy. Why don't you mind your own damn business." He laughed and left.

    Having been the first deaf person to attend the town's high school since the school's founding, I became somewhat of a celebrity. I use the word "celebrity" not in the usual sense of one possessing grandeur, but as one who was different. It didn't take long to become well known in the small town. There were those willing and anxious to help. There were others who looked upon me as a freak. It was the latter group who avoided me whenever possible, and if I were to speak to them, they would stare at me without answering or simply turn and walk away. I was fortunate in having teachers who were willing to help and who appeared to show genuine interest. I believe, in retrospect, that they were learning as much from me as I was from them. They would discuss an occurrence relating to something they had discovered in working with me. Since they had never before been in contact with a person unable to hear, I could feel their amazement each time they called upon me and realized that I could understand the spoken word without benefit of hearing. I was fortunate to have the same five teachers all through the four years.

    Mr. Potter would come to my desk frequently in study hall and keep me informed on class assignments and make suggestions relating to reading material. One morning, shortly after the start of school, he came into the study hall and motioned for me to come into his office. As I was leaving my seat, I noticed that all eyes were on me and I was curious as to why they should be watching as I followed him. Entering his office, he asked his secretary to leave the room and closing the door, motioned me to a chair. Sitting on the edge of his desk, he unsmilingly passed a piece of paper to me. I at once recognized its contents and turned a deep shade of red, then just as quickly replaced that color with a chalky white. The weekend before I had come across a piece of wit which I decided to take to school. After passing it to one of the boys in class, I had forgotten about it. It was not of a lewd nature but was nonetheless gross. Apparently it had found its way through the student body and into the Principal's hands. He had traced it to me and asked if anyone in the school had given it to me. When I replied in the negative, he asked where I had gotten it. I told him it had been given to me by a cousin in another town and he suggested it would have been much better to leave it in that town. He looked at me silently and with disapproval for an uncomfortable lapse of time. Finally, he asked if I would ever do such a thing again while in school and I assured him I wouldn't. He appeared disappointed and had a hurt look in his eyes. Finally, he straightened up and seeing that I was on the verge of tears with remorse, he broke the silence and said he could not permit a repetition of the incident and would hold me to my promise that it would not happen again. A faint smile came to his face and his eyes lost their unfriendly glint and their usual twinkle returned. Saying the incident was closed, we returned to study hall. The significance of this session has remained and served as a psychological turning point in my outlook. He demonstrated that understanding and forgiveness are more effective than vengeance and punishment.

Any misgivings I had harbored in the beginning and

fears that had plagued me were lost after a few weeks following the opening of school. Class assignments were not difficult as long as I studied the texts and understood what I was reading. My prime concern was in class recitation. I was not sure of my speech and tended to talk so softly and fast that my readings were unintelligible. Speech therapists were unheard of and anyone with a speech defect simply lived with it or worked it out by himself. Mrs. Bohon, the English teacher, realized that my conversational speech was acceptable but that I could not control my volume when before a class. She was understanding and could see that it was difficult to stand in silence and talk to a group not completely in sympathy with the problem, and who could laugh at the slightest provocation. Her solution was to explain to the class that my handicap made it difficult for me to read essays and she proceeded to read them for me.

  During the noon hour, my freshman class would sometimes go over to the grade school a couple of blocks away and play ball with the eighth graders. Bud Kirgan was the captain of our team and one day he chose me to play. One of the players protested that I couldn't play because I was deaf. That brought an angry response from Bud and he said that if I couldn't play, we would go back to school. Bud was much like his dad, friendly and helpful. One evening after school I was walking down the street, the bus wouldn't be there for an hour or so. I met Bud and his brother Pete and he asked my why I didn't go see a movie while waiting. I told him I didn't have any money. He reached in his pocket and gave me a quarter. I said I would repay it and he said, "No, I'm giving it to you."

  Basketball games were the highlights of entertainment during the school year. It was a diversion I could enjoy without hindrance. I was happy at the games. Afterwards couples would go to the Atlasta, a favorite gathering place on the edge of town. I would ask some of the girls to go with me but none would. Finally at midterm one of them, Helen Biles, agreed to go to a game with me. I was excited, since it was the first date I ever had. The bus was to remain in town until after the game and would pick up the riders later in the evening. The afternoon before the game, Wayne had come into town for a load of supplies and livestock feed. It was late winter and the roads were bad. He planned to come back into town that evening for the game and had stopped at school to pick me up and take me home for supper. I didn't want to go as I was afraid something would happen and we wouldn't be able to get back in time. I was too embarrassed to tell him I had a date so I decided to go home and come back later. It was an eighteen-mile trip one way on unpaved roads. The truck became mired several times from the late winter thaws. We arrived home late but with yet time to return to town for the game. Wayne had become discouraged with the roads and decided against a return trip. I begged him to change his mind, arguing that the roads wouldn't be as bad with an empty truck. I couldn't tell him I had a date and began crying. The family couldn't understand why missing a game would affect me so adversely. This missed date was the first and last I was to have during the four years in high school, although a family friend, Virginia Hale, agreed to go with me to the Senior Prom after getting her parents' permission.

  From the beginning of my high school years, I was able to find the time, here and there, to make friends of some of the merchants. Wilma and Dwight Edwards had opened an auto parts store, the Western Auto Associate

Store, at about the same time Dwight was drafted into the Army. Wilma was able to keep it going alone for the years during the war, and after his arrival home, they opened a much larger store and had a branch in Rolla. I would always find time to stop by and they found time to talk for a while. As they grew older they retired from the store and Wilma opened a gift shop, which she still runs. Laura and I always stop to see them when in town. Another place I liked to find time to spend time was the service station owned by Herbert Dewing. We became good friends and he would fill me in on the happenings around town. He once told me to speak louder and not so fast. He was killed in an automobile accident at the age of twenty-eight on New Year's Eve of 1940. The entire town closed for the funeral. In the next edition after his funeral, Bill Ruggles, the owner and editor of the St. James Leader, included his and most of the townspeople's sentiments in the following.

The little green service station with the orange trim
Isn't quite the same as it has been.
There's something missing when you go there now.
It's the man who never frowned because he didn't know how.

Just prior to my beginning the second year in high school, it was announced that school transportation into town would no longer be available from our area that was geographically in another district. Although licensed, the thought that I might drive into town to school each day was unheard of. I fervently hoped a solution would surface which would enable me to continue as before. As the time for school to open drew nearer, it became apparent that I would have to transfer to Steelville High. It was necessary for Dad to take me for a conference with the Superintendent, Professor McIntosh, a graying gentleman who readily agreed to my entrance. There was no hassle with the Board, as we had the previous year, so the transition went smoothly.

Mr. Brenton, the Principal, was also my advisor, and in later years we became friends during his four terms as a member of the State Legislature. It was Mr. Brenton who taught me the proper pronunciation of meningitis. My brother Raymond who worked as a state official was familiar with happenings in the various branches of government. He said that Mr. Brenton had a nickname of "Mr. No" because of his refusal to accept bills that he did not approve of. The teachers at Steelville High were unfamiliar with my problems and were unable to cope, being totally unlike the ones I had before in St. James. They made no allowances for my shortcomings and ignored my inability to hear. Although it was extremely difficult to fit into the curriculum, I was able to make a passing grade. The school bus went by the house each day so transportation was no problem. I looked for an excuse to drop out with the intention of reentering St. James the following year. The break came after several weeks when I discovered that my parents were in arrears on payment of the bus fare which amounted to a dollar a week. I used this as an excuse to quit school for that term. The bus fare was later bartered with some freshly butchered meat.

The remainder of the year was spent on the farm. I had some textbooks that my brothers had used and spent my evenings poring over them. Perhaps the fact that I was able to give these particular books so much attention could be attributed generally to a lack of anything else to read. It was during this winter that a new brother, Howard, joined the family. At the beginning of the following school year I was fortunate in finding a family who let me live in their home in return for after-school work about the premises which allowed me to return to the former school.

The Campbell Home

The family consisted of a middle-aged couple and their daughter. The father was away from home during the week attending to his business in St. Louis and help was needed around the large spacious house. Their daughter, Dorothy, was also attending high school. I was fortunate in having the same teachers as during my first year. The students with whom I had started were now a year ahead of me and I found it rather difficult to make friends with the new group as easily as I had with the class two years before. However, in time the difficulty passed and I was able to form a rapport with the majority. Work about the grounds and the chickens kept me busy most evenings. I was happy to have the opportunity to earn a place to stay and was eager to finish my work and return to whatever homework had to be done. The Campbells lived on the outskirts of town necessitating a long walk each morning and evening and in between at noon when I returned for lunch and to feed the chickens. Mrs. Campbell was a calm woman who rarely became angry. She was a sister of Walter Miller, the manager of the Farmers' Exchange. She spoke with an air of firmness. She expected people to do as she asked but was very understanding in most areas. Whenever they had guests, I would eat in the kitchen, although at other times I would eat with the family. For the most part, things would run smoothly. Earl Taylor, another student, also lived there.

One evening I was returning to the house around six o'clock and in passing the high school, I noticed a group of what appeared to be my classmates in a small parkway beside the school. There were tables and chairs and I could see them eating ice cream and cake. Although a distance away, I could see that most of them saw me as I passed by and seemed to grow quiet in their activities. The next morning at school, some of them appeared to have a guilty look, but nothing was said about the evening before. They were all friendly enough in school, but I had only one or two friends on the outside. I came to take this as part of a deaf world.

At the beginning of winter, Mrs. Campbell told me one morning that it would be necessary for me to find another place to live as the family had decided to move to a farm they owned several miles from town. She suggested that I stay with a family which had recently moved into St. James and which was currently in the process of organizing a retail auto parts store. She had made their acquaintance and had approached them with the proposal that I would be able to help around the store in return for part of my keep. Jim and Mabel Banks lived next door to the store, which made the situation convenient. They accepted me as part of the family and I enjoyed the comradeship that they displayed and which had up to that time been virtually nonexistent in my world. My parents helped with some of the living expenses, however, I was unhappy with this arrangement. I felt it was an imposition on them and one that I should in some way alleviate. During midterm I decided to attempt to make extra money.

On weekends at home I would dig around in the garden for horseradish roots which were usually left in the ground during cold weather and would grind them up and prepare them as my parents had done in Detroit. It was difficult to find enough jars on the farm for the finished product but this shortage was solved by selling what I could and asking the customers to save their empty jelly and pickle jars for me. In this way I was able to earn enough money to meet most of the year's expenses. I thought I could do even better if I were to make up a large lot and take it into St. Louis with Wayne on his trips into the city on weekends to sell eggs. My first attempt was successful. I promptly sold all I had brought with me in the immediate area of the boarding house where two of my brothers lived along with several other young men. I became ambitious and decided to try for bigger stakes and made up an extra large batch. When the owner of the boarding house saw that I was planning to make more frequent trips into the city for the purpose of selling horseradish, he told me I would have to pay for the time I was staying at his place. I had been going under the assumption that I could use up the time which my brother was not using and eating meals which he was not eating while he was at home on the farm preparing for another load of produce. However, other ideas took precedence and after deducting what I owed for the time I spent there, I found it was more than I could make in the two days. This realization brought a swift demise to my first business venture in St. Louis.

It was after I had been in high school for a while that I discovered there was another deaf fellow in town. Henry Hughes was a young man who could neither speak nor read lips. He used the sign language but there were only a few in town for him to communicate with, although I could make some signs that he could understand. He was also the butt of some crude signs. His brother Arthur was a year ahead of me in high school. He was a shoe repairman and had a reputation for doing good work. As he became older, he was a volunteer fireman for many years. Upon his retirement, the town had a ceremony for the fire department in the Louis J. Donati Auditorium and awarded him a plaque for outstanding duty. His brother interpreted the service for him. It made him very happy and proud.

Shortly before the opening of school for my third year, I had a letter from Mrs. Campbell asking that I consider coming back to live with them again. They had finished building a new home near where they had lived before. Dorothy had dropped out of school to be married so her mother was alone and needed help with the house and grounds. Mr. Campbell still spent the weekends at home after taking care of his business in St. Louis during the week and would try to accomplish something worthwhile during his short stay, but it was generally something that he would start and leave for me to finish. During later years I came to realize how frustrating life must have been for the mother. It was due to this and possibly other subsurface circumstances that made it difficult to understand her varying moods which resulted in strained relationships and injured feelings. She would appear to be happy when their youngest son Alphonse, or Al, would make infrequent visits home. I enjoyed those visits as well. Earl, my brother, and Al were good friends and I would sometimes see Earl at the Campbells' home in St. James while I was living there. I remember one evening when Al and his dad surprised Mrs. Campbell with a new Pontiac. They had sold the Ford. Sometimes they would go to visit Al's sister Dorothy and her husband Paul Hoff in Rolla for the night. Their friendship lasted up to the time of Earl's death in April 2001. I had written a long letter to Al when Earl died. He answered with a welcome letter. He had been a Lt. Colonel in the Army and his wife had died a number of years before after more than fifty years of marriage. He told of how much he misses her and how he was able to get through it with the help of his daughters. He is the last of a family of five boys and one girl. There was Emory, Edwin, Lee, Clarence, Alphonse and Dorothy. I knew them all before they started passing away. The Campbell boys and Dorothy were all popular in town in younger years. Edwin, or Eddie as he was known, had an orchestra for many years and later became a chiropractor.

The home was situated in a densely wooded grove known as the Campbell Grove. It was fun to burn fallen leaves in fall and clear the undergrowth around the trees. Squirrels and rabbits were abundant and it was common to see a neighbor's dog chasing a rabbit through the snow in winter. There was a large fireplace in the living room that necessitated felling trees for fuel. I had learned the use of a double-bit woodsman's axe on the farm and enjoyed cutting whatever trees were necessary in order to keep an ample supply of fireplace wood on hand. Chain saws were, at that time, unheard of so the work was tedious but rewarding. There was more to be done at the new home than there had been at the first house. The chicken house was much larger than what they had before and more time was needed for cleaning and feeding. Perhaps it was because of the change in environment that made living in the Campbell's home the second time more unrewarding. Mr. Campbell seemed to be in a difficult mood on his return home weekends and there appeared to be an impasse which never seemed to right itself. An added burden in the arrangement appeared early when Mrs. Campbell informed me one Friday morning that it would be necessary for me to come to town early enough in the mornings on Monday to dispose of the chores before going to school. She had been attending to the chickens and adding coal to the furnace on weekends, but she said that in the future she expected me to take care of this on Monday morning the same as during the rest of the week. I was also asked to stay Saturday mornings so that I could help clean the house and do the laundry. I asked if this extra work would mean that I would be paid a small amount and she became indignant. This had become upsetting to the schedules at home on the farm. It became necessary to get the chores finished an hour earlier on Monday and necessitated a trip to town on Saturday morning at about noon to get me. On occasion, I elected to walk the eighteen miles home in order to save the family an extra trip to town.

There were only two bedrooms in the house. A corner of the new basement was made into an extra bedroom, used to accommodate guests and family members who visited on weekends and which became my room while staying there. I was happy with the arrangement, but could sense annoyance when Mrs. Campbell would have to come down and wake me each morning, a situation that I decided to eliminate. With some crude switches and an old key-wind alarm clock, I was able to rig up a contraption that would turn a light on when the alarm went off. A long extension cord terminated at the end with a large bulb attached to my hand, with a stocking slipped over the bulb. The bulb nestled in the palm of my hand and the stocking was tied around the wrist with a handkerchief. The resulting heat from the bulb woke me promptly and at times it was a race to remove the stocking before it burned my hand. Everything went well until one morning I awoke to the smell of burning cotton. I was horrified to find that I had removed the light in my sleep and laid it aside where it burned a hole through the sheet and into the mattress. I tried to cover the incident by hiding the sheet and sewing a patch over the hole in the mattress, but when Mrs. Campbell asked me one morning about the missing sheet, I decided to tell what had transpired and took her down to show her the damage. She appeared angry at first but when the true significance of what had happened dawned upon her, she seemed unsure whether to laugh or cry. She regained her composure and told me I could not use the light in that fashion again. She was glad the damage was minor and she was grateful the house had not caught fire. From then on I hung the light from a hook in the ceiling directly over my head, which worked very well. In later years, she and I would laugh together over these incidents when I would go back to visit them.

Once someone gave the Campbells a beautiful dog. It was a cross between a chow and a police dog. From the beginning it barked at night but they thought it would become accustomed to its surroundings and calm down a bit. After more than a month, there was no change so Mrs. Campbell called the town marshal to take it away and destroy it. He refused to do that and then she asked me to do it. We borrowed a twelve-gauge shotgun from a neighbor and I took it out in the woods. It took a while for me to get up enough nerve to shoot it and to this day I can see its eyes as I pulled the trigger. I shot it again to be sure it was dead and then I buried it. I have never since killed any kind of animal.

The last year of high school was uneventful. I had taken a second year of Bookkeeping and Accounting in addition to the regular curriculum that included Typing. I had written to Miss Muller, the class sponsor, regarding subjects. She was vacationing in the north woods in Canada. She said she would help me with Physics and said that she thought Chemistry would be out of the question because of the many details that I would miss. Homework was extensive. By the time I had completed the chores and homework assignments, I was usually ready for bed. As

Graduation time drew near, there was the usual excitement and exchanging of graduation name cards. I imagine there had been numerous parties although I never knew of any with the exception of the class banquet. The usual class day exercises started with little excitement on my part. Mr. Potter was making announcements and giving awards. I wasn't paying much attention until I was elbowed by Tony Mingo and told that Mr. Potter wanted me on the stage. At first I didn't believe it but when I looked up, I was surprised to see a motion being made for me to come. Walking a bit unsteadily from the sudden excitement, I approached the stage wondering why he would ask me to the center of attention. After a short speech, which he was careful that I understood, during which he said that I had attained a very good average grade, he presented me with the annual Scholastic Medal of Achievement. I protested that I did not feel I had earned it, but he smilingly assured me that the Senior Class had voted that I receive it. It represented the second highest honor in class. The highest, the Medal for Citizenship, went to Bill Cowan the class president for all four years. On graduation night, announcements were made naming the recipients of the year's various awards and medals. I was very proud.

      I have always considered Mr. Potter and Mr. Donati as mentors. Mr. Donati and I had always included personal messages with our Christmas greetings until two years before he died. Laura and I had gone to visit him in the nursing home at Rolla about a month before he died but he was out that day and we left a note. He wrote us a letter thanking us for coming and added that he wasn't used to the present accommodations and expressed a hope to be able to return to his home in St. James. I have never been able to call Mr. Potter and Mr. Donati in any way except as

Mr. and Mrs. Charles E. Potter,
coach and principal during my high school years
at St. James High School.
Taken at high school reunion in 1969.

Professor and Mrs. Louis J. Donati,
taken at my class's 50th reunion in 1990.
Superintendent of St. James High School, 1948-1978

"Mr." Most people in town called them Ed and Louie. My decision to call them "Mr." was not based on formality, but a feeling of deep respect that I had always had for them and still do. While co-owner of Arcy Manufacturing Company, I presented a business-type desk to Mr. Donati while he was Superintendent. He was very proud of it and mentioned it at the fiftieth reunion banquet. He had taken it to his home upon his retirement as superintendent.

The fact that I was able to attain high grades throughout my four years in high school was due directly to the faculty's ability to recognize my need for assistance. Besides being the first deaf student the school had ever admitted, I was also the first deaf person the teachers had ever made contact with. Their performance was exemplary. They would not visibly go out of their way to help me but I could sense their recognizance of the need and it was offered at the crucial moment. In the beginning I would sit with another student and as long as general lectures were in progress, I could glean enough to be able to follow the subject. This was fairly easy since I had studied the texts several times and knew what was to be discussed. The difficulty arose when it came time to take notes. I would attempt to copy off my seat-mate, but it was a laborious and trying process as the one being copied off of would often skip parts of what was given or would miss it entirely. At times I would merely pretend to be writing, then after class would ask someone for their notes in order to copy them, but ran into the same obstacle as I found when trying to copy in class. It did not take long for Mr. Donati to recognize my need. He realized the importance of my being able to get the notes as they were given out. He would motion for me to come to the front of the room and sit at his desk. As notes were given out, a finger would be on the one in question and I would copy it off his notebook. Most of the other teachers had various methods of their own which were brought into play whenever they could see that I was having difficulty. Mr. Cahill, the Math teacher, would become exasperated with some of my solutions in his arithmetic class. He told me once that I had arrived at the correct answers in all of the test problems but that he was at a loss as to how I had done it and asked me to please do the problems in a more acceptable way in the future.

I want to add that there were two girls in my class that helped me more than they would know. Maxine Steen was the daughter of the custodian who incidentally was at the door each morning to greet the students. She and her brother Merle were especially friendly and that more than most other things was a big help. Laura and I have seen Maxine and her husband frequently over the years. Maxine and Bill had a party for us when we returned from out trip through the west and California. Many that I had known in high school had since become friends. The party was at their beautiful country home north of town. The other girl was Davene Williams. She would often come over to sit with me in Study Hall and we worked subjects together. Davene was the high school band Drum Majorette and was beautiful in her red and white uniform and jaunty hat. She has said that I helped her pass Algebra but I don't recall much of that course. Her father owned a variety store in town and I was always welcome to stop by to talk with him. Davene married Bud Kirgan, the fellow who insisted I play ball and he is the son of Marshal Roy Kirgan, the man who later did a lot for me of a legal nature. I still exchange correspondence with Davene and Bud occasionally besides seeing them at five-year reunions and occasionally inbetween.

The principal was also in charge of Accounting. Although I had devised my own ways of solving arithmetic problems, I was able to follow the rules of Accounting and enjoyed the work. A few weeks after graduation, tentative arrangements were made for me to enter a business college. Mr. Potter, the principal, felt that I had the potential to become a C.P.A. and he thought the work would be compatible for one with my handicap. Mr. Potter and Mr. Cahill had made the arrangements on their own that I enter Springfield Draughon College and made repeated trips to the farm to talk with my parents. I hoped for a way that would enable me to go to college, but I knew that Dad wanted to build a new barn to replace the one lost by fire a number of years before. In light of other obstacles that were obvious during the years of the Great Depression, I decided my entrance into the school was not feasible and knew further education was out of the question at that time.

Mr. Hodge, the superintendent had included along with our diplomas a poem that offered a great deal of inspiration and which has stayed with me to the present day. He wrote:
> You have each been given a bag of tools,
> A shapeless mass and a book of rules
> And each must make ere life has flown
> A stumbling block or a stepping stone.

I cried on graduation night. After going to bed, I lay thinking over the past four years and found it hard to believe that I was a high school graduate and that I had earned honors. Commencement Day purportedly commemorates a beginning, but all I could see after the excitement of the last days of school was a dark and uncertain ending. The thought of going out into a strange silent world amongst strangers and seeking employment having no idea what I would be able to do or where I could find work left me in a state of depression. I was looked upon as being different and knowing that others thought of me in this manner left me with a renewed feeling of inferiority.

    A few weeks after graduation, the family had gone to a funeral home to see a cousin who had died. I was sitting across the room from Dad and some of his friends. I looked up in time to see Dad motioning to me and saying to the people grouped around him that I was one of his boys and that I was deaf. Arising from my chair I turned and left the room not caring to remain for anything further. Dad was especially guilty of tormenting me in this way. I realize that he had no intention of hurting me and that he was merely stating a fact as he knew it to exist. His total ignorance of what he was accomplishing was frightening. On another occasion he and I had gone to a distant farm to buy a load of baled hay. I was in the hayloft with the owner of the farm helping pull the bales to the front for transferring to the truck. I was telling him an instance of how something had happened in the past, whereupon Dad interrupted and said impatiently that I was deaf and that he shouldn't pay any attention to me. The farmer became embarrassed and smiling uneasily motioned for me to resume the work at hand. Burning with frustration, I finished loading and, climbing down from the hayloft, went to wait in the truck while Dad settled for the hay. The trip home was made in silence. I wanted to say something that would help Dad to see what he was doing to me, but decided that anything I could say would be accepted in the wrong way so just kept quiet and hoped the situation would one day improve.

    Later in the summer our great-aunt Minnie came to

the farm for a few weeks. She was a vivacious talker and one of her favorite subjects was her late husband, Uncle Albert Zinke, and his shoe repair shop which had remained in the same location in South St. Louis for a quarter century. She would ramble on endlessly of how he had repaired shoes for a goodly number of St. Louis' famous people including the Mayors. She would tell of how he enjoyed talking to them when they came in to pick up their shoes. One evening after supper, after the dishes had been cleared from the table, she was relating these tales of yester-year. She was sitting across from me and would wave her hands while describing her late husband. I was enjoying it all immensely. Suddenly Dad came in and interrupted and told her she was wasting her time talking to me as I wasn't able to understand a word she was saying. She became flustered and lamely finished a sentence she had started and turned her attention to Dad. I was on the verge of tears and could only lower my eyes and ask myself why life must be as it was. After tracing patterns with my finger on the floral oilcloth table cover in the dim light from the kerosene lamp, I went up to bed.

    On another occasion, the family was eating Sunday supper when my brothers hurriedly finished and dashed upstairs to change. A singing revival was being held at the Benton Creek Schoolhouse and they were anxious to go. Finishing my meal, I started upstairs when Dad asked me where I was going. I told him I wanted to go with my brothers. He sarcastically reminded me that I was deaf and that he didn't think I should be going to a singing program and he thought I should stay home. Being too numbed with hurt to protest something that I knew to be true, I went to my room.

Rehabbing the Farm House

The summer before finishing high school was spent in its entirety remodeling the farmhouse. While not as challenging as future construction of the barn would be, it opened up many avenues of learning which were in themselves a degree of sophisticated education. The house was originally constructed of logs somewhere around the turn of the century. Additions had been built by Johnny-come-latelies and the result was a crude abode which provided shelter but little else. The floors were of oak boards worn smooth by years of scrubbing and use. Cracks were covered in winter with straw and this in turn was overlaid with rag carpeting tacked around the edges. The resulting insulation afforded a surprising amount of warmth. Heat was provided by a large woodburning stove that stood on a square metal-covered board. Sparks would occasionally pop out of the small draft door at the base and would require extinguishing by stepping on them. How the house survived as many winters as it did is amazing but not surprising since this was a way of life and dangers were accepted as the norm. This stove was the cause of a terrible accident one winter when Frieda was two years old. The stove was fastened by quarter inch bolts to the four legs that supported it. Mom was in the chicken house and I was watching Frieda. Suddenly one of the bolts broke, the stove fell and the teakettle on the stove fell into the crib beside the stove scalding her middle and legs. I ran screaming for Mom. Dad was in the fields. Uncle Harry happened to be there that day with the car and they took her to town to Dr. Henderson. She had terrible scars resulting from those burns.

    The remodeling project consisted of laying new

The farmhouse after total rehabilitation in 1939

The farmhouse after further rehab added a guest room on the corner in 1945. My parents in the yard on their last day on the farm before retiring to Cuba, Missouri, in 1968.

tongue and groove floors over the existing ones and adding new windows and doors throughout. New electric wiring was installed and the log walls covered with insulating board. The exterior was shingled and in general the house took on a look of decency and livability. I reduced the size of the back porch by half and constructed a half bath, in this case meaning a tub and wash basin. Lacking a sewage system, the outhouse survived several more years. It was about twenty years later that I decided to devote my weekends to trips to the farm and enlarged the room sufficiently to accommodate a toilet, installed the necessary sewer pipes and put in new plumbing and a water heater. I also completely wired the house for electricity. The REA had brought in the new 110-volt system and the 32-volt system was discarded and new wiring was needed. It was at this time that I decided to add a new set of kitchen cabinets. Although happy and with a feeling of accomplishment at the culmination of the summer's work, I was glad to see it end and again return to school.

Trip to California

That fall, shortly after the beginning of my final year in high school, Wayne told me one weekend that he was planning a trip to California to the World's Fair. The year was Nineteen Thirty-Nine. He asked me if I would like to go along, but since I had already started back to school I felt that taking off a month would put me to a disadvantage and make it difficult to catch up. I discussed the problem with Mr. Potter and he said there would be no difficulty and that he would help me to make up anything necessary in order to bring me up to date and he said it would be an advantage for me to make the trip. I asked Dad if he would give me money for the trip and he assured me he would. Plans were made and all preparations taken care of. We were to be accompanied by a neighbor friend, Arthur Howald. The Sunday for departure arrived and the car, a two-year-old Chevrolet, was loaded. Mom had prepared a large amount of food for us including canned goods, several loaves of bread and an entire smoked ham. Dad had not yet given me the promised money so immediately prior to departure I asked him for whatever he had decided to give me, whereupon he reached into his wallet and gave me *five* dollars saying it was all he had. Not knowing how much the others had between them and being too dumbfounded to tell them what I had before we left, it was several hours later at a rest stop that it came out that we possessed a total of eighty-five dollars. I thought Dad would give me about forty dollars but since he didn't, I told them that if we could make the trip on what we had, I would pay them back later out of any money I could make. Since gasoline was only about ten cents a gallon and we had provisions for camping out at night besides staying with friends and relatives along the way, we fared well and arrived back in Joplin, Missouri, a month later stone broke. After spending the night with them, our Uncle Bill gave us ten dollars for the remainder of the trip, a distance of three hundred more miles.

The California trip had been an interesting and educational one. On the way out, we came upon a meteor crater in Arizona. Arthur Howald and I decided to explore it and asked Wayne to come along. He decided to wait for us. It was much deeper than we had thought and was nearly a half-mile across. The temperature was over a hundred degrees and it took over four hours to get back out. Our exploring days were over. We spent two days in Yosemite Park and marveled at El Capitan, which at that time had no trees to block the view.

While in California we spent some time with Russell Bell who was working in the vineyards of his Aunt and Uncle, Dolly and Arthur Balch at Fresno. The grapes were cut in bunches and thrown into a galvanized steel tank on a large truck. Usually it would take a day to fill one truck, with several people picking in the hot blazing sun. They would set overnight and be on the road to the processing plant by four in the morning. It was about noon before the load could be dumped since about two dozen trucks were lined up waiting their turn in the hot sun. Russell helped us climb up the side to the top of their truck tank before it was to be dumped. By this time, the entire top of the load was covered in maggots, which were included in the fermenting of the grapes.

Returning to Los Angeles, we drove around a lot and went past several movie studios but couldn't get in. We spent an afternoon with Emory Campbell and his wife, the oldest son of the family I would be staying with in St.

James while going to high school. After leaving Los Angeles, we went up to the Fair at San Francisco and stayed in the area for four days. We stayed with a friend we had known in Detroit, Wilma Bodenbach, at San Rafael and spent time on the bay. Wilma was my age and we had played together in Detroit. She had always been feisty and the first morning at her place in San Rafael, she put salt in the sugar bowl and waited anxiously to see my reaction when eating my cereal. It was in San Rafael that I learned about ocean tides when one came back swiftly and caught me up to the knees.

At the fair we saw Sally Rand, a famous fan dancer of the time. We also saw our first television. After a few repeated trips to the fair, which cost only twenty-five cents to enter, we went on to the Redwood Forests and Muir Woods. We have a picture of Wayne and Arthur Howald sitting on the car in the hollowed out redwood. Several years later, the tree fell. On the return trip we stopped in Las Vegas for a night. At that time Las Vegas didn't amount to anything in the way of entertainment. We found a small cabin for the three of us for the night for one dollar. At about three in the morning, Wayne heard someone knocking on the window. Pulling back the blinds, he saw three girls. He asked them what they wanted and they said they would stay the rest of the night for fifty cents each. He told them no and they said twenty-five cents apiece. The answer was still no. That was our first experience in Las Vegas. I have often wondered if the decision not to let them in was solely related to the lack of money.

In Colorado Springs we decided to drive up Pikes Peak. In those days cars didn't have the kind of cooling systems we have today and there were water faucets about every mile on the way up. By the time we stopped at one, the radiator was boiling and we had to wait for it to cool a bit before adding water. We were driving a 1937 Chevrolet in 1939. This brings to mind my Uncle Harry Riefenstahl. He was one of the last to get a new Chevrolet in 1941 before the government forced them to stop production for the war. He and his wife, Aunt Inez, and her sister, Hazel Bell, and brother, Bud, made a trip out west in 1942. They went up Pikes Peak as we had in 1939 but for some reason he let the car overheat badly and ruined the motor. When they got home, he sold it. It still looked like a new car. He found some kind of old car, which he drove for a few years. It was in 1945 that he found a 1941 like the one he had before. The motor was good but the body was in bad shape. He took it to Oscar Schebaum in St. James who painted cars on the side. I drove him down to get it and asked him why he hadn't put a new motor in the good one he had before. He looked like a deer caught in the headlights and said, "I never thought of it."

    The months on the farm following graduation from high school were unbearably lonesome. While in town I was surrounded with motion, things moving and people to talk to. In contrast, only an occasional car passed the farm and days would go by before one would stop. Neighbors would drop in from time to time, but only for a moment to inquire about something and then leave. I could not use the phone or listen to the radio or hear the natural sounds of the farm animals. There was nothing to read except old copies of papers that occasionally found their way to the farm. I would write to girls I knew in town. Although they would not go out with me while we were in school, I thought perhaps that since I had graduated with honors their attitudes may have changed, so I wrote asking them out. Out of maybe a half-dozen, only one answered, declining.

This situation is related to one regarding a student in high school. Emil Saroch lived about three miles south of town and although a school bus went by his home, he didn't have enough money to ride it so he walked the distance each day through all four years of high school. Often he was the butt of jokes about his clothes and chopped up home haircuts. He graduated with a high rating in 1936 and entered Annapolis where he graduated with honors. The town of St. James paid for some new clothes and the two-way ticket for his mother to attend the ceremony. He became the commander of a ship during the war.

My brother Wayne, (on right) and friend, Arthur Howald, in Redwood Forest, California, 1939.

My First Job

Shortly after graduation I was visited by a neighbor and family friend who asked that I assist him in his annual operation of shearing sheep for farmers in the surrounding areas. Mr. Cain was middle-aged and lived with his sister and brother-in-law. He was generally available whenever a farmer found that he was short of help. He possessed a manually operated shearing machine. Hand operation was necessary since electricity had not yet come to many farms. The agreement was that I furnish the farm truck for transporting the equipment and getting us to the job sites; he was to furnish the machine and do the shearing while I cranked and took turns shearing. We were to split the fees equally. It was a dirty and greasy job. His nephew, Arthur Howald, had helped him for several years until being drafted into the Army. A sheep is protected from the weather not only by its thick fleece but also by an additional layer of lanolin on the skin. Our clothes became saturated with the smelly oil within minutes, but since it was all part of the work at hand, we accepted it. It was my first real job and I was making money and I was proud. We were in constant demand as we were the only sheep shearers in the area. The work lasted through June. As happy as I was to have employment, I was glad to see it come to an end before the hottest part of summer arrived. Handling greasy wool in hundred plus temperatures can become a most unpleasant task. The summer months were spent in the fields cultivating the crops and harvesting hay. The work was performed with teams of Missouri mules as I have mentioned previously, and it was generally a tie as to whether man or mule did the greater amount.

One of the distant neighbors had purchased a large

threshing machine powered by a huge steam driven tractor. He would go from farm to farm threshing oats and wheat. All the neighbors would follow him to help each other, and large dinners were prepared by the farm women. No money was involved as all help was voluntary and the owner of the equipment took his pay in a percentage of the grain, which he sold. Some farmers who had no grain would volunteer to work in return for the large dinner.

      It was during my first summer of helping that I met Rev. Watson Thornton at his farm. He had been a missionary to Japan before coming to our area as a minister. He would hold Sunday services in the Benton Creek schoolhouse and there were carry-in dinners afterward. We became close friends and would talk a lot about his travels. He would never accept money for helping a neighbor and was loved by everyone. He was instrumental in helping me to accept my handicap and did much in leading me to have faith in God.

Building a New Barn on the Farm

That fall saw the beginning of the new barn. Mr. Cain, also a skilled stone mason, was hired to help Dad with the foundation work consisting of twenty-inch thick walls of stone-faced concrete, three feet underground and rising ten feet into the air. All he wanted was a dollar and a half a day and his dinner. Variously hued flat sandstones were for the taking alongside the road. They had been blasted out with dynamite when the road was built the year before. Gravel was hauled by wagon from the river. The actual mixing of concrete was done with a gasoline-powered mixer that performed erratically but served to lessen the labor involved. The Louden Machinery Company in Iowa had furnished a complete set of blueprints. In return, we were supposed to buy a hay hook from them but we never did. We got it from the Farmers' Exchange at a lower price. The dimensions were thirty-six by fifty-six feet, a size arrived at in order to accommodate a hundred tons of processed hay. The structure atop the massive walls consisted of green oak timbers that had been cut off the farm. Having completed the skeletal framework before winter set in, we left it exposed to the weather until spring with the result that the seasoned oak developed tremendous strength before installing the channel steel roofing. Since money was in short supply, it was decided to eliminate the customary weather vane-topped cupolas that adorned most barns of this type. I was able to convince the family that I could make them if I had the materials so it was agreed that extra sheet steel be purchased along with the roofing. Using a picture from a Sears Roebuck catalog as a guide, I set about constructing a full-scale replica from cardboard. When I was satisfied with the design, I spent every evening after farm chores had been finished working on what I was confident would be a beautiful finished project. Using the only tools available--a pair of rusty snips, a hacksaw, a hand drill and blowtorch for soldering--I was happy that I had something to fill my need for a challenge. Tinning flux was made by dissolving zinc jar lids in muriatic acid, and I discovered that by designing and building the cupolas with a free hand I was laying the groundwork for what was to become a way of life as the years passed.

      When Dad realized that I was capable of designing and fabricating my own ideas and when he saw that the results were fully acceptable, he let me go ahead and do what was needed to complete the barn using what materials we found available. The heavy twin haymow doors were a real challenge. Each one was fourteen feet high by six feet wide and weighed several hundred pounds. After constructing them and obtaining the necessary help in hoisting them to the top of the barn, a distance of approximately forty feet, they would open and close with one hand. Lacking the necessary weights, I decided to use stones. I selected a goodly sized stone that I thought would be appropriate and secured it to the heavy ropes. However, I found it too heavy so I proceeded to chip away at it until the balance was sufficient to hold the doors in place but which would allow opening and closing them with a slight tug on the ropes. I was happy and satisfied with what I had accomplished and pointed with pride whenever visitors came to the farm. The new barn was a great improvement over the old one, although my lack of hearing played a part in the operation of the hay fork. We had always had to put hay in the loft by hand, pitching from the wagon to the loft. In the new one, we had installed a hay fork which had a

My father and I loading hay in the new barn using the hay fork.

The cupolas I made atop the new barn.

track attached to the top of the loft. The hay fork had four "arms" which were pushed into the load on the wagon and the team had been unhitched from the wagon and hitched to the rope from the hay fork which went to the other end of the barn. On signal, the horses would start up, pulling the hay which by now was taken up by the hay fork and lifted to the top of the barn. When it had rolled back far enough, a trip line was pulled, releasing the hay. When Dad gave the go-ahead to the horses, they were to stop when the signal was given to pull the trip line. I had fashioned a rope on the trip line so that I could stand at the side of the barn and pull it when Dad said to, but I didn't always see him, resulting in the load of hay going back too far. My last summer on the farm, we stored one hundred tons of hay in the loft. Dad had meticulously recorded all monies spent on constructing the barn. The total for those depression days was twelve hundred dollars.

Central Institute for the Deaf

In desperation for companionship, I wrote to an agency for the deaf in St. Louis. They responded promptly and suggested that I write to the St. Louis League for the Hard of Hearing. My spirits rose and I felt that perhaps at last I had found an avenue of relief and wrote asking for information. I received an immediate reply from the social secretary. A young lady, Ann Marie Rich, herself deaf, wrote that a party had been scheduled for the next Saturday evening and she was insistent that I come. A feeling of excitement and relief passed through me as I felt sure that I had found an answer to prayers and that friends would soon be found. I arranged to go into St. Louis that weekend with Wayne on his egg truck. The evening of the party was in early summer. The group had gathered on the patio at the side of the League building, which had previously been a residence in a well-to-do area, Westminster Place. Lanterns were hung and a soft breeze was blowing through the overhanging trees. I found it difficult to realize that I was with people who shared my handicap and that they were to become my friends. The Committee arranged that we all wear name tags so as to facilitate introductions. After becoming acquainted, we went downstairs to the game room and played games and in general had a very enjoyable evening. I was sorry to see it end as I knew that, like Cinderella, I would be going back to a world of reality and that the evening's memory would fade. I was determined that there would be other evenings and that I would see my new friends again soon. This was to be the beginning of events that were to culminate in my leaving the farm. This was where I met Ann Marie Rich and Russell DeHaven. We have remained friends to this date.

The summer passed swiftly. I had not seen my new St. Louis friends since the party although Ann, the secretary, and I corresponded almost weekly. She kept me up to date on what was going on in the group's activities and she made me feel as though I was already one of them. I had never before had a feeling of belonging so her letters were an inspiration. I lived for the time when I could join in the regular weekly meetings and explored every available avenue of possible employment in the city. Life on the farm was becoming more difficult with each passing day. I felt trapped. It was as though I was living in a glass enclosure where I could see out and watch things in motion but with no sound coming to me or with no outstretched hand offered in encouragement. I repeatedly asked my parents to subscribe to one of the St. Louis dailies so I would have something to read at the end of the day, but they steadfastly refused to do so. The mailbox was a mile away across the river. I would often run over at the noon hour after I knew the postman had gone, and sneak the paper from a neighbor's box and read as much as I could before returning home to dinner. The neighbor, Mr. Bell, would sometimes come to get his mail while I was reading his paper and I would refold it and give it to him. He never appeared to mind and would often drive me home.

One day in early Autumn Dad and I were finishing some work on the roof of the new barn. I was on the ridge forty feet in the air when I suddenly lost my balance. Although I tried to grab hold of the ridge cap, it was too late and found myself sliding down the steel roof off the edge and into a pile of leftover stones thirteen feet below which had been used in constructing the walls. Dazed, I tried to rise but momentarily couldn't move. In the meantime, Dad had scrambled down to come to my assistance and helped me to my feet. I felt a stabbing pain in my left side that necessitated a trip to town to the doctor. Examination revealed several broken ribs and a highly nervous state. The doctor advised that I take a couple of weeks rest. In retrospect I realized my condition was not a result of work but was an outgrowth of emotional suppression. I decided to go into St. Louis to stay with my brother Leonard and his wife, and looked forward to being able to once again see my recently made friends. I had saved some money from the sheep shearing venture and felt that I would be able to relax and enjoy my stay in the city.

In her letters Ann had frequently made reference to a private school for the deaf located near her home. Some of her comments were antagonistic and critical because sign language was not permitted. I was curious and one morning boarded a bus for the long ride from the county where my brother lived into the inner city. After a number of transfers and having no idea where the school was located except that it was on South Kingshighway, I got off the bus at what I thought should be the approximate location but found that I was too far south. Not wanting to spend more money on bus fare, I decided to walk the three or so blocks to the school. Walking into the lobby, I was impressed with its formality. A lady came out of the front office and asked some questions. She was rather old with her white hair piled on top of her head. I later came to know her as Miss Taulby, a retired teacher. It was difficult to understand her. After several attempts to get through to me, she wrote out the message, which was "Are you deaf?" I laughed and asked why she would ask me that when I had had so much trouble understanding her. Another lady, Mrs. Sharp, the secretary, took me into the office of Dr. Lane, the principal. This was our first meeting and my first

Central Institute for the Deaf,
818 S. Kingshighway Blvd., upon my arrival in 1941.

(Courtesy of Central Institute for the Deaf)

Helen S. Lane, Ph.D., CID Principal 1941-1972.

(Courtesy of Central Institute for the Deaf)

experience with a Ph.D. I had never before known a woman doctor and was a bit confused. She was very warm and friendly although aloof in a strange way which I eventually discovered was par for professionals. My teachers in high school had always been strict when necessary but at other times they were friendly, never aloof. They knew how to hold the line between friendliness and familiarity and I learned it early. It didn't take long to learn at the beginning of my association with professionals that the air they possessed was a bulwark against familiarity. It was recognized at once that I had a speech impediment that she felt would respond to therapy and asked if I would like to take lessons at the school. I replied that I would but that I had no money for private lessons. She laughed and told me that by coincidence their dishwasher had quit that morning and said that if I would like to take the job she would arrange that I have two private hour-long speech sessions per week in addition to my room and board. No money was involved. I became excited and assured her that I was interested and asked for an extension of two weeks so that I could finish some things I had started on the farm. I knew in my heart that once having left, I would never again return to the farm to live. This was the beginning of what was to become my long association with the Central Institute for the Deaf, which was to culminate in disappointment fifty years later.

My arrival at the school opened up an entirely new life and afforded a fresh outlook. I had come into St. Louis with Homen Marshall on his daily trucking service. Leonard had taken me to the school at about nine in the evening. Mrs. Beulah Guseman, the head of housekeeping and mostly everything else, met me and took me to a room and made the bed for me. I was naïve enough to think she would be doing that every day, but I learned fast. Chores in the commissary were unpleasant and tedious. There was a machine that washed the dishes but each piece had to be hand-dried. There were perhaps one hundred in the dining room for three meals each day. Each person had a full setting consisting of two forks, a knife, two spoons, a cup and saucer if coffee was served, two glasses--one for milk and one for water, and a dessert dish, in addition to the regular plates and serving bowls. Pots and pans in the kitchen had to be done before the meals were served and this necessitated being on the job by seven in the morning. The heat from the machine would break an average of ten glasses a day but Mrs. Guseman, the supervisor over the kitchen and custodial help told me that the previous dishwasher had broken twice that many and a lot of other things besides. By the time each piece had been washed, dried and put away it was almost eleven in the morning and time for the maids to take them out again and start setting the tables. It was also time for me to attend class at eleven on the Tuesday and Thursday mornings assigned for my speech sessions. Besides the dishwashing, there were the large garbage cans that were emptied three times a week by a St. Charles hog farmer who used the garbage as hog feed. They had to be scrubbed and set out in back of the kitchen to air out. This was before the advent of garbage disposals and plastic can liners. Every other day the kitchen floor had to be scrubbed. The dishwashing chore had to be started again immediately after dinner which kept me busy until four in the afternoon. Supper dishes were somewhat less and I usually finished up by eight-thirty. Thursday afternoons and evenings were free as well as every other Sunday all day. Sometimes the school valet, Henry Keener would relieve me for perhaps a half day. On one of these half-day relief times, I decided to explore the neighborhood. About two blocks from the school I passed a small florist shop, The Euclid Flower Shop. I stopped and walked back to admire the window display. The owner, Arnold Kriemelman saw me and stepped out to say hello and introduce himself. I went inside with him and met his wife. That was the beginning of a friendship, which lasted until their deaths. The lived a few blocks away on Forest Park Avenue and I was welcome to drop in to see them at any time and was often invited to eat with them. They had two boys and a lovely daughter all under ten years of age. After our marriage, Laura and I spent almost every New Year's Eve with them. At our wedding reception, they furnished all the table flowers as a gift.

In spite of the long hours and demanding work, I was happy in my surroundings after the many years of virtual confinement on the farm. When I was through in the evenings, I would go into the school lounge and become acquainted with the college students. Some of them were reluctant to talk to me and I sensed it was because I was deaf and a part of the commissary staff. I felt that perhaps I shouldn't be in the lounge in the first place, and from some of the looks I received from my supervisor, I decided that my out-of-place feelings were justified but I kept on going as often as I could.

I had never before experienced the deep feeling of happiness that I found in just being able to talk with girls. All college students were of normal hearing. It was here that I developed a friendship with one that had endured over the years. Norma Allen, a college student, had the duties of keeping the office open in the evenings and answering the phone, but she always had time to talk and told me many things all of which I devoured eagerly. She spoke of her parents and especially of her father who was a Captain in the Army during the war years. Her home was in Muscatine, Iowa.

Norma was the first real friend I ever had. She was sympathetic and a good listener. We talked endlessly. Although I asked other girls in the college to go out with me later on in the year, I never asked her to go out. We were content with our conversational rapport and I came to love her for what she was. She graduated the following spring and on the day she was to leave school, I ran several blocks in the rain to a drug store to buy a bottle of "Evening in Paris" perfume as a graduation present. I arrived back at school just as she was getting ready to leave. When I gave her the gift, she cried and kissed and hugged me and told me she would miss our long talks and that she would write. After her marriage, we continued to correspond regularly and would exchange pictures and long letters at Christmas time. She passed away after more than fifty years of friendship. I had become friends with her parents one summer after her marriage while driving through Iowa. They asked that I return some weekend for a longer visit. A Christmas card from them asked that I come for New Years. The day before I was to leave, an ice storm came, but I was determined to go. I was driving the new DeSoto and had chains on it so I made the trip without incident, although I could see electric lines falling beside the road. New Year's Day, Norma's father, Mr. Allen who was president of the First National Bank there said he wanted to go to the office for a while and asked me to go along. After going through the bank, we came to the vaults. He opened one and asked me to come in. I suppose I felt a bit honored with the bank president taking me into the vault, which appeared to have perhaps several million dollars arranged on shelves. After spending the day and night and after a very memorable visit, the ice was melting and I had a better trip home.

Being a college student in training to become a teacher of the deaf, she was my first verbal contact with anyone displaying an interest in helping me to fulfill my need for social adjustment. The college students received their training at the Central Institute's college, which was affiliated with Washington University. Norma would talk to me and accepted me as an equal. After leaving school, her letters to me were warm and personal but uninvolved. Among other things she would keep me informed on her progress as a teacher and would discuss some of the problems and obstacles that cropped up in her work from day to day. I realized many things from her letters, which had never occurred to me, and things which others would never think to broach, either because of a lack of interest in relaying general subject matter to one assumed incapable of assimilating such information, or simply because of a lack of desire of becoming involved with one known to be different. I have found this negative trait in many with whom I have associated, including those trained to teach or assist the deaf. I realize an extra effort is needed to carry over into a social context after the professional aspects of the relationship have been fulfilled. This not only holds true of professionals but includes laymen as well and is an underlying cause of a deep-seated feeling of not belonging, which in turn leads to a feeling of resentment and inferiority and breeds distrust of those purported to be helpful. This further leads to segregation of handicapped groups. Three years after her graduation, I received an invitation to her wedding in Iowa. I was in no position to attend, but later made her a small beautiful walnut sewing cabinet as a wedding gift. Laura and I visited her and her husband several years ago at their home in Texas. We were on our way home from Houston where we had attended the convention of the Alexander Graham Bell Association for the Deaf. I asked her about the sewing cabinet I made for her wedding many years before. She said that when they decided to move into a smaller place, she had given a lot of things to her two daughters, among them the cabinet. She said her daughter prized it highly. I was glad.

I had been able to form a niche for myself at the school, and while officially I was part of the kitchen staff, I was able to become involved in extracurricular activities which brought me into contact with teachers and office personnel. I feel that it was partly my persistence in broadening my circle of associates that brought the Principal into the kitchen one afternoon.

I had finished with a portion of the dishes and decided to take a break. I was sitting on the counter reading the paper when she suddenly came through the swinging doors. Becoming flustered, I jumped off the counter, and putting the paper aside, began stammering an apology for not being on the job when she came in. Laughing, she assured me it was perfectly all right to rest for a while, and then, reverting to her usual businesslike manner, she told me that she had been getting excellent reports on my work and that she was very pleased with what she had heard. She went on to say that she felt I would be more valuable to the school in another capacity and that she no longer wanted me living in the servants' quarters. She said there was a vacancy and they needed someone to take over the manual training department and serve as a part-time supervisor for the older boys. This would necessitate a move into the dormitory building across the street and would be a general upgrading of my living standards. It also meant that I would be eating my meals in the dining hall instead of in quarters reserved for the custodial staff. I was happy in knowing that I had succeeded, through perseverance and dedication to the work, in earning a promotion to something better, although remuneration remained the same. Part of my duties consisted of taking the older boys to the downtown theaters on weekends and often to roller skating at the Arena. The school paid all my expenses.

  Christmas arrived soon after my move into the dormitories. I had been enjoying my newly found freedom during the days and evenings and especially on weekends. The kitchen work had kept me busy and there was no time to seek out the friends I had made before leaving the farm. The supervisory tasks were of a relief nature and I was required to fill in for regular houseparents during their time off. I had never been off the farm during the holidays since our return from Detroit. School was closed and the children, as well as the college students, had returned to their homes for Christmas. I looked forward to what I thought would be a time of gaiety. However, with the dormitories deserted and the school building quiet as a tomb, I could find little to do except for one lone party at the League.

  On Christmas Eve I went home to the farm finding things pretty much the same as they were when I left. I had harbored illusions of grandeur and thought perhaps the family would accept me differently now that I was living in the city and making my own way. I had become used to the more sophisticated ways at school and had begun to develop a more genteel lifestyle than I had known on the farm. Ties and coats were required in the dining hall and grace was said before each meal. We were expected to say "Yes, m'am", "No,m'am", "Yes, sir" and "No, sir" to those in charge, and any deviation from the straight and narrow usually resulted in a summons to the Principal's office, not for censure but for guidance in what was expected.

      Christmas on the farm that year was strained. World War Two had been declared and conscription had begun several months earlier. Wayne had been drafted into the Army and it was an uneasy time. Earl was to be drafted the following spring. They were home for Christmas but each knew that it was only a matter of time until they would be sent overseas. I had received a notice from the draft board to report to the induction center for a physical but decided that a letter to them would be sufficient to explain my handicap. Return mail brought another letter from them insisting that I report, so I had Dr. Lane, the principal write to them explaining that I was a member of the school for the deaf and that I thought I was exempt from the draft. They were very persistent and wrote saying, in no uncertain terms, that I was to report at a certain date or that a United States Marshal would be sent after me. This board was in our hometown, so I sent the letter to Dad and asked him to intervene. He took the letter to town and showing it to them, asked them what in hell they were doing. Since they all knew Dad, and knew he had a deaf son, they were surprised and asked if I was the one. After assuring them that I was, they told him I would be placed in the proper classification. This sort of thing left me with mixed feelings. While it would be understandable that I should be relieved that I would not be expected to serve in the Armed Forces, I was left with a feeling of inadequacy and inferiority. My brothers and many of my friends were leaving for what they were beginning to realize would ultimately lead to overseas duty.

    Rachel Dawes Davies, the coordinator of the teachers, was a lovely person of perhaps fifty and was liked by everyone she came in contact with. She had a perpetual warm smile that was contagious and she was always available for help when asked. She and Mr. Davies lived just down the street from school. On summer evenings they could be seen walking toward Forest Park, across the street from the school. She usually wore a light flowered flowing dress and a wide brimmed hat. Her husband always had on a white linen suit and bow tie with a Panama hat and white shoes. He usually carried their cat, a beautiful Persian, on his arm. I never knew what he did until the following happened.

    One afternoon after school, I met Mrs. Davies on her way home. She said there was a piece of furniture in the house that needed some work, and she asked me to come to dinner that evening and look at it. Their home was beautiful and contained several antiques. She had prepared a delicious dinner and I felt completely at ease with both of them. After dinner she showed me the piece of furniture in question, a lovely walnut chest that she said had been in her family for many years. One of the drawer bottoms was loose and I told her I would come by in a day or two and re-glue it. She said she wanted to pay me, but I told her it was so minor that I couldn't accept anything for it. We went to sit in the living room and Mr. Davies asked me what my plans were for the summer. I told him that I had done painting for the school the last year at vacation time and that they may ask me to do it again that year. He then asked me if I would like to work at the Curtiss Wright Aircraft Company, a current war plant, making Navy Hell Divers. I found it hard to believe that he asked me if I wanted to work at a place as large and famous as that. I asked him if he thought they would hire me, seeing as I was deaf. He sort of smiled and said "Oh yes they will hire you." I then asked him if he worked there. With a trace of embarrassment he smiled and said he was the president of the company. He said that as soon as my duties at the school were finished for the year to come to the factory and ask for him and he would introduce me to the head of the department where I would be working.

It would be a lie to say I walked back to the school that evening. I floated. I had never dreamed of finding work in a place like that. The Chevrolet plant had been taken over by the government for building the planes.

I explained my intentions to the Principal and she worked out a schedule that permitted me to remain at the school. After returning from work each evening, I was to take the boys to manual training shop after supper and on Saturdays, thereby putting in the same number of hours as I had previously and still having time to serve as a relief supervisor. After about two years working at the plant, the war ended and Curtiss Wright moved to Buffalo, New York. All the workers were offered work with the newly formed McDonnell Aircraft. I decided against joining McDonnell at that time although I did many years later. I remained living at the school teaching manual training and doing various odd jobs until I found other employment.

My speech had been deteriorating steadily since graduating from high school. Loneliness on the farm and a total lack of social life coupled with frustration brought on by the realization over the years that I was deaf and further realizing that chances of recovering my hearing were moot, if not impossible, frequently made my speech incoherent. With the disappointments brought on by each passing day, the hope I held out in the beginning had begun to diminish. There were times when frustration and hopelessness would leave me in a dazed state of exhaustion. I would try to rationalize and whole days would be filled with silent prayer. Prayer was the only thing left for me to turn to since it was impossible to find anyone capable of understanding the horrendous change which deafness had wrought in my life. I was unable to sympathize with anyone who had a handicap that I thought to be less than the one I had to live with. I felt that almost any situation would be bearable if hearing were present. Even the blind were envied since they were not cut off from communication. They could converse normally; they could laugh and sing, they could enjoy music and radio, and use the phone. But gradually I decided that blindness would not be a preferable alternate to deafness no matter how great or maddening the frustration would become.

  I was able to realize that there were different degrees of handicaps and limitations and that no one specific lack need remain as a permanent deterrent if the will to overcome and the ability to visualize were present. In addition to the inner forces destroying my speech, there were circumstances over which I had no control and that infuriated me. Individuals would stop to talk to me and our conversation would be meaningful. Halfway through a sentence a third party would come upon the scene and with no indication of apology, would interrupt and dominate. The one I had been talking to would turn away and give full attention to the new arrival, ultimately ignoring me completely and walking away with the one who had interrupted. Unnerved, I was forced into a desperate try to finish what I had been saying before being interrupted. This led to almost unintelligible speech where the words would run together. I knew others were having difficulty in understanding me so I would lower my voice and hope no one other than the one spoken to would be able to hear me. The result was chaos. Some would pretend to listen to me and nod or shake their head before I had finished, hoping that either an affirmative or negative answer would satisfy me. Sometimes I could accept that and let it go. But there were times I would persist and keep at it until a response was aroused. One happened not too long ago while at a memorial service for a friend. I was talking to the husband of a teacher I was acquainted with. I greeted him and remarked that it was a shame that such a nice person had to go. I then added that two of my brothers had died recently. He didn't even pretend to have understood but instead started laughing and walked away. Those kind aren't worth pursuing. It was at the school that I found someone who really understood the problem. It was Mrs. Davies who explained that I talked too fast in order to say it all before being interrupted.

There are millions of deaf everywhere and only a very small percent are fortunate to attend pricey private schools which teach speech and lipreading. Many of the poorer ones are shunted into state schools or other places where the sign language is taught, although these private schools have scholarships for the deserving, and the rest are left to fend for themselves as best they can in a society totally ignorant of anything they might need for survival. This latter group generally stays out of the limelight and is hidden from view. The sign language is well and good in its place. It has been called the natural language for the deaf, however, it can only be used with other deaf or in the schools that promote it, or perhaps with the hearing interpreters. The deaf have striven for years, even decades, for recognition and as soon as successive generations have assimilated some of the teachings, they will die out and it will have to be done all over from the beginning. As in all things, survival of the fittest will prevail. Some of the passages in this book will appear to be cruel or frightening or both, but they show how a large number of hidden deaf must live. I was one of them until I found a helper and was able to overcome most of it, although memories remain.

It was at the height of this phase of my life that I found the Institute and began a reversal of what had become an impossible situation. The road back was slow and tedious. Progress would be made and my confidence would rise only to be dashed to pieces when the inevitable third party would arrive, which I have found to exist everywhere and has continued to today.

In spite of discouragements, life at the school was fruitful and rewarding. It was generally from the resulting improved lifestyle and newly found companionship that life began to take on more meaning and became more bearable. The realization that I was different was ever present. There was no escaping the hard cold facts of total deafness. The school gave me a feeling of protection and served as a cushion from the constant blows of unacceptance found in the outside world. There was the feeling that no matter how great the disappointments of the day would become, there was always the warmth and acceptance at day's end and from understanding companions. Regardless of whatever shortcomings may have been present, either real or imagined, I could always feel that I would find emotional shelter within the brick walls that comprised the Central Institute.

There are two friends that I have had since they entered the training college at Central Institute in 1946.

Bill Hartwig was a teacher at Central Institute for about ten years when he moved to Columbus, Ohio, and was the head of audiology at the Ohio School for the Deaf. Upon his retirement, he and his wife Betty moved into a beautiful retirement village in Waverly, Ohio. We keep in touch and visit occasionally. The other one is Irvin Shore and his wife Elaine. They remained with the school. He was a teacher for several years and went on to be the head of the audiology clinic. Still later he became principal of the school. Upon leaving the school, he entered the business world for a few years until he and his wife both retired. They live very close to us and we see them often socially. We enjoy them very much.

S. Richard Silverman, Ph.D.
Director of CID 1947-1972

(Courtesy of Central Institute for the Deaf)

S. Richard Silverman, Ph.D.

It was at the school that I first met the man who was later to become the head of the school. He was only a few years older than me. He headed the lipreading department and, as a part-time supervisor, played football with the older boys. Since the death of the school's founder, Dr. Max Aaron Goldstein, a few months before my arrival, the Principal relied heavily upon him for assistance in management. Shortly afterward he became the Business Manager and was looked upon as the one to go to when help was needed. His manner was demanding and it was difficult to misinterpret his intentions. He spoke with decisiveness, firmness and finality. He was respected and, unfortunately, sometimes feared. When approached with a specific matter, he would become concerned, would listen intently, and any advice he offered could be accepted and followed with complete confidence. A few months later he received his doctorate from Washington University and shortly afterward was appointed Director of the Institute by the board of managers. He later became a world leader in deaf education. His name is Dr. S. Richard Silverman. He served as director for over thirty years.

Few other men have had such a lasting influence on my life. He has been critical, and at times almost cruel, but always there has been a lesson learned and an improvement made. He has angered me and disillusioned me, but over the years I have always found enlightenment and progressiveness as an end result of my association with him. Once, shortly after he received his Ph.D. degree, he asked me while in his office about a project he had asked me to do a week or so earlier. I apologized for not having done it and added that I would get on it right away Mr.

Silverman. A bit haughtily, he stopped me and said "It is <u>Dr.</u> Silverman to you, <u>Mr.</u> McCann" and smiled.

One day at Central Institute, the school was host to a group of international electrical engineers. They were having a week long convention at the Chase Hotel and accepted an invitation to use the nearby school auditorium for a day. Dr. Silverman, the director, was naturally in charge. The school was very proud of their ability to teach deaf children to talk and lipread. He wanted to make an exception of me and explained that I had lost my hearing at an early age and he wanted to give a demonstration of how well I could understand and speak. He proceeded to ask me questions and I answered each one. A very professional looking gentleman of perhaps fifty stood up and asked for permission to come to the stage and talk to me. Dr. Silverman asked me if I was in agreement and I told the man to come up. He asked some rather simple questions, then asked one of a smart alecky nature and I replied in kind. He became embarrassed when the entire audience laughed and thanked me and went back to his seat. Later in the dining room where they were having refreshments, Dr. Silverman took me aside and with a scowl on his face asked why I had embarrassed that man. I said I didn't mean any harm and simply went along with what he had said to me. Then Dr. Silverman asked me if I knew who the man was, and of course, I didn't. It turned out that he was the president of the International Telephone and Telegraph Corporation in New York City. I sought him out and told him I wanted to apologize but he laughed and said he had it coming.

Dr. Silverman was proud of his membership in the Cornell University Alumni. In fact, when he bought his first home in University City, a suburb of St. Louis, he chose Cornell Avenue as his new address. He moved to Florida a few years after his retirement. He and his wife Sally had one daughter, Rebecca, or Becky as everyone called her. She is married to Dr. Richard Howard, a transplant surgeon at the University Hospital in Gainesville, Florida. Becky has earned her Ph.D. degree and they have two sons. Dr. Silverman was very proud of his family and would always write a long letter to Laura and me at Christmas time until a year before his death, always signing them 'Dick and Sally Silverman.' He traveled extensively around the world in matters relating to deafness, and could speak perhaps half a dozen languages fluently. I have always treasured the friendship of Richard Silverman. In his world travels, he would always bring a doll from each country for his daughter, Becky. I made a cabinet for them when the number neared a hundred. Becky was very happy with it.

Having known Dr. Silverman since he was in his late twenties, I feel that I am one of the few who have seen him outside of his staid decorum. The state highway department had been widening Highway 40, which separated the school from the research building. There was a fear that the highway would take the research building instead of going around it in a curve, but that's what they did, probably as a result of some stiff urging from powerful school board members, many of whom were lawyers. Another thorn in the side of the Institute was a pedestrian bridge across the highway connecting the two buildings. When the road was originally built about fifty years before, the new road divided the school property and the state had erected a steel covered bridge over what was then a two lane highway. When the new four-lane highway was put in, there was much indecision about the feasibility of building a footbridge of that length. An overpass half a block away could be used by pedestrians, although there was no doubt it would be a great inconvenience to the Institute personnel. I was with the aircraft plant at the time and hadn't been following the progress. One day I was driving down the street from the school at noontime and saw Dr. Silverman walking up from the hospital where he sometimes went to eat lunch. (The rest of the time he carried his lunch in a Snoopy lunchbox.) He saw me and waved for me to stop. He was in a jovial mood and I asked about the bridge. He was elated when he told me that they had won and that the bridge was to be put in. He laughingly said that they had gone to sleep in a pile of horseshit and had woken up smelling roses! It was one of the times that he and I could drop our seriousness and laugh together.

It wasn't long afterwards that I was driving through the area of the bridge on the way home from McDonnell at about two in the morning. I was rear ended by an eighteen wheeler loaded with new cars driven by a drunken driver. The blow from the rear end crash had damaged my sacro joint and after thirty years I still have pain and difficulty walking. I sued for twenty thousand dollars. The case dragged on for three years and finally came up in federal court since the man who hit me was fired and left the state.

The trial was held in the court of Federal Judge John K. Regan, a friend of my friend, Roy Kirgan, the marshal. Before the trial, the judge asked if we would like to talk about it in his chambers. My lawyer and I went with him and found Mr. Kirgan in the office. It was a bit comical to see the six foot plus, white-haired, sixty-ish judge unzip his robe and offer cigarettes before sitting at his desk and putting his feet up on it. He started out,

"Arthur, do you mind if I call you Arthur?" And I said, "Of course not." He said that being the judge he wasn't supposed to talk to me but that Roy had told him all about it. He added that while he could understand a damaged back, the jury couldn't see anything wrong with me and they might think that being deaf, I may be looking for sympathy. He suggested keeping it from the jury and settle it with the lawyers and himself. They finally decided on ten thousand. After paying the lawyer fees and medical expenses and car repairs, I came out with four thousand, two of which I put on the deposit on my first house in Richmond Heights.

Most of the teachers at the school were understanding and sympathetic although there were those who would go overboard in their zeal to further their cause. Among these was a dedicated teacher-supervisor in charge of the speech clinics, Mildred McGinnis. She had never married and a lot of her mannerisms were typically old maidish. I had never had direct contact with her since most of her work involved the clinics and my speech sessions were under a private instructor, Mary Lou Rush. Miss McGinnis was very critical of the progress being made by those under her and would leap at any chance that presented itself in order to correct flaws in speech uttered by anyone within earshot. This particular trait did not especially endear her to the victims of her onslaught, and sarcastic remarks regarding her methods were common. It was during my fifth year at the school that I had a run-in with her in this category.

Speech clinic sessions were held on Saturday mornings. Afterwards the teachers and students, mainly children other than those residing at the school, along with their mothers, would mill about in the lobby. It was a wintry day in December and snow had fallen the night before. Fresh snow had always appealed to me and I enjoyed being out in it. Before going into the dining hall for the noon meal, I had taken one of the college students aside and asked her in a low tone of voice if she would like to go for a walk in the snow that evening and later to a show. Before she had a chance to reply, this teacher was upon us. Berating and displaying her displeasure, she said she could not hear what I was saying and that I was not talking loud enough. She always made it a point to see that everyone around her talked in normal tones that were pleasing to her as a speech teacher. I protested that I was talking to the girl and that I didn't want others to hear what I said. She stamped her foot and demanding to know, told me to speak up. I became angry and told her that it was none of her damn business what I had said. She glared at me and walked away.

    The following Monday morning I was called into Dr. Silverman's office and he brusquely asked what had transpired the past Saturday with Miss McGinnis. After telling him the story, he suggested, with a faint smile, that there would have been more genteel ways to tell her what the situation was, and he further requested that I apologize to her. A few days later I chanced to meet her in the hallway. She had an impish smile on her face that suggested that she had talked with Dr. Silverman. I told her that I had been asked to apologize and she said, "Well, I'm waiting." Then I said, also smiling, that I was sorry but that it wasn't any of her damn business what I had said to the girl. We both laughed and after that she was a bit more respectful of muted conversations which she had come to feel were not for her to interpret. We later enjoyed an amicable friendship. Mildred McGinnis was an institution

in herself.
    Total deafness generally suggests manual communication, more commonly known as sign language. A complete lack of association with other deaf individuals during my school years forced me to rely entirely upon lipreading, at which I became very proficient. Having no formal instruction in lipreading other than the short period of time in the Detroit School for the Deaf after I finally discovered that there were deaf students in the school other than myself, I had been forced to "do or die" in communicating with my peers. Basically, learning to "hear" visually was relatively uncomplicated. Although not fully aware of what total deafness meant, I realized early that there was something about my life that made me different and forced me to glean whatever I could in the way of spoken information by following the movements of the speaker's mouth and by closely observing the facial expressions accompanying the lip movements. It was not necessary to follow each word in succession. The speaker could talk for several moments and I hadn't the faintest idea of what was being said when suddenly a key word would come into the picture and my mind would flash back over the lip movements and the full meaning would suddenly become clear. Once I had mastered the gist of what was being said, the rest was easy to follow. The teachers with whom I associated at the school were not familiar with this method of communication and would suddenly stop in mid-sentence and demand to know what had been said. Usually I couldn't tell them since they hadn't gone far enough for me to catch up and they would show exasperation at what they thought was my inability to read lips as well as they thought I should be able to.
    Sign language at the school was strictly taboo.

Even normal hand gestures were frowned upon. One Saturday during the noon meal, a deaf girl of perhaps seventeen was excitedly telling others at the dinner table something which required quite a bit of hand waving and gestures, but basically no formal sign language. It happened that the recently retired Principal, Miss Connery, was visiting the school for a few weeks and was in the dining room that day. Without a word, she arose from her seat and crossing the dining hall, firmly grasped the startled girl by the arm, leading her to a supporting pillar at the center of the room. She forced the girl to stand with her nose on the pillar and wave her arms wildly. The girl was fiercely embarrassed and stopped waving her arms after a few moments whereupon she was prodded to continue. This went on for the duration of the meal. The girl became hysterical and incoherent and had to be helped from the room. With a look of triumph on her face, the former Principal returned to her seat. She would tolerate nothing suggestive of the signs. That was the last time she was to visit the school before her death a few months later. I have never been able to say that I was sorry.

Because of episodes such as the foregoing, I never attempted to learn the signs. I was taught to look upon them with contempt and thought that only the very stupid deaf required them to converse. It was many years later that I was to discover the importance of this type of communication which most deaf adults use as a supplement to lipreading. However, I had relied upon lipreading for so long and had such limited association with other deaf people that by the time I realized my life would perhaps have been richer had I been able to communicate with the deaf, interest in learning the language had been lost. I had been told by Dr. Silverman and Dr. Lane in the beginning that signs were mostly for uneducated deaf people who were not capable of learning lipreading. In later years, they would both rescind this opinion.

For many years lipreading was thought to be the only worthwhile communication method for use in teaching the deaf. The general idea appeared to be that if deafness were ignored sufficiently, it would go away. If only the deaf could speak and read lips, lo and behold, no one would know they were deaf and they could take their place in the hearing world and become productive members of society. Parents of deaf children sent them to the finest schools which taught lipreading and speech and would expect miracles. When fantasy began to change into reality, the numbing facts would settle into perspective and whatever could be accomplished in the way of making the child talk and understand would be accepted gratefully. It must be remembered that not all so-called deaf children are totally deaf. Many have a limited amount of residual hearing that, coupled with a hearing aid, serves them well in learning to speak and read lips. This residual hearing may be of varying types, often supplying only sound that cannot be used to distinguish words.

Dr. Hallowell Davis – Research

    Dr. Hallowell Davis, M.D. came to Central Institute from Harvard Medical School where he had been a professor. I knew Dr. Davis and had a great deal of respect for him. He, along with Dr. Silverman, founded the Research department as it is known today. After several years of intense research, he developed a method that made it possible to know if a newborn child would be deaf. Several states have made this into law and recently a federal law was passed making it mandatory that every state perform this test at birth.
    In recent years a device known as a cochlear implant has become a popular technology in oral schools for the deaf. It is implanted inside the skull behind the ear, and small children, either born deaf or having lost their hearing, have been known to understand very well with listening and lipreading. As they become older, their speech improves remarkably. This would not benefit me much at this late date, and like me, many other totally deaf adults elect to bypass it. This was developed by a research group other than Central Institute. There is a leader of a deaf group that vehemently disagrees with the cochlear implant saying that it deprives the deaf of their natural lifestyle.
    I will not attempt to go into the technical aspects of something with which I am not familiar; however, I have remained in complete disagreement with professionals in the field who say there are no totally deaf people, but that everyone possesses a certain amount of hearing. A child will respond to sound, which has been amplified, whether or not the sound is actually heard. Even vibration-free sound will reach the eardrum and set up a sensation that a

totally deaf child will hopefully mistake for sound and which, in turn, the tester could mistake for hearing. This has been argued back and forth for many years and will continue to be, although in recent years strides have been made in distinguishing between the two.

Many hearing aids are sold by unscrupulous testers on this basis, saying that with time the sound will become distinguishable. By the time the user realizes how futile the thing is, they are too disillusioned and chagrined to attempt to return it. My parents were sold an aid while I was in high school and I was forced to wear it for several months. I hoped that by some miracle the tingling sensations I could feel would eventually transform themselves into actual sounds and I looked forward to once again hearing music and being able to dance, which would make it possible for me to get a date. Gradually I began to feel that I looked ridiculous wearing the thing since everyone in school knew that I could not hear a sound. Whenever I saw anyone glancing in my direction and talking to someone and laughing, I would imagine they were talking about and laughing at me which they may very well have been doing. One night, in total dejection and anger, I destroyed it. I hid the pieces in a box in my dresser drawer and whenever any member of the family would ask about it on weekends, I would tell them I had left it at school. As time passed, it was recognized that the instrument had been useless.

In recent years a controversy has arisen as to the actual benefits of lipreading and speech in educating the deaf as compared to a newer version of the signs called total communication. Total, as it is referred to, is a combination of signs and gestures coupled with lipreading and speech, making it possible for the child to use whatever he or she is capable of in communicating with both the deaf and hearing. I personally lean towards the system since I realize it would have been a great help in my education, which was restricted to lipreading. I already possessed communicative skills and had acquired a vocabulary comparable to that of any nine-year-old hearing child when I became deaf. It was this that enabled me to learn lipreading so easily and effortlessly. I had acquired full speech so the usual problems and obstacles in teaching the deaf were not present. When a child has been born deaf, it does not have the advantages I retained in the beginning, so it is obvious that an early introduction to lipreading and speech would have an advantage over the manual method during the formative years. After the stage of learning to speak and communicate had been mastered, there are advantages to be found in the total system since higher educational institutions have recently been required by law to furnish interpreters both oral and manual. Because of this, I feel the system should be taught in the last year of elementary education in both private and public schools for the deaf whether or not they are restricted to lipreading and speech. Oral schools are not in agreement with this.

Maxwell Aaron Goldstein, M.D.,
Founder of CID in 1914.

(Courtesy of Central Institute for the Deaf)

Dr. Max Goldstein, Founder of CID

Before the advent of lipreading as a medium of communication, a number of the deaf were committed to institutions and many were considered insane. Since they were unable to speak and could not understand the spoken word, even the signs were meaningless to them. It was after leaders in the field had been able to reach them by demonstration and gestures signifying word meanings that they began to respond to lip movements and became aware of sound by feeling the side of the throat of the speaker. Dr. Max Goldstein, the founder of the Central Institute for the Deaf was one of the pioneers in this method. The ones doing the teaching were learning as much from this slow process as were the ones being taught. It was mostly a matter of mutual cooperation between teacher and pupil which evolved into a perfected method of lipreading as we know it today, and which has enabled the deaf to communicate with hearing people. But like with all handicapped groups, the crutch afforded by lipreading has not brought complete freedom and independence to the deaf. It is generally used for communication with the hearing, but for ease and speed the deaf will usually revert to signs when talking among themselves, the exception being oral groups which prefer speech and lipreading although being familiar with the signs.

It was in 1914 that Dr. Maxwell Aaron Goldstein, a surgeon at the Jewish Hospital, saw the need to do what he could to help the deaf. There was space above his office on Vandeventer Avenue in St. Louis that could be utilized as classrooms and he set about organizing a school for the deaf which was to be called the Central Institute for the Deaf. Dr. Goldstein, along with his office assistant, Julia

M. Connery as his Principal, worked diligently and headed the school in two other locations until they both retired in 1941. I have repeated that I never knew him although I feel that my life would be richer if I had met him. He died three months before my arrival at the school. He purchased a plot of land farther west into the city which at that time was pretty much open space. By today's landmarks, this plot of land would be bounded on Euclid Avenue, although at that time it was called South Kingshighway Boulevard. The name change came about when Kingshighway was routed through Forest Park and Euclid, which formerly ended two blocks to the north, became extended south to the front of the Institute. The north and south borders were Clayton Avenue to the north and an alleyway between West Papin Street and Chouteau Avenue on the south. It extended east halfway down the Papin Street block. When the three-story building was built in 1916, a large front yard was left open with plans in mind to erect a much larger building there. This came about in 1928 when a beautiful four-story, block-long French renaissance design building arose for the school, which served well until 2000 when plans were made for a complete new complex which included classrooms, clinics, a research center and a teacher training college. In 1951 a four-story research center was built on property that the school owned across highway forty which was part of the land bought originally and was later divided by the highway in the early 1930s. It was in 1968 that a beautiful residence hall down Clayton Avenue from the school relieved the crowded conditions that had been developing in the confines of the school building. It was Dr. Goldstein's dream that each child be able to speak. On each of his birthdays to the present, the school observes that date with a program in which each child recites a short sentence. After his death in 1941, his widow, Mrs. Goldstein remained active in the school until her death about twenty years later. I did many things for her and enjoyed being with her. Once when she was in her nineties, at an alumni banquet with Dr. Silverman, she was very frail and a bit bent over. I put my hand on her arm and said, "Do you remember me, Mrs. Goldstein?" She looked up and shaking a finger at me said, "I'll never forget you, Arthur McCann."

Dr. Goldstein was a well-known man in St. Louis in his own right besides being the head of Central Institute. Upon his death in 1941, there was an article and picture in the St. Louis Globe Democrat. The headline stated *Dr. Max Goldstein, a man outstanding in his field, has died.* Dr. Goldstein owned a large farm in western St. Louis County and he sometimes took some of the students there on weekends. The day after this announcement, a deaf boy of perhaps six or seven came to his teacher and exclaimed excitedly, "Dr. Goldstein isn't dead!" When the teacher said that he was, the boy said, "No! No, he is out on his farm standing in his field."

While Dr. Calvert was director, which he assumed upon Dr. Silverman's retirement in 1972, he had visions of a new building. When I returned to the Institute in 1973 at Dr. Calvert's invitation, plans were being made to purchase all the property on the south side of Clayton Avenue. He told me that a beautiful building would be built there but it would not be during his lifetime. He died about four years after his retirement at the age of 62. Had he lived another ten years, he would have seen the new complex finished after thirty-four million dollars had been raised for its construction.

Since Dr. Calvert's retirement there have been a

number of directors. The first one to serve was Dr. Richard Stoker who was himself deaf, but was able to serve very well with the assistance of Yvonne Churchwell as his administrative assistant. It was after a number of years that he was summarily removed by the Board of Managers. A reason was never made public. At that time Dr. Ira J. Hirsh, the retired Director of Research, was appointed as Interim Director until a permanent replacement could be found. In a few years, Dr. Donald Nielsen arrived, and shortly after, active plans were being made for the complex which became a part of the Washington University Medical Center a block away. A number of years after my retirement and with Dr. Nielsen's arrival, changes were being made throughout the Institute. It was Dr. Nielsen's dream to have all the outlying departments incorporated into one unit, which became a reality after the necessary funds had been raised.

Dr. Maynard Engebretson, the Assistant Director of Research and one who had complimented me many times on my dedication to my work and the Institute and who always had time to talk when I was in the area, had resigned from the Research Department and joined Washington University until his retirement. Once, when I did not understand him, he wrote out "You're the most impressive person that I have ever known." Administrative changes were made, and Jean Moog, a veteran of perhaps thirty-odd years, was replaced as principal. The teachers were upset by Jean's removal and staged a walk-out for several days. In the end, perhaps fifteen of the Central Institute teachers and her secretary followed to her newly established school, the Moog Center for Deaf Education. With her husband Alva on the finance committee, the school has become remarkably successful and they have recently built a new building in West St. Louis County. As I have remarked before, I was very fond of Jean and Alva while working at the Institute and have wished her well in her new venture. While Jean was principal, we worked together on many of her "pet" projects. We made a playground on the flat covered roof of the fourth floor, and remodeled most of the classrooms with built-in desks for the teachers. At the culmination of one project, she sent me a letter with the words *Thank You Thank You Thank You* repeated across and down the full length of the page. I was always welcome in her office and would often chide her on the disarray of her desk. Once I asked her why she didn't have a Ph.D. degree and remarked that I though she was better qualified than most of the ones that had them. She said she was too busy being the principal to bother with that sort of thing.

    The greatest obstacle in lipreading is to be found in the hearing world, including the very professionals who advocate the medium. The average deaf are unable to speak well. Their speech is often halting and unsure. The one being spoken to will like as not, nod approval at almost anything that is said although not being followed well enough to understand. The deaf sense this and become confused which in turn affects their ability to read lips. Seeing that they have not been successful, the deaf will repeat until the listener will finally make a concerted effort to understand. This is more the rule with those who know they are talking to a deaf person, and is not so frequent if the deaf can succeed in communicating with a hearing person prior to revealing the fact that he is deaf, thereby proving that he is capable of communicating although in a limited way. Many hearing people are afraid to speak to the deaf unless they are familiar with the problems involved. They shy away and their speech is restricted. They speak in a way that says they know they are talking to a deaf person and that they are not sure of being understood. This unsureness confuses the deaf and leaves them with a feeling of inadequacy. This is brought about by a mental block on the part of the hearing. My speech has been considered exceptional since it is not entirely the speech of a deaf person. However, many professionals with whom I associate will look at me intently and listen with apprehension when communicating with me. They realize the extent of my handicap and react accordingly. The handicap applies to both groups; to the deaf because they are different and to the hearing because they are unable to accept the deaf without a disguised display of rejection.

I once was told of an American in Tokyo, Japan, who was lost. He came upon a Japanese policeman directing traffic and asked him for directions. The policeman kept on directing traffic and pointing to his mouth and shaking his head. He could only say "No speaka English." The American very slowly said that if he would put his brain in gear and listen, he would know that he was speaking Japanese. After that they got along fine. This is the same problem the deaf have with hearing people.

During my second year at the Institute I decided to take preparatory courses at Washington University prior to enrolling in engineering school. Since the early days on the farm when our first electric generating plant was installed, I had sustained an interest in electricity and had become adept at servicing the system. I did an extensive amount of house wiring and enjoyed taking motors apart and cleaning them and putting them back together. I had read manuals on electricity and its production and decided to study electrical engineering. It was during the first semester at the university that World War II took on a new intensity with rationing, light dimming at night and increased production in war goods. The War, coupled with a lack of funds and inconsistencies of communication, brought on my decision to do what I could to help the war effort and found employment, as mentioned previously, with an aircraft corporation, abandoning my plans for higher formal education.

Curtiss Wright Aircraft Company

It was with a great deal of apprehension that I started my first day in the war plant. Mr. Davies, the president, had introduced me to the head of the assembly department and further assured me that there wouldn't be any problems. The local Chevrolet factory had been hastily converted to Navy Hell Diver manufacture and the set-up was rather crude although effective. I was the only deaf person in the department and was eventually placed in charge of driving exploding rivets. An exploding rivet is used when there is no room behind the part being riveted to position a bucking bar. The rivet is filled with powder that explodes with heat from a soldering gun, swelling up behind the plates being joined. It was thought that this was an ideal place for a deaf person; however, each explosion was nerve shattering. Since the physical makeup of my ears is normal, the reverberation on the drums, coupled with the fact that my equilibrium along with the nerves had been partially destroyed when deafness set in, left me a nervous wreck by the end of the day. Being grateful in having the job, it never occurred to me to try to explain my agony to my superiors since I was sure they would not understand how noise could affect a deaf person.

It was at the plant that I met Jim Holden, one of my foremen who took the time to explain procedures and plant operations in a way that left little doubt. I admired him and his cheery disposition. He would stop at my work area from time to time and offer any encouragement that he felt was needed. A friendship ensued which endured for many years after the War ended until his death. Jim was one of the few who were able to recognize my need for encouragement and assistance over the rough spots in daily living during those early years. His influence stayed with me and his lifestyle helped to mold my acceptance of life for whatever it had to offer.

    Once while sitting in the restroom I had fallen asleep with my head down. Suddenly I was awakened by a security guard and given a note to report to the office. I went to Jim and told him what had happened. Sleeping on the job was a rather serious offense and called for some sort of punishment. Three various offenses in a year meant dismissal. Jim told me he would take care of it. Arriving at the security office, the guard and his superior were there. Jim asked him why he thought I was asleep, and the guard said he had called to me several times before he had to shake me. Jim said that I was totally deaf and was simply sitting there with my head down. Since the guard couldn't prove much, he tore up the note and, giving me a dirty look, walked off. On the way back to our department, Jim laughed and cautioned me not to let it happen again.

    After the war ended, he and his wife moved to Yucaipa, California, where he founded and headed a real estate development corporation. We visited them and they spent four days showing us around the area including his developments. They took us to Newport Beach where we had dinner at Coco's and saw the yacht in the bay where John Wayne lived. We had made plans to return in two years and go to Hawaii with them, a place they enjoyed visiting each year. We were shocked to learn of his death from cancer the following year. Yucaipa was in the process of building a large lake with recreational areas and upon his death, named it after him.

    The time I spent in the aircraft plant was rewarding. There were many opportunities to learn the various aspects of airplane design and construction. Planes were being shot down as fast as we could build them and were being sent from the plant with only a prime coat of paint. This served to expedite delivery as well as cutting weight that allowed for extra maneuverability. Although my handicap posed no problems so far as doing my work was concerned, I was reminded constantly of being different which resulted in the old feelings of inferiority returning to haunt me. There were instances of being ignored when speaking to someone who was aware of my deafness and of having them turn and walk away without responding to what I had said. These experiences had been rather common over the years and I was becoming callused to them. I knew these occurrences were a result of fear and ignorance of the unknown on their part. This type of individual would usually respond to having observed others conversing with me. I had learned early in life not to begrudge this trait in those who displayed it but to wait for an opportunity to speak to them again after I knew they had become more tolerant of those less fortunate than themselves.

    The hundreds of pneumatic rivet hammers produced a continuous din that served me in good stead unintentionally. Whenever I could not understand when being spoken to the first time by one unfamiliar with my problem, I would ask them to repeat which resulted in the one speaking to me raising their voice and speaking more slowly, making it easier to read their lips. I also found that I was obligated to raise my voice and speak slower in order to be understood above the noise, all of which proved to be a great help in my speech rehabilitation.

    It was at the plant that I learned a lesson in promptness and in keeping my word once given. One of the hand tools I was using was not performing as it should. I took it to a foreman other than Jim and explained the problem. He told me to take it to tool repair and ask that it be repaired that day. An hour before the end of the day, the foreman asked if I had gone for the tool. I said I would get it in the morning. A bit upset, he told me that if I didn't get it now, that the next time I asked for fast service, I wouldn't get it. When I went to pick it up, the shop manager said that they had put other work aside to do mine. I thanked him, and reported this to the foreman who reminded me that I had learned a lesson. I thanked him for that.

Granvil Bates

It was during my tenure at the plant that a cruel disappointment arose that left a scar on my emotional well being which took many years to heal, if indeed it ever did. A brother, Earl, had been shipped overseas early in the war and was in North Africa attached to a service group serving the Air Force. We corresponded regularly; he kept me informed as well as he could and my letters contained information that I thought would interest him. In one of his letters he told me that I might as well go down to the farm and remove his car from the blocks he had left it sitting on when he was drafted expecting to return in a year or so. He said the car wasn't doing anyone any good where it was and if I wanted to bring it to the city and drive it and buy it, to do so. Mom and Dad protested when I went to get it saying that it should be left where it was, but after I convinced them that I had been asked to take it, they reluctantly agreed to its removal. The car was a three-year-old 1940 Deluxe Chevrolet Tudor in excellent condition. Cars were no longer being built since the beginning of the War and good ones were at a premium. I wrote and told him I wanted to buy the car and would put money into his bank account each month until it was paid for. I gave it to Granvil Bates, the manager of Hoehn Chevrolet Company, who had sold the car to Earl and asked him to do whatever necessary to put it into first-class condition. Granvil was a family friend. He had some small dents in the fenders removed and painted, tuned the motor, put on new seat covers and two new tires and polished the car. I told him of my intention to buy it, which resulted in his seeing that the car was taken care of properly. The title to the car was in a safe deposit box in the bank at home and I was planning to have Dad get it out and consummate the sale. I was driving the car to work and using it socially and planning to have the final details taken care of. Granvil had charged only for two new tires.

    Wayne had come home from camp where he was attending Officer Candidate School in Virginia, and coming to me asked if he could use the car for two weeks while he was home. I readily agreed as I knew he was soon to be sent overseas and I was anxious that he enjoy his leave. He drove the car to the farm and to visit friends and relatives in Owensville, Missouri. I was inconvenienced without it as I had become used to driving it to work and had to make arrangements to ride with others. I was unable to use the bus since I had to be at school to assume my teaching duties right after work. I anxiously awaited the time when the car would be returned and was glad when the day arrived that Wayne said he would bring it back. It was about nine in the evening on the day he promised that he came to the house. He had on odd look on his face which told me something was wrong and I uneasily asked if he had wrecked it as I noticed he was driving another one. He told me the car had been sold. I was on the verge of tears and protested that I had planned to buy it. He told me Dad had decided that I didn't need the car and that it should be sold. I never knew the details until later. Dad had power of attorney and decided on the sale of the car without asking me.

    This was an unexpected blow that left me unnerved and confused. I was unable to comprehend a reason and was visibly shaken. When our uncle saw the nearly new car, he asked Dad if it was for sale and Dad said it was. Being a dealer and with the war on, he couldn't get good cars to sell. He knew this car was a "cream puff." Wayne said that Dad should talk to me about it before selling it and Dad replied that " Arthur doesn't need that damn car." Without saying so, it was apparent that Wayne was extremely sorry for what had transpired while he was in possession of the car and said he would loan me the money, interest free, to buy another one. I was without transportation to work and dependence upon others for a ride was erratic. I went to Granvil and told him the story. He was appalled and could not understand why the family would take the car from me and dispose of it since it was apparent that I needed it. I thought he was going to cry. It being impossible to replace the car with one of like quality, he said he would find something and for me to wait a while. Within a week he called and said he had a nice sport coupe coming in from a doctor who qualified for a new car. It was a six-year-old Chevrolet but a very nice car and I was happy to find it. This was the beginning of a friendship that lasted until his death many years later. When I went to take possession of the car, he wasn't there but had left a note describing the car. The note said:

1-12-44
Arthur,
I bought you a 38 Chev. Sport Cpe. today. Not just a plain cpe. This one has a rumble seat. So it will cost a little more but when you get ready to sell it, it will be worth more. Here is what I can do: I can sell it for $485 plus tax (as it is now). Now Arthur here is what I believe it needs: the clutch is just a little bit grabby, not bad, and the tappets are noisy and one or two pins are pecking. So you can be the judge. It may use some oil. I don't know. The pressure is very good. If you want to, I will overhaul the motor and clutch, replace rings, pins, grind valves, etc. and

Granvil E. Bates, his wife, Ara, and son, John

My new 1947 DeSoto

replace clutch – on a 50/50 basis. This is, you pay half of the bill. I would say the bill would run close to $75 to $100. That means it would cost you close to $35 to $50. Whatever it would come to. And I could put that in the payments if you want to and they would be about $3 more per month. Depending on the cost of overhauling. I drove the car. It seems to drive ok so if you want the car, give Dennis or Frank the order and everything will be ok.
G. Bates

He told me later that when the war was over, he would have a new car agency selling DeSotos and Plymouths. He said he would get me a new one as soon as they came out. I drove the Chevrolet for three years and it was a very good car.
    One Saturday morning a call came to the school office from Granvil. He told the secretary to tell me he had a new car for me. I had forgotten that he had promised me one three years before. I hurriedly drove to his agency in Clayton and went in. The showroom was empty and he was on the phone in his office. Not wanting to bother him, I went back into the service area and saw only one car – a new 1947 DeSoto -- a beautiful maroon coupe with fog lights and chrome wheels. I knew that wasn't mine so I went back to his office and found he was off the phone. I asked him if he had called to say he had a new car for me. He said, "Yes." I asked where it was and he said it was out in the shop. I asked if he meant the DeSoto and he said, "Yes, it's yours." I said, "Oh hell, Granvil. I can't afford that thing." He laughed and said, "Of course you can." Then he tossed the factory invoice to me, which showed nineteen hundred. He asked how much I had paid for the Chevrolet and I told him four hundred ninety-four. He said

he was taking that amount off the nineteen hundred, which came to one thousand five hundred and six. He asked if I could handle that and I assured him I could. I asked him how he could do that and he said he would sell the Chevrolet Monday for a thousand dollars and added that he could sell the DeSoto for three thousand five hundred, but he promised it to me and that he valued my friendship. Very few cars were available in 1947. He asked that if I were unsatisfied with the car in a year or so, would I please bring it back to him. I said I would and it happened that within a year, I felt it was too big and too powerful so I went back to see him. He asked what was wrong with it and I said nothing except that I was afraid of driving it too fast. He asked what I wanted and took me out back where he now had several cars. He showed me a new gray Plymouth with the same equipment that the DeSoto had and asked if I liked it. I said I did and asked him how much it was. He said, "You have a 47 DeSoto and I have a 48 Plymouth. They are worth the same so it's an even trade."

I bought other cars from him in later years. He had a reputation of being one of the most honest automobile dealers in the area. He later moved to California and opened another agency. Several years later, he and his wife Ara came to our wedding reception in St. Louis and a year later we drove to California and spent several days with them. They took us to Disneyland and the Queen Mary ship as well as other attractions, such as Forest Lawn Cemetery where many movie stars are buried. He always loved telling jokes and some of them bordered on things that brought looks and cautions from Ara. I can honestly say that I loved him. We visited them at their marina on Table Rock Lake in Missouri. He died of a heart attack at the age of 68. I was probably too naïve to realize at the time, but I know he was trying to make up for the treatment I had earlier from my family. I had come to love him as a friend.

When dad was about 65 years old, he had been working in the field with a mare that was used principally for breeding. She was a beautiful Belgian and unused to field work although teamed with a gentle mule. Dad was making a turn with the riding hay mower when she became excited and kicked him in the leg below the knee. She had just been shod with new shoes and the leg was numb from the blow. Dad had been kicked before and thought it would feel better if he got down and walked on it. As soon as he touched the ground, his leg collapsed. It was broken all the way through. It was Sunday morning and he was alone in the field and began calling for help. He was behind a hill from the house and Mom couldn't hear him. He kept calling for about two hours, getting weaker as time went by, when finally a neighbor across the river told her husband that she had heard him but wasn't sure what he was saying. They drove over and found him about to pass out. They took him up to the house and took him and Mom to St. James to a doctor. They first went to the home of Dr. W. H. Brewer and he went out to the car to look at him. He was dressed in a white suit and told them he was on his way to church and couldn't help. They then went to the home of a lady doctor, a Dr. Hammar, who immediately went to work and applied a tourniquet and told the driver of the ambulance to go to Waynesville about thirty miles farther and not to worry about being stopped for speeding. Dad had lost a lot of blood but once in the hospital, Dr. Hammar did what she could until the regular surgeon, Dr. Eamil Stricker, could be found. Dad was in a cast for over a month at home.

My brothers and I would go out every weekend to help with the farm work. It just happened that I had taken delivery of the new DeSoto the week before. I had worked late that Saturday and left St. Louis at about eleven in the evening. It was a hundred miles to the farm. It was raining and when I got to the Meramec River which was a quarter mile from the farm, I found the river to be flooded and over the bridge. I have mentioned the trough bridge before but it had been replaced not long before with one of concrete footings and heavy timber troughs. I had crossed it before in daytime when the river was over it, since the rippling water over the troughs showed it was alright. I had a spotlight on the car and shone it across the river, about sixty feet. I could see the water rippling, so drove onto the flooded bridge at two o'clock in the morning. Driving very slowly so as not to flood the motor, I found that I was going deeper into the water than I thought it would be. I didn't know that the bridge was lower in the middle and could feel the swirling water rocking the car. When I finally got across, I stopped to look and found that the water had been halfway up the door of the car. Later I returned to St. Louis by another way, forty miles farther to a high bridge, much wiser than when I went down.

Work at the plant and evening duties at the school continued to keep my schedule filled although there was always time for social life. Until the time I had commenced working at the plant, I had shied away from getting dates except for a few movies and sports events with some of the college students. Now that I had a full-time job and was making money and had a car, I was able to assert myself more fully and became less self-conscious in asking for dates. I was still looked upon as a member of the deaf student group by several of the girls; however, there were others who accepted me as a regular date and responded accordingly. As would be expected of one who had gone for so long without female companionship, having these dates was exhilarating and it was not long until the girls began to accept my advances and return them. Generally, they made it clear from the beginning that their boyfriends were overseas or some place besides that place. While they were willing to accept me for their purposes, they made it very plain that they were not interested in anything more that would bring them to break off with their intended. Sex, while new to me in itself, was something that I had grown up with on the farm and while familiar with the procedures involved, had never before been able to broach the subject with a girl. Being free to discuss and indulge in it with partners who were hungry for it themselves opened up a totally new world and brought about a maturity that had long lain dormant.

Castrating pigs, lambs, calves, and even colts was an everyday occurrence on the farm in season although I never realized the reasons behind it nor was information ever offered to explain why it was done until much later. Fred Morrison was usually called upon for this task. Lard and turpentine completed it. Transporting female animals to neighboring farms for service with their male counterparts was also an accepted procedure with which I was familiar but, strangely, I never compared animals with humans in this category. Perhaps it could be said that as a farm boy I grew up with a negative attitude towards sex, which presented no real difficulty in waiting for its appearance and in being able to perform. In Dad's absence from the farm, there were times when I would assist a young heifer in giving birth to her first calf. Breeding would be at an early age and the body was not naturally ready for delivery and had to be assisted when the calf would be halfway out. Without assistance, some of these young cows would die in the field, so it was imperative that they were kept near the barn when they were due and watched closely so they could be helped. For some unexplained reason I never associated these same problems of birth mentally with a pregnant woman. Perhaps this could be attributed to parents who looked upon pregnancy as something to ignore and not talk about.

    I had become acquainted with the parents of some of the girls I dated and felt that the majority of them considered me a student from the school that their daughter was being nice to and certainly I am sure none of them suspected what was transpiring between us. Of course there were instances where the girls were doing just that-- being nice, and a date would consist of a walk through the park on a Sunday afternoon. I harbored feelings of inferiority since I was aware that most of them were taking advantage of an obvious opportunity which had presented itself and which they found, under the circumstances, hard to resist. It was this newly found feeling of masculinity that made it difficult to live realistically. I was naive and gullible. I had retained the simple trusts I had known as a hearing child and felt that no one was going to harm or take advantage of me. I had illusions of grandeur and could see only what I wanted to see in the future. I still looked forward to the time when my hearing would return and did not accept life seriously. The Institute was in the process of opening a new research center and I felt it would be only a matter of time until something would be accomplished which would prove advantageous. In the meantime, I felt the present was temporary and when the change came I could assume more of life's pleasures and responsibilities.

I lived in a world of make-believe with the college girls as the center of my existence. For some, having been away from their boyfriends for so long, they found in me what they needed as well as a freedom from any feelings of involvement. Actually, only three girls were involved.

It was many years later, during my first short marriage, that I was to discover that precautions ordinarily taken to prevent any undesirable consequences would have been unnecessary. The ravages of cerebro-spinal meningitis had left me sterile.

One Sunday after dinner at the school, a friend, a medical student, asked me what I was going to do that afternoon. I told him it was a free day and he asked if I wanted to go down to the hospital to watch babies being born. I protested that I would get into trouble and he laughed and said I wouldn't. He gave me a white gown and mask and we watched three babies come into the world. It was a charity ward and they were colored. It was a good experience and was different than what I had seen with animals.

There were three Washington University medical students working at the school as supervisors of the older boys. I relieved them when they were off duty. At times one or the other of them would have me ask them questions from their notes before examinations. I enjoyed this and learned some things I would have had no way of knowing otherwise. Two of these friends went on to become famous doctors. Don Sweazy became the head of the Mental Health Department of the state of Illinois. He died a number of years ago. George Prothro owned a children's clinic in Clovis, New Mexico for many years and later headed the Health Department of Tulsa, Oklahoma. He met his first wife, Anna, when he was a medical student and working at CID. She was the night nurse for the residential students at the school. They raised two children and enjoyed many years of marriage before she died. He and his current wife, Joy, have become world travelers. Laura and I visit them occasionally.

The end of the War brought with it an end to my employment in the aircraft industry. I had become adept in several phases of airplane manufacture and was a bit sorry when the end came and the country gradually resumed a peace-oriented atmosphere. The soldiers were returning home to the jobs they had left and employment was at a premium. It was at this time that I discovered discrimination involving the deaf. I applied for employment on the assembly lines at Chevrolet but was told the work was too dangerous for a deaf person. The same held true when I inquired about the possibilities of employment at a cooperage plant that manufactured barrels. They were leery of having a deaf person operating machinery.

I decided upon an aptitude test to see where my talents lay. It was found that I had the necessary skills to become a dental technician. Inquiry through a dentist friend led to employment in his laboratory. I quickly learned the necessary procedures and it was not long before I was making dentures from the dentists' impressions of patients' mouths, and later was doing castings of gold bridges and inlays. The work was exacting and demanding. The pay was average and it would be reasonable to assume that it would have led to a permanent career had I stayed in the field. Not being satisfied with doing just one thing, however, I was accepting small jobs on the side in my spare time.

McCann and Company

Upon completing some furniture repair work, I was asked by one of my customers to join a small firm which he, along with two other partners, was organizing for the purpose of constructing scale models of machinery and buildings for designers. Since I felt this type work was more in keeping with my talents, I left the dental laboratory and joined the newly formed firm. Basically, this move was a mistake from the beginning. There was more talent than work available and it wasn't long before the members were forced to disband. I stayed on with one of the remaining partners, Joe Tanaka, for a short while until deciding to go into custom cabinet and furniture manufacture for the trade, which consisted of working with design and decorating departments of furniture and department stores and interior designers. I had been able to accumulate enough capital to purchase the needed machinery and equipment and rent a building. McCann and Company was thus formed.

The company never became very large, usually three to four employees, but a considerable amount of work was turned out and most of our customers were well pleased with the superior quality. Most contacts come by word of mouth and commercial accounts. Besides owning the company I was the sales agent and discovered early that my handicap was in many ways more an advantage than a hindrance. The majority of clients were warm and friendly and tended to admire what I was doing. There were instances where I would have to convince a customer that I was deaf. Many of them had their own impressions of the deaf. Since my lifestyle did not add up to what they thought went into the makeup of a deaf person, I was sometimes forced to explain in detail why I was able to speak and read lips as well as I could. I obtained enough work to keep my employees busy, but because of the nature of the work, too much time was required to produce individual pieces of furniture that were custom built. The work was highly competitive and I was forced to offer an attractive price in order to get the work I needed. I very seldom showed a worthwhile profit which I realized early was not the accepted way of doing business, but which I adhered to in order to protect the company's name and reputation for detail.

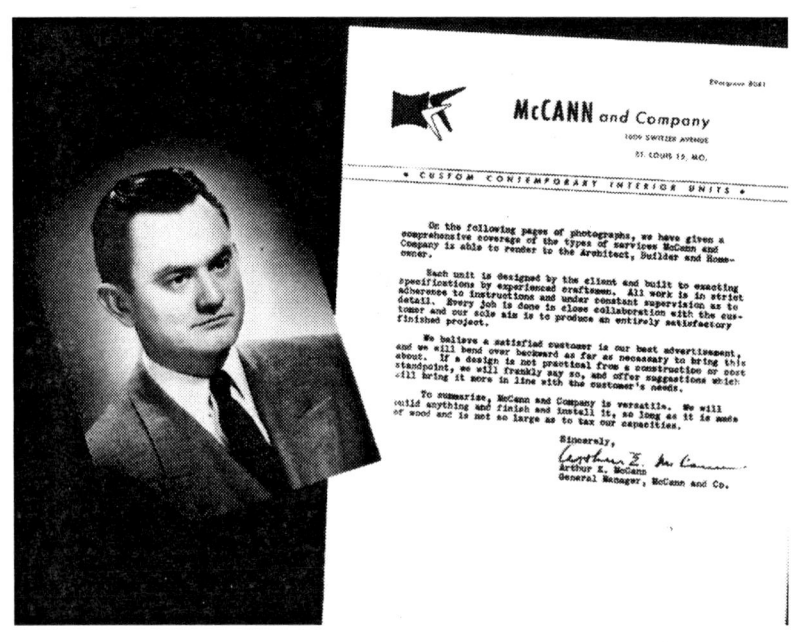

Face page of McCann and Company brochure about 1951.

(Courtesy of Paul Piaget Studio)

One of numerous custom-made pieces of furniture
made by McCann and Company

(Courtesy of Paul Piaget Studio)

One of numerous custom-made pieces of furniture
made by McCann and Company

(Courtesy of Paul Piaget Studio)

Mrs. Spencer Tracy

The work of producing custom furniture and related units had its lighter sides at times. One day when the office girl was out, a phone call came and one of the men went to the office to answer it. Coming back into the shop area he came to me and said that some dame was on the phone who said she was Mrs. Spencer Tracy, and laughed at what he thought was someone having some fun with me. I told him that if she said she was Mrs. Tracy, then that's who she was. He stopped laughing and asked if it really was and when I assured him it was he went back to the phone and a bit more respectfully asked what she wanted to tell me. She said that she had arrived in town the night before and that she would like for me to join her for lunch at the Chase-Park Plaza hotel at twelve and I assured her I would meet her then. After going home to change I drove to the hotel and found her in the lobby waiting for me. I had met her a few years before when she was at the Central Institute on a speaking tour and we seemed to have a lot in common. She and Spencer had a deaf son and she asked many things that I was able to give her advice on concerning life in a deaf world. She had organized a school in Los Angeles for mothers of deaf children and was anxious to learn all she could outside of the academic teachings she had gone through which she told me were mostly the intentions of those who had never experienced deafness. She hoped we could get together again and that the next time she was in St. Louis, she would call me. I was happy that she had remembered. We were shown to a table in the dining room and after giving our order, she arose and asked to be excused for a minute. I immediately became aware of everyone in the dining room looking after her and talking to one another. I did not realize the significance of this interest in her until she returned to the table and explained that she had been paged and apologized that she hadn't told me before she left the table. I asked her if that was the reason everyone was looking at her and she laughed and said that she supposed it wasn't every day that Mrs. Spencer Tracy was paged in the room. We talked at length and she told me of the disappointments in their lives in their inability to do more for their son John who had been born deaf. Unapologetic, she said that she had no idea how many millions she and Spencer had between them but that if there were any way that the money could be used to find a way to make John hear, they would not hesitate to give it all. In spite of her status as a celebrity, I felt completely at ease with her. She was dressed in a plain gray suit with no jewelry except a very conservative necklace and a plain wedding band. She wore a hat which appeared to be a part of her and her manner was matter-of-fact. She mentioned what was generally known about her and Spencer's separation and his involvement with Katherine Hepburn, and how she did not feel free to give him a divorce, although she added that he often said that he didn't want one. They were both free to pursue their other interests and she admitted that since John had been born deaf, her dedication to helping him had been the chief cause of the deterioration of their marriage. As she put it bluntly, she said that concerning their marriage, he may as well be a monk. As I mentioned before, she and I seemed to have something in common. I could sense right there what it was. She refused to admit that there was no cure for John's deafness and until recently, I have harbored the same feelings about mine. We talked for about three hours before saying good bye, hoping that we would have an opportunity to meet again. Although we exchanged letters a few times, I never saw her again. In one of my letters, I mentioned the son of my friends in Clayton and told her he was in Hollywood after going to drama school in New York. I asked if she might be able to make contacts for him. She wrote back, thanking me for thinking that she may be of help but added that since Walt (Disney) had died, she had lost all interest in the movies and further added that there were thousands of hopefuls in Hollywood waiting for a break. Many years later my wife and I were in Los Angeles and I attempted to look her up but was sorry to learn that she had passed away a few years before. She was a wonderful person and her work lives on in her school. I am sorry that I have never been able to meet John and I do not know whatever happened to him.

    An account of note while operating McCann and Company was with a famous architect, Bernard McMahon. We would build store fixtures of his design for stores he was engaged in building throughout the United States. Some were of conventional design and served their intended function, while others were of a nature that had the effect of bringing customers into the stores. We also built several pieces of furniture for his beautiful home in a suburb of St. Louis. Mr. McMahon had built several buildings in Clayton, which is the hub of county government for St. Louis County. There was a restriction in the city on the height a building could be, which was two stories. After a lengthy fight with city officials in the early 1950s, he won and built a four-story office building. Today there are so many skyscrapers going up giving downtown Clayton the appearance of continuous buildings bonded together that the mayor recently proclaimed a halt on future buildings until further notice. Another account upon which we depended rather heavily was the Dolan Real Estate Company. We designed and built fixtures for offices they were building in various locations in the city. Clients would come to the offices to look at displays of homes for sale, which were arranged on our fixtures that were built in the shape of a house. Once a sale had been made we were recommended to the new homeowner for special built in units, such as bookcases and room dividers, and occasionally a special dining room set. Another company with which we enjoyed a good working relationship was the Lammert Furniture Company. Lammert's was the most exclusive furniture company in the city at the time and many of the clients were from the surrounding wealthy suburbs. Often there would be a request for a specialized unit that the company couldn't supply and I would be called in to confer with the customer. I was once asked by the Lammert Company to go to one of their clients in Clayton, a wealthy suburb. I met with a very nice couple who was in the process of redecorating their home. After discussing their needs, extensive changes were made in rooms that were outmoded having been built many years before. They had a number of things they wanted done and explained each one in detail. When I began to explain how we would proceed, the husband started to interrupt and his wife told him to be quiet so that I could tell them what they needed. Once while we were installing a combination bar and bookcase for them, the wife's mother, a very wealthy widow who lived across the street, came in and asked her daughter if she thought we might have a piece of sandpaper. Her daughter asked her what she needed with a piece of sandpaper and her mother said sarcastically, "What do you think I need it for, to wipe my butt?" At that, my helper who happened to be my brother-in-law, Jim Roller, started laughing. The mother was mortified and said, "Oh my God. I thought they were both deaf." Over the years I became friends with the family. I continued to do work for them for many years and they did many things to help me.

It was also through The Lammert Furniture Company that we did considerable work for the home of August Busch Jr. and some special pieces for his office at the Anheuser Busch brewing company which he owned. They were in the process of renovating the mansion prior to moving in after the death of Mr. Busch's mother. An amusing incident came about one day while another man and myself were installing a large outdoor swing we had made for Mr. Busch. He had always wanted a swing like his father had before him when he lived in the mansion, but which had long since fallen apart and had been disposed of. It was designed by one of Lammert's designers to Mr. Busch's specifications. It was a hot July day and after we had been at work for about an hour installing it, Mrs. Busch came out with two glasses of cold Budweiser beer and told us that it looked as though we needed something cold to drink. After thanking her, we continued working and not long after she came out again and asked if we would like more beer. I told her that we would appreciate another and jokingly asked if she could bring us some Falstaff beer this time. She laughed and replied that they didn't have that kind in the house, and brought more Budweiser. Both Mr. and Mrs. Busch were affable people and the kind I enjoyed working with. Besides the aforementioned incident, we made a number of other projects for the home. One was a huge upholstered headboard for their eight-foot bed. Later, the designer from Lammert's, Mr. Stephens, brought in plans for a clothing wardrobe, about eighteen feet long and floor to ceiling, for the guesthouse across from the mansion. The sliding doors were of an ornate design and were hung from the top on a track with rollers. Units of this nature were assembled in parts in the shop and transported to the destination for installation. Two men were with me putting it in place and were installing the doors. One of Mr. Busch's daughters was visiting from out of town and seeing the upper track, protested that the doors should be on tracks on the floor. I told her that this was the way her father wanted them and it was too late to change. She persisted in her insistence, so I asked the men to pick up their tools and go back to the shop. Shortly after arriving back at the shop, Mr. Stephens came running in, very upset and wanted to know what had happened since Mr. Busch had called him. I explained it and he called Mr. Busch back. The next morning, Mr. Busch called and apologized for his daughter's behavior and asked us to come finish the work and said for us to not worry about her since he had put her on a plane and sent her home to New Jersey.

Another project in the Busch's home was a heavy pine breakfast hutch in the living quarters on the second floor. The huge formal dining room was on the first floor and the kitchen was too large for regular use. Mrs. Busch was very proud of the addition. Before her marriage to Mr. Busch (his third), she had lived in her father's villa in the Swiss Alps, which is where they met. And yet another project was a seven-foot long coffee table of solid walnut for Mr. Busch's office at the brewing company. He was always pleased with our work and would either thank me personally or have his secretary send a letter.

An incident came up one day that resulted in a dark day for the city of St. Louis. A company in St. Louis had invented and made gliders in a wing of the Arena which were to be loaded with cargo for the military and pulled by planes. The idea behind it was ostensibly to save fuel since the plane doing the pulling was a large cargo plane, which kept troops supplied. The first one to be completed was very newsworthy and it was taken up on a Sunday afternoon at the airport. St. Louis Mayor William D. Becker and other high ranking city officials as well as a number of company executives went up on the maiden flight. Everything was going according to plan until suddenly the glider banked and broke away from the plane, crashing and killing all aboard.

The president of the board of aldermen, Aloys P. Kaufman, then became mayor. One of the fellows that worked for me, Ronald Johnson, also deaf, told me his father was the service manager of the Buick company that serviced Mayor Kaufman's Buick and they were friends. The mayor served two terms. Work was a bit slack at one time and Ronald asked his dad to mention to the mayor that we might be able to use some extra work and wondered if something around City Hall may be available. Mayor Kaufman told Ronald's dad for me to get in touch with him. The next Monday my office girl was out so I asked one of the men to call the Mayor at City Hall. The secretary wouldn't let him talk to the Mayor, so the next morning I asked the same fellow to call the Mayor's home before my secretary came in. The Mayor answered and when told the reason for the call became upset and asked, "Why in hell are you calling the Mayor at home before he has had his breakfast?" When the fellow mentioned Mr. Johnson's name, he calmed down and listened and asked me to come to his office at City Hall at eleven o'clock that morning.

I apologized for calling him at his home and

explained the situation, telling him what type of work we did. He smiled and said he wished he could help but that such a thing would have to go through too many channels of politicians and he didn't believe it would be worth considering. He arose from his chair behind the desk and came around and shook hands with me saying he was sorry he couldn't be of more help. Laughing, he added that it wasn't really a good idea to call the mayor of the city at his home before he had his breakfast. Mr. Johnson told me later that they had talked about it the next time the mayor brought his car in and laughed.

Another incident occurred after moving the company to North Broadway. I had been buying plastic laminate, better known as Formica, from the McCready Supply Company a few blocks away. Once while I was there picking up some material, before I could take care of charging the order as I always had done, the phone rang and Mr. McCready's secretary told me it was my office and they wanted to tell me something. I told her I couldn't take the call because I couldn't hear. When her boss heard that, he wouldn't give me credit for the order. He wanted cash. I didn't have the cash – about two hundred dollars – on me and told him I would have to make other arrangements. My office manager, Mr. O'Conner, went over to talk to him, reminding him that we had been buying from him for several years and paying on time. Mr. McCready told Mr. O'Conner to have me come pick it up and sign for it and he apologized.

While involved with McCann and Company, I came into contact with several men of Japanese ancestry. They were all professionals and friendly with me and for the most part overlooked my shortcomings.

There was Joe Tanaka. Joe was one of the partners

in the model-making venture that I had joined. Joe's parents had a restaurant in mid-town St. Louis. It was called "Little Tokyo" but when the war started, they changed the name to "Pig Meat Restaurant." Joe's father couldn't pronounce pork chops. Another partner was Harry Shelton, the owner of a large company that made machinery for crushing limestone and other crushable stones. He was murdered one Christmas Eve outside of his office while locking the door and his luxury car was stolen. The third partner was Don Putney, an interior designer. They all worked well together, but I fear there was more talent than work and it led to disbanding before long as I have mentioned before.

Dan Sakahara was a landscape architect and had created beautiful landscapes for numerous large corporations including the Botanical Gardens' Japanese Garden. His hobby was woodworking and he asked to be allowed to work in my company without pay for the experience. After about a month, he came and told me he would be leaving because he felt that he was taking work away from my regular employees.

Then there was Kimio Obata who owned an advertising agency. He had several artists who would draw advertising pictures that were greatly enlarged and displayed on billboards. Television wasn't yet a medium. He would design office fixtures and I would make them and together we would install them. Once we worked all night to finish a project and were leaving at four in the morning. We were walking towards our cars and I was lamenting my problems. He stopped, turned to me and said that he was tired of me bellyaching about my lack of hearing. He and his family had been in the camp in California during the war and his left arm was injured in some way that slightly shortened it. He said to look at him. He said his left arm wasn't much good, and using both hands to stretch his eyes, he added that he was also one of those "damn Japs" as everyone called them. He was later instrumental in bringing in the account of Emerson Electric Company when they expanded, which resulted in us getting our new company, Arcy Manufacturing Company, to a good start with an order for 30 desks. We also made steel display boards for Emerson that had numerous products built in, and later he made the drawings for the three story Sutter Medical Clinic downtown for which we made most of the equipment. Today it is owned by Washington University Medical Center. Another of our accounts was Phillips and Standard Oil Company for service station equipment. I lost track of Kim after I left the partnership and went to McDonnell Douglas. It was about twenty years later that I met Mr. Charles Knight, the CEO of Emerson Electric Manufacturing Company. His daughter, Ann, a teacher at Central Institute, was having a party at their home. I mentioned how I had been involved in making equipment for them in past years and, since I knew that Kim had brought our company orders from Emerson, I asked if he had known Kim. He said that he had put Kim in charge of their Tokyo operations, then added that he had died a few years before from cancer. I was sorry to learn that. I had first met Kim at a party at Alfred Morioka's home. His brother Gyo was also there. I first met Gyo when he was a partner with George Hellmuth and George Kassabaum on a boat in the Mississippi River located about where the Gateway Arch is now although it wasn't there at the time. They were in advertising and architecture. They eventually formed a world famous architecture firm known as HOK in St. Louis which Gyo still heads today.

I first met Alfred Morioka through our friend Joe Tanaka. We became friends from the beginning. He was a student in the St. Louis University Dental School and the school was very near the Designers and Builders location where I worked. I sometimes stayed late in the evening and he and his wife Asaka would drop in to see me and watch what I was doing. After he became a dentist, I made most of the fixtures in his office, charging only for materials, and he furnished me with dental work, charging me for precious metals used, until his retirement. One day he came to our house with a cabinet top that he wanted me to cover in laminate. I told him I would call when it was ready. When we called him, his wife said he was in the hospital. I had known he had cancer but didn't know it was very serious. Later, she called and I expected him to come by to pick up the top but she said he had died. She added that he was anxious to get home so he and I could go out for lunch. I had lost a friend, one that I loved.

I don't want to forget to mention two other unofficial members of the group who called themselves Designers and Builders Association. One was David Haven who was a freelance designer but had not invested with the original three. Due to some misunderstanding, he was asked to leave. Another member whom I believe contributed heavily to the treasury was Phillip Cady. His grandfather had been the owner of the old St. Louis Browns baseball team. He left to become an official with Hussman Refrigeration Manufacturing Corporation. I asked Dave Haven to come into McCann and Co. in the beginning. He was in no position to invest money but we thought that his designs would serve a purpose. In the beginning we had very little work or money so we agreed that he should leave. It wasn't long before work started coming in. By that time he had other employment.

The years spent operating McCann and Company were educational and profitable in ways other than material. Many friends were made and some were lost. The venture proved beneficial in experience and in knowledge gained, affording an insight into aspects of human nature that would have been lacking had I accepted employment with others. Some life long friendships were formed during the ten years I owned the company. Al Moore was the owner of Parkway Chicago, dealers in real wood laminates. He would be in St. Louis occasionally and would take me out to dinner. Once, while I was in Chicago on business, he took me through his plant and showed me how they manufactured the laminate. I lost track of him in later years and would sometimes write to tell him of my current progress. He always answered until a few years later. I heard that he had died. He was a man whose friendship I valued. Two other personal friends whom I had known before going into business and who later offered considerable help and advice, and still do, were Elmer Meyer and Frank Petelik. Laura and I see them and their wives often socially and enjoy their friendship.

It is doubtful if there exists a more formidable way to discover who your friends are than to have everyday dealings with them involving commerce. There are those who are willing to lend a helping hand if they can see there is need for it with no thought of monetary gain. There are others who will come to your aid if they feel that in doing so there will be a profit involved. During my tenure in business I discovered how greatly the former outnumbered the latter.

U.S. Deputy Marshal Roy L. Kirgan, Sr.

Chief Deputy U.S. Marshal Roy L. Kirgan, Sr.

An incident happened one day which could have turned into a tragedy were it not for unexpected assistance from a long time friend. I had a contract from a subdivision builder to furnish the needed cabinets and laminated tops for the kitchens and bathrooms in the homes he was building. A letter had arrived from the Internal Revenue Service demanding payment on delinquent withholding taxes on my employees for the last quarter. Because of the urgent nature of the letter, I sent a check which I knew to be several hundred dollars short, but thought that the work on hand would be completed in a few days and the contractor always paid on delivery. From past experience I had found that a check sent to the Revenue Service in Kansas City usually took a week or so to get back to the bank, and I decided that things would work out if I had the money on hand in a few days. How wrong I was! Three days after I mailed the check, two men dressed in dark suits and wearing gray hats walked into the office. I knew right away who they were and became uncomfortable since I realized that the situation was a serious one. They asked if I was Mr. McCann and I said I was whereupon they both produced badges identifying themselves as Treasury Agents and one of them reached into his pocket and brought out the check that I thought would take much longer to reach the bank. They asked if I knew that the check was worthless and I admitted that I did and explained that I had sent it as a result of the urgency of the request for payment and knew that I would have the money to clear it in a few days. Apparently they had called my bank to see if there was enough to cover it before sending it on to Kansas City. They were typical unsmiling, somber Revenue men, and said that they had orders to get the money that day, or that they would have to close me up and sell my equipment to cover the check, which was in the amount of two thousand dollars. I asked them if I could give them the name of a man in the Federal building that would vouch for me to make the check good. They rather sarcastically asked who in the Federal building would vouch for me. I gave them the name of Chief Deputy United States Marshal Roy Kirgan. They asked if I knew him, since he was their superior and appeared to doubt that I knew him until I told them that I was a personal friend and had known him for most of my life, and asked them to call him at his office, which they did. I could tell immediately that Roy was telling them to give me time to clear the check since the man on the phone repeated "Yes, sir, Mr. Kirgan! Yes, sir, Mr. Kirgan!" and when he hung up the phone, they were more friendly and told me that I would have ten days to make the check good. I told them I would have the money to them within a week, whereupon they smiled and shook hands with me and left. That evening Roy came to my home. I had been to his home and he had been to mine before but this time I felt a little uneasy after what had transpired that day with the agents. I immediately apologized for having the men call him and thanked him for getting me out of a position which could have become rather serious, to which he laughed and said that it was something that happened every day and that I shouldn't worry about it. I made some coffee, and after talking for a while, he arose to leave and asked if I would be able to have the money as promised. I assured him that I would. He said that if anything should come up and that I wasn't able to get it to call him and he would pay it for me and I could reimburse him when it came in. I thanked him and assured him again that the money would be there. He asked me to bring it down to his office when I got it so that I could sign some papers showing that there had been no intention to defraud the government. If I had anticipated a problem, I could have gone to the bank and borrowed the money to cover the check.

Roy was a handsome, heavy set, stocky man with an ever-present smile. I first knew him in St. James while I was in high school. He was the father of Roy Junior and Charles, better known as Bud and Pete. I was in school with both of them and they were always friendly to me. It was Bud who had insisted that I play ball at noon at school. The family owned a grocery store in town and while I was selling horseradish after school, Roy asked me to bring what I had to his store and he would sell it for me and give me all he got. I thanked him but told him that I only had enough for my regular customers in town and didn't want to make too much of it. Home delivery was an era of time when storekeepers had the comfort of their customers in mind. The small black closed truck, emblazoned with "Kirgan's Market *Phone 12*," could be seen flitting about town all hours of the day. One of my best customers was Mr. Hodge, the superintendent. Almost every week he would come into study hall and motion for me to come to his office and ask me to bring him more horseradish. Another steady customer was Miss Muller, the class sponsor. She and her sister lived together with their mother. Shortly after my graduation, she resigned her position as teacher, which she had held since finishing school, and became the head of the James Memorial Library.

Before becoming Chief Deputy, Roy had an active life in law enforcement. He once went to California to bring a wanted murderer back to Missouri. This was before planes were used and he was bringing the man back on a train. Somewhere in Colorado, while they were handcuffed together and asleep late at night, the prisoner knocked Roy out and took the keys to the handcuffs and jumped out of a window of the train as it was crossing a trestle over a river. Roy had the train stopped and dove into the river, captured the man and brought him in. Another time, his picture was in the St. Louis daily paper showing him making a running tackle to bring down a prisoner who made a break for it during a murder trial.

     When Roy's wife died a number of years before his death, I went out to St. James, Missouri, to the funeral. I was standing at the entrance to the chapel, unsure as to where I should sit. There were a number of personnel from the Federal Building in St. Louis, including some federal judges. Mr. Kirgan came up and taking me by the arm led me to the side that is usually reserved for family members. When I protested that it was the side for families, he said, "Arthur, you are a member of this family." This man's warmth and friendliness has stayed with me and has had an effect on my life.

Sister M. Lillian McCormack, S.S.N.D.

One of the more pleasant aspects of owning a business came about while engaged in building custom furniture. A call came to the office one day from Sister Lillian McCormack, the founder of St. Mary's Special School for Exceptional Children. An appointment was made for the next morning. Arriving at the school in northwest St. Louis, I was impressed with the huge four-story building, which had at one time been an orphans' home. Sister Lillian met me at the door. She was perhaps forty-five, dressed in a conventional habit which I presumed would be uncomfortable in the hot weather but it seemed to have no effect on her smiling, happy countenance. We became friends and I did many projects for her for many years. We made several fixtures for the classrooms and chapel and cloister. She always had something she wanted done, and my prices were always agreeable with her. She called the projects "labors of love."

One year she called two weeks before Christmas. I went over to see her and she excitedly told of how Monsignor Elmer Behrman, the head of the St. Louis Archdiocese and associate and resident in the school, had told her and the other sisters that he would pay for a much needed dining table for their cloister. It was to be made of walnut laminate, twelve feet long and four feet wide with alcoves built into its six inch thickness all around for holding prayer books and beads during meals. She said it had to be finished for their Christmas breakfast. I had previously built some huge walnut bookcases for Father Behrman's office at the school. I was under no obligation to complete it in the two weeks before Christmas, and protested to her that I had men on other contracts and couldn't see how we could also do the table. She put her hand on my arm and said, "Arthur, God never says how or when. I know you can do it for us." I told her I would do all I could to have it for them for Christmas morning.

I immediately set about getting the necessary materials and went over to Granite City, Illinois, across the river to my sister and brother-in-law's home. Jim Roller had been working for me in the evenings after his work at the Granite City Steel Co., and after telling him the story, he agreed to help me. He came over every evening and sometimes brought our friend, Bob McKinney, to help us. We often worked until midnight and could see the huge table taking shape. It was supported with two pedestals three feet by one foot. Two days before Christmas we started to cover it all with walnut laminate, also called Formica, which is precision work and slow to avoid damages.

The day before Christmas, Jim called her and told her it would be there but would probably be after midnight. She laughed and said she didn't mind the time. They would be waiting for it. It was one in the morning when Jim called again and said we were loading it on the truck and asked if anyone would be there to help carry it up the steep flight of steps. She laughed and said they would help. It was about two in the morning when we got there. About eight young nuns in full habit came running down in the snow and lifted it off the truck. She told them that if they dropped it, to fall under it. She laughingly said that their bones would heal but the table wouldn't. We had it assembled at about three Christmas morning. They all held hands and danced around it singing Christmas songs. I have never regretted the extra work involved in making it for them.

Sister Lillian once asked me to have lunch with her and Sister Dona, her Principal. She said that most of the hundred and fifty students were downs syndrome, and she asked if I had ever seen a happier group. I admitted that I hadn't. They were always smiling and would sometimes come and hug me. I enjoyed being around them when working there. Then she said, "Arthur, you are deaf and it seems that you can do anything at all and you always seem happy. Maybe God brought this about so that you could show others that some so-called handicaps are really an advantage.

A number of years later she left the school and opened another one, St. Michael Special School, in New Orleans. She and Sister Dona came back to visit St. Mary's one time and called Laura and me to come visit with them. After a couple of hours, we got up to leave and I told her we would be in New Orleans some time and would take them out to dinner. I was glad to see that they both now wore more conservative dress-type habits. She said, "Is that a date?" I said yes.

Several years later we were in New Orleans. We had called ahead that we were coming. They were as happy to see us as we were to see them and took us all around the school, which they said had two hundred students. She showed us an album of her family, brothers and sisters and parents. She was born in New Orleans. I was teasing her and said that after seeing her family, she was the prettiest one and asked her why she had never married. She laughed and said she had been "jilted." I have wondered if that may have been the case. We reminded her of the promise to take them to dinner, and I added that since we had the camper van, we would call a cab for the four of us. She said, "No way. We have our own car." We went to a very nice restaurant on the bay. For years she had sent us flyers about a fundraising event which she planned at an exclusive downtown hotel and it always said "Black Tie Only." We would send her a check and add that I couldn't come because I couldn't afford a black tie. When the bill came, I reached for it, and she grabbed it saying, "You can't pay for this. You can't even afford a black tie." and laughed. She insisted on paying for it.

Since the visit, we have been sending them a sizable donation each month. She has always responded with a lovely letter. In her last letter a year ago, she told of how their prayers were answered. They had needed money for building repairs. Celebrity New Orleans Chef Emeril had won a hundred twenty-five thousand dollars in the celebrity version of *Who Wants to Be a Millionaire* and had given it to them. Two weeks later, Sister Dona wrote that Sister Lillian had died suddenly of a brain hemorrhage. We were very sorry to learn that. She was eighty-five. We loved her and miss her.

Another incident involving McCann and Company came up one day at noon. A call had come in early that morning from the city Fire Marshal who had been in the day before when I wasn't there to do an inspection and the call said he would be back at noon that day. I had been out on a call and he was in the office when I got in. I looked at him and asked him what he was doing there, and he asked me the same thing. He was Kenneth Sturdevant, the Fire Marshal but I didn't know he was with the city. He saw the company name but didn't know I was the owner. He said that if he had known I was the owner, he would never have turned in his report which he said wasn't serious and that he would say that it had been corrected. He was one of mom's many relatives at City Hall. Another one of her relatives was a cousin, Robert LaBaube, the chief of Internal Revenue in the federal building. He had served at a different time than when I had a problem with the check.

There were times while operating McCann and Company that resulted in comical incidents. I would sometimes visit a club run by the deaf for deaf members. I wasn't a member but enjoyed the company. There was a young deaf Mexican, rather short in stature and able to speak and read lips with difficulty. He came to me at one of these parties and asked me what I did and I told him I was a cabinetmaker. He asked for the name of the company and I told him. He did not know my name. A few days later he came into the shop where I was with some of the workmen. He asked me if I liked working there and I said I did. He then asked if he could work there and I asked him what he could do. He was embarrassed and said "not much of anything." I told him to come into the office. When we got there, I asked him to sit down and I sat behind the desk. He looked around and said that if I would talk to the boss for him, he might be hired. Then he looked around and asked, "Where is the boss?" I said, "I am the boss. I own the company." He didn't say a word but got up and walked out.

The way in which I had been forced to grope through life during my formative years in the deaf world -- never knowing for sure from day to day whether I was being accepted, always hoping for a better tomorrow -- shows graphically how the loss of hearing at an age where life has begun to instill customs differs from deafness at birth.

At age nine we are beginning to awaken more fully

and becoming conscious of our surroundings. We begin to take an interest in what life has to offer and become curious to the point of asking questions. We are acutely aware of sounds. Each new one registers and becomes an indelible mark in our learning process. I remember each sound made by the farm animals, from the lowing of the cows at milking time, the bellowing of the bull calling to his mate, the grunt of the pigs and the whinny of horses. Each had a sound foreign to the others but each had its place in the general scope of farm life.

Later in the city came sounds never heard before. There were the sounds of the trains and announcers at the stations, there were the sounds of cars in the streets with their horns and loud mufflers. The factory whistles told us what time it was. The rumbling and crash of thunder told us to go indoors to wait for the rain and winds to subside. These are the sounds we remember. The voices of loved ones remain with us in the sounds we hear constantly in our minds long after they have gone.

Professional educators and those working with the deaf are pitifully lacking in any underlying knowledge of the actual problems faced by those who have lately become deaf as compared to those born into a world without hearing. This can only be learned from actually living it, not from reading about it in books or listening to instructors. The two groups are combined since they share a common handicap although living in totally different worlds. Those born deaf have never known sound. They have never heard the chilling quiver of a bow being drawn over taut strings of a violin. They have never known the beauty of a strummed guitar, or the piercing notes of the trumpet. They feel the throbbing of the drums and assume all music is of this nature. The lilting notes of a lively tune from the piano are gone, and in their place is a rhythmic vibration.

Once, while talking with a woman deaf from birth, I was extolling the advantages of life in the hearing world. With a look of puzzlement, she asked if being able to hear was really all that wonderful.

There are times when situations arise which reverberate into comical endings. My father was in a hospital for several weeks with tuberculosis and I would drive my mother to see him, a distance of two hundred miles. Upon arriving at the hospital on a Sunday afternoon in mid October, we proceeded to his room on an upper floor. Once in the elevator, which was operated by a young girl and which was crowded with visitors, Mom remarked to the girl that I was her son and that I was deaf, but she added that I was a lipreader. Now, I am sure that none of the ones in the elevator had the foggiest idea what a lipreader was but all eyes were on me. I was 40 years old and felt like an imbecile being led around by my mom. Later, outside in the car, I became very angry and asked why she thought it necessary to announce that I was deaf. She replied that if someone tried to talk to me behind my back, I wouldn't be able to understand them. Actually she thought she was doing me a favor, but I reminded her that after that, no one in the elevator would try to speak to me, and further, told her that if she ever did that again, that I would do something she would regret. She became flustered and asked what I would do. Whereupon I told her that the next time it happened, I would tell everyone around that she walked with a slight limp because she had a bad case of hemorrhoids. She angrily replied that she had nothing of the kind, and I said she couldn't prove it. It never happened again. On a more serious side of this incident -- There are times when someone will introduce me to another and immediately announce "He is deaf." That statement practically leaves me dead since anyone hearing it will usually make no attempt to talk to me. I have to lamely explain that I am a lipreader, which sometimes helps and sometimes doesn't, depending on the nature of the one involved. For this reason, I never tell anyone that I am deaf. I explain that I have a serious hearing problem and that lipreading helps me to understand. This usually brings about a concerted effort to help.

Deafness is an invisible torment that is ever present, affording no release. Modern educators have coined phrases and words that make it sound as though prestige is attached to the damning lifestyle, but there is nothing that will alleviate the facts associated with total deafness. They use such terms as "hearing impaired" and "profoundly deaf" which they feel cover all facets of hearing defects including total. They say students who are able to attend regular schools have been "mainstreamed." They are but they need interpreters. They use professional jargon and often lose sight of what they originally set out to seek, specifically, a way to help those less fortunate than themselves. They are like the fellow who, when he found himself up to his ass in alligators, remembered that he was supposed to drain the swamp. Numerous associations bearing alphabetical titles have been formed to which they travel internationally for conventions among other organizations. They have the Alexander Graham Bell Association for the Deaf and have added a sub-association for the oral deaf--those able to communicate orally. While attending conventions, these oral deaf members are issued separate badges branding them, which leads to "mouthing" on the part of regular members.

Alexander Graham Bell, other than inventing the telephone, was purported to be a famous teacher of speech and lipreading. I am in no position to dispute this contention; however, I do find it extremely difficult to visualize in light of the fact that all his pictures show him with a full, flowing beard and mustache. I have learned from painful experience that it is virtually impossible to lipread a person whose face is covered with "foliage." My grandfather wore a full mustache, which prevented any form of communication between us from the time I lost my hearing until his death thirteen years later. All I could see was his mustache bobbing up and down, although I could make out a general meaning from eye expressions which, along with facial changes, serve to identify the primary essentials necessary for speechreading.

Several years ago my wife and I were in Nova Scotia, Canada, and visited the home and laboratories of Alexander Graham Bell. There were displays of numerous of his inventions and most were interesting. We looked for whatever was in evidence pertaining to his work with the deaf, for which he was especially famous. We found pictures in a corner that showed him as a teacher. There were many movie screens in various rooms showing his work. We asked an attendant why they weren't captioned for the deaf and were told that they couldn't afford it even though the entire layout was worth in the millions.

In spite of numerous obstacles strewn by the wayside of life, deafness has offered advantages far above any which would have been available had I been journeying through life in a normal way. I have been fortunate in having been gifted with an understanding nature. Regardless of how densely the pathways of life have been strewn with stumbling blocks, I have striven to convert the majority into stepping stones. I have remembered Mr. Hodge's departing message as I graduated from high school.

Life has dealt some extremely disheartening blows that have landed well below the belt and left me reeling. Struggling to regain my composure, I have always found a gleam of light shining through which has eventually evolved into rays of encouragement and renewed hope.

Except for the time I sought employment at Chevrolet on the assembly lines and the cooperage plant and found rejection due to my deafness, I have never applied for a job through regular channels. Each position I have held has been proffered and each time I have been free to accept or refuse. Some, including the aircraft plants, have come about through recommendations from within the organizations, or relatives and friends.

Arcy Manufacturing Company, which I co-owned for three years.

A 12-foot bending brake operated by James H. Roller.
One of the numerous machines at
Arcy Manufacturing Company.

Arcy Manufacturing Company

During a recession in the late fifties when I was having some financial problems, I was having dinner with some friends I had known from doing work for them. I mentioned that I would have to let my office man, Mr. O'Connor, go since I couldn't afford to keep him. Mr. Herbert Worth motioned to his wife and said, "She can take the phone for you." I said I couldn't pay her and he said, "I wouldn't let you." She came down from time to time. She liked the arrangement since she had never worked outside of the home. They owned a large furniture company. Not long after, I was approached by a man who was interested in forming a partnership to manufacture steel office furniture, service station equipment and some hospital and restaurant fixtures. Since I already had the building and most of the necessary equipment, I abandoned my custom furniture venture and went into an equal partnership. At one time we employed fifteen men. The name was Arcy Manufacturing Company.

This was another mistake from the beginning as I later found he was the type of person who leaned toward harassment and considering my handicap, I was unable to cope with his methods. It was after about three years that I discovered some unsavory practices he had been engaging in, namely buying stolen property to use in our manufacturing, and mentioned them to a friend one evening at his home. I first became aware of it when I saw several very expensive stainless steel stirrups used on examining tables and asked where they came from. He admitted that they had been stolen by a foreman at the factory where there were made and that he had bought them among other things. He lamely tried to justify the practice by saying that all businesses did that. I had initially been unaware of his practices. He had taken care of the business and I most of the manufacturing. His wife took care of the bookkeeping and typing. This was before Xerox and copy machines. He would often give me the fifth carbon copy, which was too dim to read and other harrassments. This friend was Roy Kirgan, the Chief United States Deputy Marshall, whom I have mentioned before. He told me of the dangers of remaining in the partnership, explaining the possibility that if he were to be called upon to arrest him, in his position as United States Marshall, he would have to arrest me as well. He suggested that I look for other avenues of endeavor. It was at this point that we initiated the dissolution of the partnership. Since we hadn't been in business long enough to satisfy the seven-year book value requirement, it was necessary that I relinquish all the machinery, equipment and tools that comprised my half of the business. Because I also owned half of the three-story factory building, that was also involved in the seven-year clause, and I emerged with a considerable financial loss. It was at one point in the dissolution that he asked the lawyer involved if my car, a new Chevrolet Impala, was included, to which the lawyer, showing disgust, answered, "Of course not. That's personal property." It was at this point that I contacted my younger brother, Raymond, who was director of personnel of the state division of employment security. He suggested McDonnell Douglas aircraft manufacturing and arranged an appointment for me with the personnel manager, with whom he was acquainted, before I left Arcy. It was a very successful interview at which I was given a job in the Engineering Department as a Mock-Up man and Precision Toolmaker. Roy expressed a desire to come to the factory on my last day, if only to see what sort of person I had been in business with. I introduced him as Mr. Kirgan. The fellow asked him all sorts of questions, some personal and in the end Roy just said, "I am Arthur's friend." Later, out in his car, he told me he had been in Federal law enforcement for over twenty years and had never met a worse son of a bitch than the one I had been in business with. Roy said he was glad that I had found employment with McDonnell Douglas. I became so engrossed in my work at McDonnell Douglas that about a year passed. I had wanted to see him to tell him of the new work. I was shocked to see his picture in the morning paper announcing his death. I was unable to go to the funeral but went to the funeral home in St. James to see him the day before the funeral. I stood by his coffin and said a prayer for a man I loved and called my friend.

I had always been rather close to my Uncle Bill Kampman, Mom's brother. In later years, after his wife Aunt Thelma had died of a brain tumor, we would visit twice a year. A number of years after her death, he married a friend whom I came to know as Aunt Jessie. They would come to my home on Labor Day and I went to their home in Joplin, Missouri, on Thanksgiving. Laura and I continued this after our marriage. It was at one of these visits that I told him of the partnership dissolution and the loss of all of my assets in the firm. He expressed regret and reminded me of the perils of doing business with strangers.

It was with a great deal of hesitation and soul searching that I decided to include the following in this autobiography. As I have mentioned previously, my parents could never accept me as an individual other than as "a deaf kid." I had struggled for several years to build my business, McCann and Company, to a worthwhile endeavor. Outside of loaning me a couple thousand dollars to help start up, they never showed much interest in my work. It was after about five years that all my siblings had gone from the farm and this left my parents without help. They came to me one day and suggested that I give up the business and return to the farm to help them and to work off what I still owed them, less than a thousand dollars. When I protested that I had three men working for me and plenty of work on order, they simply said to let the men go, sell my machinery, and let someone else take over the work. As ridiculous as it sounded, they were serious. I finally got through to them that what they were asking would be impossible. It was some time after that that I was telling Uncle Bill of how I was repaying the loan from my parents that he became angry, considering all the work I had continued to do for them of which he was aware. Since Mom was his sister and knowing that his temper flared easily, I decided to withhold the part about asking me to give up my business. He went to them and although I do not know what was said, my next trip to see them resulted in them not only canceling my note including the one I had at the local bank, but Wilma and Jim's and Howard's as well. Howard had borrowed from them to convert the farm from horse-drawn to tractor and other power equipment. Nothing more was ever said about it. Not long afterward, they sold the farm and moved to Cuba, Missouri, where they spent the remaining years of their retirement.

It was on Uncle Bill's death a number of years later that his lawyer approached Laura and me after the funeral and told us Uncle Bill had left me twenty-five thousand dollars in a tax-free CD. He had been a postal letter carrier in Joplin for forty years. His act of compassion and love has stayed with me and I have tried to equal it whenever an occasion has arisen.

McDonnell Douglas Aircraft Corporation

  My appointment with the personnel manager went well. Arriving at the appointed time I went to the desk at the front of the room and told the receptionist that I had an appointment with Mr. Whittington. There were several hundred in the room. The Gemini spacecraft mock up was just beginning. She asked me why I wanted to see Mr. Whittington and I said, "for a job here." At that she handed me an application form and asked me to wait my turn. I protested that the appointment was for ten o'clock and that I didn't want to keep him waiting. She was still skeptical and I asked her to call him. His office was right behind her. She called and before she hung up the phone, he appeared in the door and motioned saying, "Come in, Arthur." He explained the operation of the plant and assured me there would be no problems concerning my deafness. He said he had already checked my qualifications and that I would be working in Engineering Mock Up. I asked for a two-week extension so as to dispose of the business I was in. When I rose and reached across the desk to shake hands with him, he took my hand and pushed me back into my chair. I asked if something was wrong and he said he had been head of that department for fifteen years and no one had ever left the office without asking how much they would be paid. I told him I purposely had not asked him that. I told him that I had a job like his at one time, although in a much smaller way. People would come to my office and ask how much I would pay. Sometimes I would say "nothing" and send them away. I also told him that Raymond had told me of the pay scales and work classifications. I added that I knew I would be on a twenty-day probation period and after that he could decide where to put me, or ask me to leave. He exclaimed, "I'll be damned. I like your attitude. You are to be a top grade journeyman Engineering Mock Up man and precision toolmaker. The only way you can make more is when the company and union decide on raising the rates." I thanked him and left his office. I met him a few weeks later in the cafeteria and he asked me how things were going. I told him that I liked the work and he said he had received reports from my foreman commending me.

    Mr. Whittington's assurance that no difficulties would arise in relation to my handicap notwithstanding, they came on loud and clear from the beginning. It is human nature to assume any handicap, especially total deafness, carries with it a certain degree of occupational risk. Supervisors are reluctant to assign responsibility, resulting in resentment and feelings of inferiority. Handicapped individuals are often more capable of dependability than their so-called normal contemporaries, but their capacities must remain dormant until an opportunity arises, allowing them a chance to prove their capabilities are valuable and of a competitive nature. Albeit most deaf are quick to grasp a given situation, they are not always able to show through oral conveyance that they understand and want to assume control.

    It was evident from my first day on the job that I was being favored with minor, insignificant tasks. The foreman watched apprehensively as I assumed operation of simple machinery. He went to great lengths to explain the operation of each piece of equipment, ignoring my protests that I was entirely familiar with their potentials and hazards. As time progressed, I was ultimately permitted to utilize my talents, but it was several months before I was in a position to fully convince my superiors, including the engineers involved, of the feasibility of giving me a free hand in development of construction procedures involving aircraft tooling projects, and permitting my operation of more complicated machinery.

The beginning of my second tenure in aircraft manufacture coincided with the inception of one of the first spacecraft. The departments were buzzing with activity in constructing preliminary models of the proposed craft and conversation dwelt mostly on the various aspects of initial procedures necessary before actual construction could be undertaken for the full-scale mock-up of the craft. The astronauts came by to inspect specifications and to supply data for precision detail work. Nothing was left to chance. Each man knew how crucial the work was and how each one's performance would affect the finished space vehicle. In retrospect, the foreman's concern for my ability in the beginning may properly be traced to his realization that, with so much depending upon the successful completion of the ship, he had to show diligence in ascertaining each new man's capabilities and performance. There is an added possibility that my handicap was immaterial. However, the fact remains that not every man was scrutinized as closely in the beginning as I was. Nor were they subjected to as complete a sifting, performance-wise, as I was required to undergo, especially considering that I was assuming duties as a top-grade journeyman and precision machinist and mock-up man in the engineering department. Upon the return of the first spacecraft, it was sent to our department for inspection. The heat shield was of foremost importance since if it burned through, the astronauts would be killed.

The lot of the deaf is a difficult one. Their fiercest drawback lies in communication. Many professionals dealing with the deaf will show a concerted effort when speaking to them, consisting of various mediums, among them an exaggeration of lip movements, hand motions and facial gyrations, deliberate slowing down of their regular speaking manner, and occasionally, abbreviating what they would normally say. As in every instance, this does not constitute a blanket coverage, but occurrences are numerous enough to bring on consternation among deaf laymen who are concerned with the methods employed. When the deaf have been accustomed to communicating with teachers, hearing friends, or other individuals with whom they normally associate in the manner described, it is no wonder they have so much difficulty understanding total strangers who are not familiar with the methods customarily used. This is not a form of criticism of individuals who work with the deaf. It is merely stating a fact as it exists. Many deaf will welcome any form of communication available. They are eager to show they can be reached and are not in a position to be critical of those desiring to help. The ones who protest these approaches and cringe inwardly when they confront them are principally the deafened who have become deaf during a later stage in life and remember how it once was.

At the plane plant I encountered an assortment of individuals within a short period that would comprise a lifetime under normal conditions. A couple of weeks after I began working in the machinist department, a number of us were given the task of making scale models of the space capsule approximately a foot high. I was attempting to put a mixture of fiberglass in a mold and was having trouble making it hold a shape. Al Sadowski, the foreman, came by and after watching for a minute or so asked me what the trouble was. When I told him, he became a bit agitated and said that I was a top grade man and ought to be able to do better. I said I could if I knew the right way. I had never done it before and had been told to do it as I was doing it. He asked who had told me to do it that way and I motioned to two men who were watching it all. He looked at them and told me to carry on and then left. Half an hour later, he returned and asked me to come to his office. Telling me to sit down, he said he was sorry he had jumped on me out there. He said those fellows were lower grade men and wanted to get me in trouble. He added that from then on to come to him when I needed help. We got along fine after that. I was naturally the butt of crude jokes, which I accepted in stride. There were times when at break time, I would be reading the paper at my workbench and would look up to see everyone laughing. Someone had blown up a paper sack and had burst it behind me. The members of my immediate department adjusted well to my presence since there were other deaf in the area, although my acceptance was varied. They had difficulty in deciding whether to communicate normally or whether to use a form of total as they did with the others who were not adept at lipreading and whose speech was difficult to understand. The majority decided to speak normally after discovering that my vocabulary warranted it. Difficulties came about when it was necessary to do "spot" jobs in departments other than the one to which I was assigned, where I associated with workmen who had no previous contact with the deaf, and who were unable to cope.

There have been several examples of ineptitude displayed by administrators of learning centers for the deaf. One which gained national attention was when the Curators of the Gallaudet College for the Deaf in Washington, D.C., appointed a female Ph.D. as president. While her education level no doubt qualified her for the position, she had absolutely no knowledge of the problems faced by the deaf, and indeed, she knew nothing about the sign language while the college predominately uses the signs. The result was a revolt by the students and finally she was removed in favor of a male deafened Ph.D. who has done very well in the position and relates to the students as one of them.

Another glaring example, displaying total ignorance was when a large research center invited a deaf author to give a speech to an audience composed of individuals interested in accomplishments of the deaf. About two dozen deaf adults, mostly college graduates, were invited to attend, along with a large hearing audience. The stage was approximately fifty feet wide and the deaf speaker was positioned at the far end of the stage. There was a screen in the center of the stage projecting his speech, and the deaf members of the audience were grouped in front of it. There were two interpreters, one oral and one signing on each side of the screen. These interpreters had difficulty hearing and therefore understanding the speaker, because of the distance, and resorted to reading the print on the screen before interpreting. When asked why the interpreters were needed, and why the speaker hadn't been placed in the center of the stage to afford the deaf a chance to observe his performance and in the event of not being able to understand him, to simply turn to the screen, the answer was that they were unsure that the deaf members would be able to read the words on the screen or understand them. This was not only a display of stupidity and total ignorance, but was an insult to the intelligence of the educated deaf. I have purposely omitted the name of the research Ph.D. responsible for this fiasco.

The greater part of my years at the airplane plant was spent on the night shift. In the beginning, this was necessitated by low seniority, but progressively, I discovered many benefits contingent with night work. After accumulating sufficient seniority to assume day shift status, I preferred to remain on nights since it left several hours of free time during the day, which was used to further contract assignments. In addition, the second shift, as it was called, paid a premium bonus, an added incentive that kept many veteran employees loyal to night work.

My newly found lifestyle afforded many advantages. Gone was the financial strain that had dominated. My colleagues were helpful and understanding. Each day became less complicated and I began to look forward to assuming a more normal life. For the first time I could think constructively and make tentative plans for the future.

As time passed, I discovered how working nights, including almost every Saturday in overtime, could bring on seclusion which resulted in the return of a total lack of social life. In the beginning, I welcomed anything which would alleviate the financial pressures I had lived under for so long, but I began to miss the companionship I had become accustomed to in former years and sought an avenue of escape from the gradual depression I found engulfing me. Being unable to use the telephone is a severe disadvantage in any form of social life, and deafness itself disqualifies the average individual from participation in almost any, except deaf-oriented, group activities. By this time, another factor was emerging which added to the already accumulated barriers I had come to accept as the norm in a deafened world. I was in my mid-forties, an age which many consider halfway, but one at which I had just begun to discover the many things life had to offer, only to find that as soon as one difficulty had been recognized and overcome, another would arise to take its place. Ordinarily, adverse situations over which we have no control, can be ignored and a hope harbored that they will go away. However, when the nature of the situation is one that defies normal reason, then we must, in retrospect, try to understand why life has dealt the cards we hold, and keep our trump for overwhelming demands.

      The total lack of social life began to take its toll. I could see others enjoying a happiness that appeared to be bordering upon fantastic compared to my limited scope of activities. I could not see nor recognize any form of obstacles that might lie in their paths. I could see only the things that were not available to me and the weight of the resulting oppression was dragging me deeper and deeper into depression. Because of a slack in work at the plant, it was not possible to get a transfer onto the day shift, which would have given me a chance to have my evenings free. In desperation, I began to contact customers I had served while operating McCann and Company several years before, with the thought of doing furniture repair and building on contract, which would make it possible to leave the aircraft company. A short time later, the tooling and mock up for the F-15 Eagle, the fastest fighter in the world at the time, was completed. Before its final manufacture, the full size mock up was displayed in its full splendor in a special room of mahogany walls and a dark blue carpet. It left those of us who built it with a feeling of pride in our accomplishment and it was a real thrill when we assembled on the ramp to see the first completed plane take off and soar into the air. When the first one was in the air, the company announced a sweeping layoff that was to affect large numbers of engineers and supporting departments. Our department was to be reduced by half, although instead of a layoff we were given the option of transferring into alternate departments until we would again be needed for engineering assistance. A layoff was an answer to prayers since it afforded a chance to leave the plant without giving up my position. I had three years of layoff status before being recalled to the plant unless they needed me sooner in my home department, in which case I would have to return or sever all connections with the company. In lieu of a transfer, I chose the layoff.

At this point I would like to recount an occurrence during the building of the F-15 full size mock up. When the contract was signed, Mr. Mac, as he preferred to be called, came into our department and explained the situation. We were competing against another company in California, which had offered a different design, and he was anxious that we complete ours before they did. He said that we would be on twelve-hour shifts with Saturday and Sunday as options. One time at the beginning of the shift, I was talking to the foreman about what he wanted me to do while standing under some scaffolding. Suddenly a good-sized piece of plywood was knocked off the scaffolding and hit me in the head. Startled and in pain, I angrily exclaimed, "Who is the son of a bitch that hit me in the head with a piece of plywood?" Hawk, my foreman, said, "Sssshhh! That is Mr. Malvern." He was the head engineer on the project. I said, "I don't care who he is!" Mr. Malvern came down and I apologized. He said, "No. If someone hit me in the head like that, I would call him a son of a bitch, too."

Generally, total deafness is difficult to understand and is feared by ordinary laymen. Very few, including scholars purporting to gain an insight into the difficulties arising as a result of the handicap, are able to fully comprehend the walk through life in silence. We look about us and see movement. Our lives become a pantomime in which we must decipher each movement into a meaning relative to a present need. We must be content with abbreviated contexts and be able to fill in missing parts resulting from monosyllable communication with individuals uninterested in supplying anything other than basic fundamentals.

Some Deaf People I Have Admired

Ever since my earlier years at Central Institute, I have known many deaf and partially deaf individuals who have become successful in later years. There are three that have returned to mind each time I think of them and have decided to bring them to the fore as examples of persistent intelligent effort. I have known all of them since they were young children and I have watched from a distance as they evolved into successful adults. They are Penelope Atlee, T. Alan Hurwitz, Ph.D., and Heather Whitestone McCallum.

Then there were two men who had striven most of their lives against obstacles in their way and each became successful in their own right in the end. They were Hillis Arnold and Fidel Lopez De La Rosa.

Penelope Atlee

Penelope Atlee, or Penny as she has always been called, has succeeded in her quest for success in spite of her deafness. Her early memories are of her father, a young soldier, taking her from their home in Iowa to St. Louis, Missouri, where he left her at the age of four at the Central Institute for the Deaf. He then went on to the induction center at Jefferson Barracks in south St. Louis County to await orders for transfer overseas. This was in 1944. He was with the paratroopers and was killed on D-Day. Penny's last memory of him was in hugging one of his legs while standing with her feet on one of his feet as he walked around. It was about fifty years later that she journeyed to France and found his grave in the American Cemetery. She said it was an emotional time for her to at last be so near to him and yet so far. She has often wondered how her life would have been different if he had lived. She had been an only child and her mother had problems of her own, so her grandparents, her father's parents, adopted her at the age of ten. She saw her mother every year until her mother's death in 1978.

I asked if she had any positive memories of her teachers at Central Institute. She said Mr. Shore, Mrs. Maritz, and Mr. Hartwig were her favorites and had helped her a lot. I can understand how she would remember Irvin Shore and Bill Hartwig. They and I have been friends for many years up to the present time. My early memories of her were seeing her in the halls of the school and her cheery smile. The school nurse would tell me when she was in the infirmary and I would take a flower or two to her room. We've kept in touch over the years at CID reunions, through letters, TTY phone calls, and now email.

After leaving Central Institute, she returned to Iowa and entered high school. She described herself as a "social butterfly" and a "go-getter," which helped her in getting and keeping a positive attitude. She feels that life in a small town was an advantage for her since there wasn't much knowledge about deafness. The high school was small and she knew everyone, even though she had problems in having others recognize her for who she was. Her grandparents arranged for several girls in her freshman class to include her in activities and it wasn't long until she was "in."

Most of her associations were with hearing people as well as some oral deaf. Apparently she and I have had similar experiences in the field of socializing, although she has succeeded in having a broader scope of friends than I have had. As she has become older, she prefers the company of the oral deaf since they probably have more in common like myself. She knows little of the signs, which she calls "broken sign language." Although ninety-five percent deaf, she is fortunate in having a considerable amount of music awareness.

She received a BSW at the University of Iowa and completed a year of graduate study at California State University. She was working full time so she went to classes in the evening. There were no interpreters in schools in those days so it took determination and hard work to accomplish what hearing students did more easily. She has had a varied work experience, including owning and operating a store. She has worked as an income tax preparer, as well as a bookkeeper and account clerk for a variety of governmental agencies, educational institutions and businesses. Her extensive and varied experiences finally led to self-employment as a mail order manager for a foundation that has a department that distributes videos and materials about oral deaf education in five languages worldwide.

She was married to a hearing man and they had two sons. One had influenza meningitis which left him with a 100 decibel loss in one ear and a 65 decibel loss in the other. She was not unduly distressed by this son's loss since she had experienced it herself. Her husband left this son's education to her and she naturally turned to Central Institute. Her afterthoughts are that she wished she had moved to a big city and had him mainstreamed from day one. Like her, he is oral. The marriage ended after twenty-three years. She said her husband was a stable hard-working man who was happy in his simple lifestyle, but did not understand how he could make it easier for her as he saw her as a very capable and independent woman. Most laymen today including the professionals working with the deaf are at a loss as to the actual needs of those in a world alien to those who profess to help.

After her divorce, she moved to Los Angeles, California. She found that the easy acceptance of her deafness that she had experienced in Iowa took a different turn and she became more aware of the handicap. She found many advantages to living in Los Angeles, including many services that were not available in the smaller Iowa town where she grew up. Also, there were more oral deaf friends to be made as well as those with normal hearing. There were more opportunities for employment where her deafness was immaterial.

I asked her if she had ever felt as though she had been cheated by being deaf. She said that she hates the fact that she is deaf because she is a people person and loves music. She also wasn't completely decided as to whether it was an advantage or disadvantage. She added that she has been made aware of many things that those in the hearing world would never think to consider. She has also found that more doors are open to an energetic, self-confident handicapped individual than would be available to her otherwise. She possesses a positive nature and is not easily discouraged. She has expressed a wish to get a cochlear implant, which she feels would help her. She has been trying to get her health insurance to cover the fifty thousand dollar cost.

With all the various jobs she has had, all except one were obtained without help. When first in California, she went to the state employment service, but after that, she is proud to say that she did it all on her own, and did not need or use an interpreter nor a pad and pen. She thanks Central Institute and the fact that she spent practically a hundred percent of her time in the hearing world. Because of all this, she learned to speak more clearly and lip-read more fluently. It is a joy to see how she handles herself in spite of her "so called" shortcomings.

T. Alan Hurwitz, Ph.D.

Numerous deaf have gone to heights thought to be unreachable considering their handicap. Many have achieved goals attained through long, hard work, only to discover, to their chagrin, that their qualifications are for positions which require certain capabilities that they lack and for which their training failed to forewarn. An example of persistent, intelligent effort can be found in the success story of Dr. T. Alan Hurwitz. Born totally deaf he attended the Central Institute for the Deaf in St. Louis, and upon graduating, delivered newspapers in his hometown in Iowa while attending high school. I first met him while he was a student in my manual training class at Central Institute. He was an excellent worker and anxious to learn.

Alan attended Washington University in St. Louis at a time when there were no interpreters and graduated with an engineering degree. He had been exasperated as well as frustrated after applying to over sixty companies and was told by most of them that his credentials were outstanding and that he would make an excellent engineer, but that he lacked experience. Many of his hearing classmates were getting offers as long as nine months prior to graduating. Finally, while talking with the CEO of a small company in St. Louis, he "blew his top" and asked where in hell he could get work experience if no one would give him a chance. He was given excellent advice and told to focus on large companies that have the resources for training and professional development on the job. He was further told that small companies do not have the resources and could not afford to lose employees after training and development. That was why they looked for experience in new employees although lack of experience could often be translated into one word, *deaf*. With some help, as I had, he obtained an interview with the Personnel Director at McDonnell Aircraft Corporation. During this interview, which did lead to his employment at McDonnell, he learned that his application had been placed in the inactive file because of his deafness. In his position with McDonnell, he experienced limitations in the workplace that many deaf people did. That was before TTYs and interpreters were available as communication aids. However, he was fortunate in having an outstanding supervisor who believed in him and offered encouragement. While working at McDonnell, he attended St. Louis University in the evenings and got his Master of Science degree.

Later he was offered a new faculty position at National Technical Institute for the Deaf, one of eight colleges at Rochester Institute of Technology in Rochester, New York. As an educational specialist, over time he grew professionally and progressively into various leadership positions, which ultimately led to his present position as Dean and Chief Academic Officer of the NTID. He has been on the faculty of NTID for almost thirty-two years. It was during his early years at NTID that he worked on and received his doctoral degree in the evenings. He and his lovely wife Vicki have done many things for the deaf and I feel proud that he was at one time one of my students, and continues to be my friend. He once came to me at an alumni reunion and said he wanted to thank me for teaching him in woodworking.

There have been many instances where the deaf have been encouraged into fields through higher education which has left them disillusioned and unhappy. This is often the result of the schools themselves or parents who do not want to admit that their offspring is handicapped. They often receive so much assistance in reaching the goals prepared for them, they are unable to cope with the actual task when it presents itself in a difficult form, and are unable to fit into the mainstream of society, never having been allowed to find out on their own what life was all about.

Heather Whitestone

Central Institute has always been proud of their graduates and occasionally one will stand out who had made their way with conscientious, persistent effort and has striven tirelessly until the goal has been reached. Heather Whitestone came to Central Institute as a young child and endeared herself to all that she came in contact with by her happy and charming ways. After her graduation from Central Institute and later high school and while she was in college, she decided to enter competition for Miss Alabama, her home state. She failed on her first try, but very determined, she entered the next one and this time she won and became Miss Alabama. As Alabama's representative, she entered the Miss America pageant. With her beauty, her charm, her poise, and with her stunning talent as a ballet dancer, she was crowned Miss America 1995, the first Miss America with a disability. Shortly after her crowning, she came to visit the school. Everyone was looking forward to seeing her. Although she had only a short time to visit and her visit was scheduled very tightly, I went to the school hoping to see her. While a student at the school, she had always given me a bright smile and sometimes a hug when we met in the halls. This day, I was waiting for her to appear at the head of the stairs leading from the preschool. Reaching the top of the stairs with an entourage of reporters, photographers and school administrators, she saw me and came running with open arms and a hug. I asked her how she liked being Miss America and laughing she said she loved it. She was carrying a small walnut box and asked me if I would like to see her crown. I told her I would love to, whereupon she removed it from the box and gave it to me to look at. Several photographers were able to catch the occasion. I was very proud that she had remembered me. Laura and I have seen her twice since. She has married and the last time we saw her was on St. Simons Island, Georgia, where she and her husband, John McCallum, have a summer home. She was with her small son. She now has two children. They reside in Atlanta. Laura's mother also lives on St. Simons Island and we were there for a week. We took the opportunity to see Heather while we were there. She is always effusive in her greetings and we love her.

Hillis Arnold
Concerning other deaf who have made accomplishments, of note is Hillis Arnold. He was born totally deaf and became a world famous sculptor. He had made many beautiful articles. Among them, he was the assistant to Carl Milles, the man who made the "Meeting of the Rivers" fountain across from the St. Louis Union Station. He also made by himself the 30-foot high marble Soldiers Memorial spire in downtown St. Louis. He has made numerous carvings in wood of religious figures and many church altars. Like myself, he demanded perfection and I was proud to call him my friend. He made a statue of a mother and child called "Learners" in marble and I made

Heather Whitestone, Miss America 1995, and the author on her visit to CID.

(Courtesy of Patti Gabriel)

Hillis Arnold's sculpture, *Learners*, and the
author's solid walnut pedestal
in the lobby of CID.

the octagonal base of walnut with a round top for its display in the front lobby of the new Central Institute campus. He taught sculpture and art at the Monticello College in Godfrey, Illinois, for many years. He was about eighty-six years old when he died of cancer.

Fidel Lopez de La Rosa

Another was a Mexican from Mexico City. He had become totally deaf in Detroit at the same time as I did. He was 15 at the time. Fidel Lopez de La Rosa had mastered English after totally losing his hearing. He told me that one time Dr. Silverman was in Mexico City and met him, telling him about the training college at Central Institute. He was told that if he were to complete the course, he would not be awarded a diploma from Washington University because he was a foreigner and deaf. Apparently it was thought that such information would discourage him. He came to the school in 1945. He lived in the dormitory in a room opposite mine. We became good friends and he spent all his spare time studying and writing at his typewriter. A classmate, Lorraine Meier, was his constant companion in school and helped him immensely. Near the end of the second year, it was found that his grades were sufficiently high for graduation but he knew they wouldn't let him graduate. He wrote repeatedly to Dr. Silverman and Dr. Reals of the University begging for a certificate but was steadfastly refused. In the end, he received a paper showing that he had successfully completed the course. He returned to Mexico City and successfully founded and headed a school for the deaf. He died several years ago at the age of 80. I am sorry he didn't live long enough to see the time when Central Institute would become more tolerant of the deafened adult and foreigners.

It has never been my intention to attempt to garner sympathy through the medium of total deafness. To say that I have striven to elicit understanding toward a minority group would be a more accurate description. I have stated before how frustrating it can become to have the term "hearing impaired" used as a synonym for total as well as partial deafness. The two are unrelated and the emotional impact upon the lives of those who must struggle through the maze of misunderstanding and toleration from their peers does not rate on any scale of comparison. Those with a degree of hearing, however slight, are capable of distinguishing sound. Their world is not limited to the use of their eyes to guide them through each day. They need not fear they will miss an impending danger. Highly amplified hearing aids are at their disposal. They need not watch mutely while others enjoy music and laughter. They do not have to watch every movement of a speaker's mouth in an attempt to understand the spoken word. They also do not need to look to see if the water is running. They do not have to display a total dependence upon others for interpretation of programs coming over the airwaves. They need not continually apologize for shortcomings and hope they will be understood. They need not fear that each word will be muted to the hearing world sufficiently to require repetition repeatedly, and occasionally, bring on rejection. And lastly, they do not need to have a dim light in the bedroom while they are with their mates at night.

I have been accused of being emotional and bitter toward some professionals. I admit that I am and feel justified in displaying animosity toward those who are living a mode of life in which they purport authority to a degree prompting rebellion from deafened laymen.

My association with educational professionals in the field of deafness began when I first came to the Institute after finishing high school. Generally, I was receptive to what they taught, and at that early date, professionalism had not reached the magnitude enjoyed by today's scholars. The scope of specialization in the field had not assumed the staggering proportions as presently embellished by so great a number of pseudo experts compared to the genuine.

Trials and disappointments have become an accepted way of life for the deafened. Happiness, feigned or imagined, consistently lacks fulfillment and often comes through imitation. Ever present is the emotional abutment. Segments of life deemed necessary for living in a world totally geared to sound have been deleted. Everywhere there are movements reminding us of the sounds we can no longer hear. Holidays and special occasions bring with them moments of despondency and despair. A certain ornament on a Christmas tree will take us back to Christmases of yesteryear and we will hear in our minds the songs our parents sang on that day, but no songs of the present are there to take their place, or to relieve the pain of recall. We remember the patriotic songs of the Fourth of July which were supplemented by fireworks and sparklers. We remember the social gatherings on the riverbanks along with the heavily laden tables and the buzz of conversation. Our celebrations today have shrunken to watching flashing lights and mingling with people whose mouths move, whose eyes display merriment, but from whom we are unable to detect any sound.

Throughout intermingling phases of living in silence there has always been an escape hatch available, but with which I was not to become familiar until I found toleration was no longer bearable. At the conclusion of each successive bout with depression, brought on by severe feelings of inadequacy, I would find myself closer to understanding the ways of God. I realized that I was being forced to understand more fully the sufferings of others with handicaps greater than mine. I could see how God had given me the combined use of my hands and brain, and how I was able to create. I realized that without the shortcomings which had become a part of my life, I would not have been able to see over the horizons of disappointment into the greener valleys of achievement. I looked forward to when my understanding could reach a point where happiness would prevail.

My life had become a skipper-less ship. Drifting aimlessly and without purpose, I searched for an anchor. Church had never been a part of my life while growing up. Religion embarrassed me and I found it hard to talk about God or anything relative to the spiritual. Any thoughts I had along these lines were hazy. Deaf people can go to church and sit through a sermon that means absolutely nothing. The music is lost. Although they can read the hymn books, the spiritual uplifting which this is supposed to bring is missing. Unless there is someone with them, they cannot find the song which is being sung since they do not know what page it is on. Unless they are exceptional lipreaders, the sermon is also lost. They cannot refer to passages in the Bible that the minister gives out.

In recent years a number of churches have included interpreters in the service. Even the music is interpreted, however this includes only the words while the actual music is missing, although there are signs that depict the rhythm along with the words. Apparently, those who have been deaf from birth can find enjoyment in this manner since they have never heard a musical instrument. I have never been able to derive satisfaction from music by merely following the words. Subsequently, going to church never meant much to me. The spiritual meaning of the Word of God eluded me. There had never been a meaningful medium. Even the interpreted services weren't within my reach as I knew no signs. Recently, closed-captioned sermons have come to television, the end result of untiring work of the deaf.

It was later that I came to realize how life can be filled with the ways of God without going to church. Although I had always possessed a degree of humility in my dealings with others, I never fully realized the depth to which one can go in reaching his fellowmen through God-inspired love until I observed it demonstrated by those who had found it and lived it.

For the past fifteen years or so, a televised program aired weekly has become as popular with the deaf as with the hearing, being fully captioned. This is the "Hour of Power," a televised non-denominational church service from the Crystal Cathedral in California, founded and pastored by the Reverend Dr. Robert H. Schuller. His ministry has never been tainted by scandal in any form and his programs are broadcast worldwide by satellite. Each week he has a famous individual on the program, each one telling of their happiness through living the ways of God. Once several years ago he had each president from Nixon to Clinton on the program, and each recounted how his friendship and services had helped them through rough times. He once had the Archbishop of Los Angeles, dressed in full robes, who told of how he watched the program regularly and said he felt humbled in being on the program with Rev. Schuller, which brought protests from

Dr. Schuller. There have been many government people, including Bob and Elizabeth Dole, and others, and several athletes including Olympic champions. And, of course, Heather Whitestone, Miss America of 1995, the first woman with a disability, hearing impairment, to be selected to wear the crown. There is a different famous personality each week, including ministers and rabbis.

We have a very close friend who is a minister. We do not attend his church but know him and his wife socially. We have owned three homes and several new cars since our marriage and each time we got one or the other, we invited them to dinner and he said a long prayer over the new house or car asking that no harm befall either. We have traveled to every state in our large camper van and into Alaska and through Canada without mishap of any kind except for the following.

We were on our way to Nova Scotia and had crossed into Canada at Detroit and followed the St. Lawrence Seaway farther into Canada. After about an hour we stopped at a parkway by the river to have lunch out of the refrigerator in our camper van. After eating and resting for a while, we started out again. It wasn't long before I started becoming very sleepy but the highway had no shoulders to pull off on so Laura could drive. There were embankments on the side of the road about five feet high ostensibly to keep the river from flooding the road. I became so sleepy that I finally passed out. I had been driving about sixty miles an hour, and the last I remembered was seeing the heavy van leave the road and start down the embankment. At that point I was dreaming that the van was going deeper and deeper into the undergrowth and small trees and could feel the right front tire digging into the embankment. I thought we would turn over and might be killed. Suddenly I became conscious of a voice in my head that repeated over and over that we would not turn over. I could feel a hand tugging on the left side of the steering wheel and I suddenly felt calm. The next thing I knew the van was back on the road and the motor was off. Laura was screaming and was terribly frightened at what had happened. I asked her if she had been pulling on the wheel and she said no, and that I hadn't been either. We went back to look at the deep rut halfway down the embankment and we were horrified at what had happened and happy that we had come through it safely. We have floor to ceiling closed cabinets in the raised top van on the left side and everything in the cabinets and refrigerator were in the floor up against the right doors. I have always believed in Jesus and God and it would be hard to convince me that one of them hadn't been pulling the wheel. Later I mentioned this to our friend, Raymond Gander, the minister, and he said, "Arthur, that is the way it works. You must believe and keep faith."

James S. McDonnell

Prior to my decision to leave the company, plans were being made by McDonnell-Douglas to build a new World Headquarters Building. One Saturday afternoon my doorbell rang, or rather the lights flashed, and I went to open the door. A well-dressed gentleman with a silver McDonnell-Douglas badge was standing on the porch. I noted that a low slung foreign sports car was at the curb and wondered what would have brought this man to my door. I knew that a silver badge meant that he was a member of the executive branch of the company. I invited him in and he introduced himself as Mr. Cain. He added that he was Mr. McDonnell's "right hand" man and went on to explain his visit and how he had found me. He said that the week before, Mr. McDonnell, Mr. August Busch, Mr. Whittington and he had been having lunch at the Missouri Athletic Club in downtown St. Louis and the discussion had turned to the new World Headquarters Building that Mr. McDonnell was looking forward to building. Mr. McDonnell had mentioned that he was interested in having a new desk made for his office in the new building, and he had been unsuccessful in finding a craftsman who could give him what he wanted. At that, Mr. Busch spoke up and said that he had some pieces of custom furniture made for his office at the brewing company as well as some for his home on Grants Farm. He said that it had been quite a few years in the past, but that he thought the man who owned the company was deaf and that his name was Mc something or other, whereupon Mr. Whittington asked if it might be McCann. Mr. Busch said it was, and Mr. Whittington told him that I was working for them in Engineering mock-up and tooling. Mr.

Whittington was the Employment Manager and had recalled our conversation where I had told him of my custom work venture. Mr. McDonnell asked that I be brought to his office to look at plans for the new desk.

Plans were made for me to meet with Mr. Cain the following Saturday at the Executive Offices. Mr. McDonnell wasn't there but Mr. Cain explained what was needed, and took me into Mr. McDonnell's private office and asked me to inspect the desk and tell him what I thought was needed in a new one. When he asked me to open the drawer and look at the construction, I protested that I did not feel comfortable opening the drawers of Mr. McDonnell's private desk, whereupon Mr. Cain laughed and said it was all right since he was there with me. The plans called for a huge conference type desk with drop leaves on each side controlled by hydraulic lifters. Mr. Cain explained that the lifters were to be made by the engineering department and that I would have to incorporate them into the construction. I told Mr. Cain that I feared that the size of the project would probably be beyond my capacities since they wanted me to make it in the workshop I had at my home, but he told me to make an estimate and see if it would be feasible to attempt it. I was asked to construct a small-scale model and when it was finished to bring it to Mr. McDonnell's office. I met Mr. Cain there and set the pieces up for Mr. McDonnell's approval. He had not yet arrived. After waiting a while I was told that he would be delayed and that I could leave and come back at another time. I asked to use the restroom, and as I was about to leave, Mr. McDonnell walked in. I had never met him personally but had seen him often when he would come into our department to see the progress on the new Eagle fighter plane mock up.

Since it was obvious that I was in the executive restrooms, I felt that I should introduce myself and explain why I was in that part of the building. I told him the model desk was in his office. He wanted to use the toilet before going to his office and I waited for him. He went into a booth but like most men, did not close the door. I noticed that he used the toe of his left foot to kick up the seat and decided that he went to the bathroom the same as the rest of us. Trouble had arisen concerning promotions of African-American employees who believed they were being treated unfairly since the ratio of factory foremen was not consistent with what the NAACP organization thought was fair. As a result there were threats of having the current contract on producing the F-15 Eagle canceled unless concessions were made. Because of the resulting unrest, the issue of the desk was apparently dropped, since I never heard anything more regarding it. Shortly afterwards the tooling work had been finished by our department and layoffs were imminent. In time, I was given the choice of taking a transfer into another department until work again became available in Engineering Mock-Up and Tooling, or take what would be a temporary lay off until work was available. It was then that I decided to take the lay off and begin what I hoped would be a home improvement venture.

Return to Central Institute for the Deaf as Building Engineer

Shortly after taking leave from the aircraft plant, and busily engaged in contract work, I received a call that was to bring drastic changes into my life. Since leaving the plant, I had made progress in building a clientele and was considering hiring employees to help me. I was no longer as lonely as I had been, but the lack of social life was still evident. I had obtained a teletype machine to which a newly invented coupler had been installed, making it possible for the deaf to use the telephone by typing out messages. A deaf engineer named Robert Weitbreicht invented this coupler. I had been openly critical of the Ph.D. electrical engineers in the Central Institute research department for having failed to bring this about long before since they claimed that their purpose was to discover things that would help the deaf. The system was limited since calls could be made only to others who had a similar hook-up, a group consisting almost wholly of deaf individuals. A relay station, where a hearing person with a similar set-up would accept calls and make contact with regular phone users, had not yet come into general use. The use of this system was principally for social contacts among the deaf and existed as a novelty to those who had never before been able to make use of the phone. Today, a greatly improved relay system has come into being that allows a deaf person to contact any person or business by telephone. This type of system has been put into place in every state almost wholly because of continued efforts on the part of the deaf community. The state furnishes the equipment free. Besides the TTY system which enables the deaf to talk to each other using the phone, there is another way that came in later. The deaf person carries a pager and gives out the pager number to friends or anyone necessary. When they receive a page with a phone number, they call back by using the TTY and the relay system. Yet another method is the text pager with which deaf people can send text messages back and forth to each other. Paul Taylor, a friend since his childhood, has been called the father of the relay system. His mother was a teacher at Central Institute while he was a student there. While living in St. Louis, he was the leader in an organization to convince the Western Union Telegraph Company to donate their obsolete teletype machines. He also organized a crew of volunteers to rebuild the machines into compatible service with Robert Weitbreicht's coupler, which made it possible for the deaf to finally use the phone. They distributed the machines to anyone who needed one and they remained in use until a small desk-type unit came into being. Today many types are available and the end result has made it possible for the deaf to use the phone independently. Today, Paul is one of the top administrators of the National Technical Institute for the Deaf in Rochester, New York.

  The call was from Dennis Gjerdingen, the assistant to the Director of the Central Institute where I had lived and worked many years before. I had been doing contract work on a small scale for them since taking the layoff from the plant and thought perhaps they had additional work for me. I had built a walnut display case for the lobby and some laminated plastic casework for the school. I anticipated a pleasant continuing relationship working in conjunction with the school's needs for specialized cabinetry. An appointment was made for the following morning.

  During my years of discovering the meaning of

having God in my life further began to take on a significance which grew in profoundness with each passing day. I became aware of the ways in which God can come to us in our daily lives as a bulwark against emotional turbulence. The spirit was awakening, but I was not ready at that time to comprehend the full meaning of spiritual deliverance. The spirit was willing but the flesh was weak. Retrogression prevailed. With the passing of time, remorsefulness dominated. I blamed my weaknesses on my handicap and thought transgressions would be overlooked because of it. I felt that God would understand and would not blame me for the ways that I had allowed my values to disintegrate. When I asked for it, an extended hand would give the renewed strength I needed.

Religion in itself is valueless. In order to live with God as a daily companion, we must go back to our beginnings and accept the things which are recognized as our source and realize how futile it is to attempt to live through our own limited means. There have been times when I have hated God and blamed Him for apparent insurmountable difficulties, which I could see, in retrospect, I had succeeded in bringing upon myself.

Gradually, I felt as though I was being pulled away from an undesirable lifestyle and could feel fears subsiding. Difficulties then became peaceful. I was able to accept adversities with resignation and no longer feared an ultimate outcome. I learned the meaning of compassion and learned to look upon my handicap in ways in which it was not a hindrance more frequently than I felt it was.

Although faith, once instilled, is difficult to lose, there are circumstances that bring on tests of its durability, and past feelings of inferiority and inadequacy will return. These circumstances were instigated in a wholly unexpected way by the telephone call that resulted in the appointment I was to keep the following day with Dr. Don Calvert, a friend from his college days at the school and newly appointed Director of the Institute.

Driving through the park that morning on my way to keep the appointment at the Institute, little did I realize the magnitude of the changes that were to begin unfolding. They were to culminate in apprehension, chagrin, disappointment and, ultimately, an acceptance of circumstances conceived, borne and nurtured by inconsistencies of communication.

The outlines of the buildings comprising the Institute began to take form against the skyline as I neared the end of the park. Memories of past years floated through my mind. I remembered taking one of the college girls skating on the frozen-over lake one night, and how in the darkness we had wandered upon thin ice and fallen through. The water was only about two feet deep at that point near the edge and we were able to scramble out without further mishap except for a case of sniffles the next day. I remembered the happiness I had found there after the difficult years on the farm, and I remembered the enduring friendships made as a result of my long association with the school. I remembered the ways in which I had stumbled since leaving the Institute, and thought of the pleasantries and security experienced at the place I had called home for so many years.

Donald R. Calvert, Ph.D.

Entering the administration building, I went directly to the Director's office. My reception was cordial, but while welcomed warmly, I could detect a trace of formality. We talked briefly about projects that had been implemented at the school, and of how there would be various contract work for me to consider. We walked through sections of the building that were being remodeled and talked of tentative projects incorporating fine cabinetry which he wanted me to do. Our circuit had taken us into the kitchen where we helped ourselves to some coffee. I noticed he was leaning against the same counter I had been sitting on when the Principal came into the dishwashing area that day many years before and told me she had a new position she wanted me to move into. He told me that since returning to the Institute a year earlier, he found it difficult, if not impossible, to find the type of help he wanted in order to keep the buildings and equipment in proper condition. He needed a cabinetmaker, a carpenter, a plumber, an electrician, a machinist, and in general, an all-around man who could take care of problems as they arose from day to day. I asked him where he thought he could find a man with those combined qualifications, whereupon he asked if I would consider taking the job. The title of the position was Building Engineer. It came with the challenge of doing what I could, supervising the rest and contracting out larger jobs. He added that the position included full benefits, a month vacation, a five-percent increase each year plus an initial increase over my present salary at McDonnell Douglas, and free lunch. I laughed and said, "You want me pretty badly, don't you, Don?" and he said, "Yes, I do." He added that if a friend or relative should stop by at noon to ask them to have lunch with me.

The possibility of returning to the Institute had never entered my mind. I was in the process of organizing a contract service but had not yet definitely decided upon relinquishing my position with the plant. Benefits contingent with employment at the Institute were essentially equal to what I had attained through seniority at the aircraft plant as a journeyman toolmaker and engineering mockup man prior to taking voluntary leave. Being in no position to give a direct answer immediately, I asked for an extension of time in order to give his proposal more thought.

Many things had to be considered. I had fifteen years seniority at the aircraft plant and enjoyed the privileges of security clearance that entailed a special badge permitting free access to restricted areas. I had earned the respect of my colleagues and foreman as a dependable worker and was admired for the way in which I had been able to surmount the difficulties concurrent with my handicap, which at times were tantamount to a rein. My opinions in matters of crafts unrelated to airframe construction were sought after and utilized. These were the thoughts that went through my mind on the plus side. On the negative side came loud and clear the issue of loneliness brought on by working hours totally alien to any form of social life. The prospects of returning to the Institute after an absence of many years and assuming a position of responsibility held merit, and the thought of once again being a member of the school family was appealing. I wondered if the administration would recognize my professional expertise in the same manner I had come to expect at the plant.

An issue is brought to the fore here which is

recognized by most members of any minority group, but which is generally unknown or ignored by employers. The majority of handicapped employees are grateful for acceptance. They realize they have shortcomings and know their performance will be scrutinized by supervisors harboring doubts as to their abilities. If a supervisor has had an adverse experience with a member of a specific group, he will be suspicious and difficult to convince when confronted with an individual possessing a similar handicap. It is necessary to become fully aware of surroundings comprising the work area and to be alert to any inconsistencies that would affect performance. This applies especially to the deaf. They know they are at a disadvantage but constantly strive for perfection or at least superiority, and in return hope for recognition for a job well done.

At the end of a week I was still undecided. It was difficult to visualize a return to the Institute. While there were many happy memories of the years I had spent there, I was forced to recount in detail the difficulties I had experienced in being accepted in ways other than as a handicapped individual. While I was now in a position where I could furnish something materially constructive to the Institute in the form of being an experienced craftsman, I was unsure as to how I would be accepted personally. From the description of the work involved, I believed I would have a free hand in development of necessary procedures contingent with returning the buildings and equipment to a state of acceptable repair, and that I would be welcomed as an authority and my advice would be sought after.

I decided to offer the solution to prayer. Included in prayer was a visit to the personnel manager at McDonnell

Douglas, Mr. Whittington, the man who had hired me. When I began my reasons for the visit he leaned forward in his chair and exclaimed, "Oh hell, are you leaving us?" I explained that was why I came to see him. After going over the proposal from Dr. Calvert, he agreed that it sounded fair and noted the percentage offered over what I was currently making plus an increase each year. I told him the school was affiliated with Washington University and that I knew all the school personnel. He asked if he could offer some advice and I said, "sure." He asked how well I knew the doctor and I said I had known him many years and although I considered him a friend, he was not the buddy type. He suggested that I have him write down all the promises and have it notarized. I did and he did. Mr. Whittington added that in the long run I might make more at McDonnell, but there were always layoffs. He said if he were in my position, he would accept it, although he was sorry to see me leave. At the end of several more days, I called the Director and told him I would accept the position, but that I would need an extension of time in order to fulfill my outstanding obligations.

  The passing of the years had not diminished my persistence that somewhere lay an avenue of escape from the deafness that dominated my life. I harbored a hope that I was being led to return to the Institute by some invisible force, and reasoned the research department might have developed, or at least, initiated a beginning of a breakthrough which would lead to release from the bondage engulfing me.

  I tried to imagine what it would be like to return to the school. There were many there whom I knew and I felt that my return would be a sort of homecoming. Although elated at my decision to resign from aircraft work and

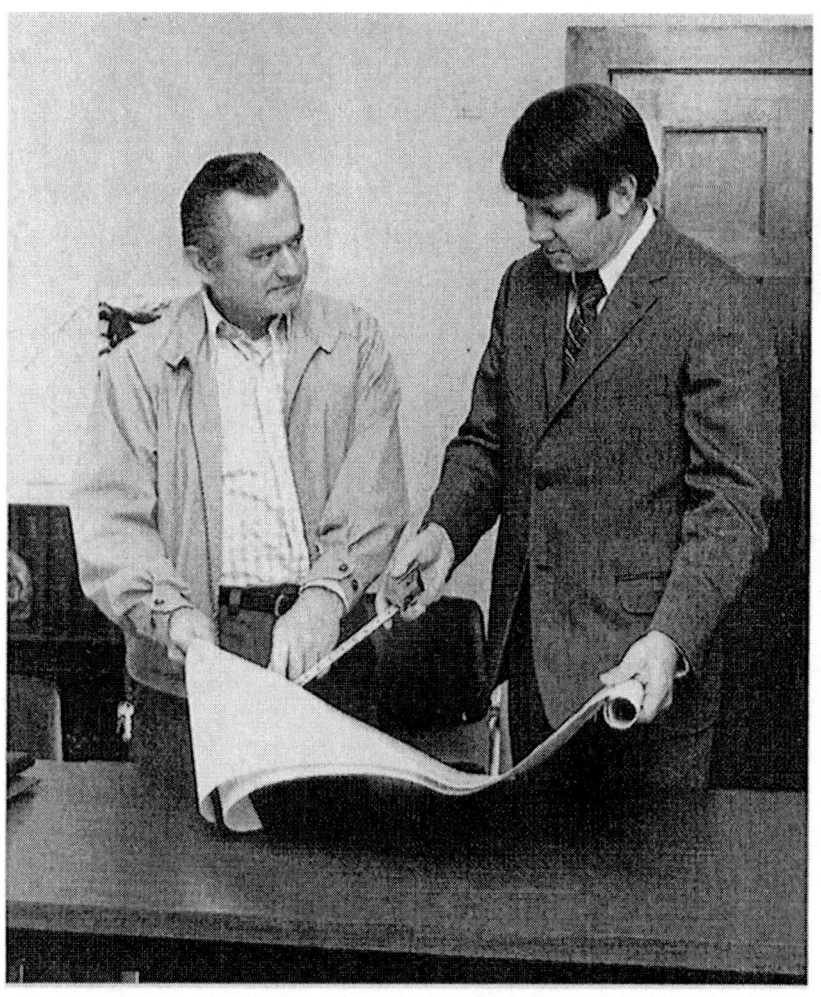

Dr. Donald R. Calvert, Director of CID, and the author going over plans for research department equipment.

(Courtesy of Central Institute for the Deaf)

Dennis Gjerdingen, Assistant to the Director, and the author, co-workers for many years.

abandon the start of a service company, I had apprehensions that difficulties would arise.

On the first day, I was met by Dr. Silverman, the recently retired director, with open arms and a "Welcome home!" A bit later I received the same from Irvin Shore, the principal and friend of many years which has continued to the present.

From the beginning, it became evident that my apprehensions were justified. With the exception of a colored custodial worker who could neither speak nor read lips and a mother of two deaf boys who served as a teacher aid, I was the sole deaf employee. I was to work under, and in conjunction with, the assistant to the Director, Dennis Gjerdingen, who had recently been elevated from classroom teaching and had a deaf son. The Institute was composed of separate but interrelated departments; and had grown significantly from previous years. All the departments, consisting of the school, the clinics, the research department, and the teacher training college, were staffed by professionals trained in their field. My work, being at-large, caring for the needs of the Institute's four large buildings, and belonging to no particular group, placed me once again in the position of a loner. I felt as though I was intruding within a group of professionals who gave the appearance of being unable to accept the presence of a deaf adult into their midst.

The term "professional" has varied meanings, each definition dependent upon the perspective of the individual defining the word. A true professional is one totally versed in accumulated aspects of a pursued subject, and whose achievements give full credence to the degree conferred. In addition, a professional should possess a knowledge, garnered from conscientious application of the fundamentals requisite of the chosen field and beyond, which enables recognition of outstanding qualifications in others, attained without benefit of higher academic coaching. Although possessing these non-collegiate qualifications gained from many years of practical experience in many fields, inconsistencies in communication steadfastly prevented my participation in administering projects within the Institute.

An attempt was made at rationalizing. I tried to reason that since I was unable to communicate in a manner which offered the least amount of inconvenience, it had been decided that my skills were predominant; and since it was my skills that had been opted for in the beginning, I was at a decided disadvantage in any capacity where communication involving decision making, or general discussions of projects in progress, held priority. The buildings had been in such deplorable condition, the task of restoration involved long-range planning. Various types of equipment had to be built, from special cabinets and desks for offices and classrooms, to custom casework for the research department. It was necessary to train, or at least attempt to train, totally inexperienced help. The assumption appeared to be that anyone could be taught to do skilled work if shown how. I found it feasible to return to the school during evening hours and on weekends in order to expedite work on schedule.

In the beginning I was given limited permission to use my own initiative and had the responsibility of designing and building equipment and purchasing needed materials. A few years later, most of these responsibilities were abruptly taken away on the whim of a newly acquired personnel during a change in administration. Limited cooperation, which had been available, was eliminated.

By the end of the second year, combined efforts began to show and it was evident that progress was being made. My duties had become varied, in categories comprising both the buildings and equipment. I was told by Dr. Calvert that in view of my favorable record, of which there was evidence throughout the Institute, I should be elevated to being a part of administration involving procedures and that at the first opportunity it would be made official. Dennis had assured me that whenever Dr. Calvert made those kinds of promises, he always carried through. A few weeks later I was invited, along with top officials of the school, to dinner at an exclusive dining room belonging to the University of which the Institute was an affiliate.

It would be natural to assume under existing circumstances that my worth was being recognized by the officials in charge, and that the extra efforts I had been making were to be brought out into the open. I was excited at the turn events were taking. The day arrived. I left work a half-hour before noon and drove the short distance home to change. Arriving back at school, I was met by the assembled group and we began the trip to the University. I anticipated a new experience as we entered the dining room where an elegantly set table had been reserved for us. I watched the conversation closely all through the meal with expectation, and became uneasy as the last course was being served. After we had finished, a few pleasantries were exchanged and we rose to leave. Nothing more was ever said regarding a promotion.

Chagrin and disappointment were generally end results of occurrences of this nature, and the psychological hurt was identical to numerous experiences during my youth. Apparently, a statement had been made spontaneously before ramifications were considered. The decision was rescinded after deliberation, recognizing a communication gap outweighing any advantage derived from my inclusion into active participation.

A situation of like nature had occurred many years before. Mr. Harrison had organized a laboratory in the school building doing recordings of the children's voices and others. He would stay until midnight recording a religious program. He had told me on occasion that he would show me the operation of the equipment and perhaps teach me how to do some of it. The end result was that all he wanted me to do was sort and file the recordings and store them in the storage area in the basement, and also to deliver current discs to the Chase Hotel for broadcast. He paid me twenty-five dollars a week for the part-time work. All this happened during my original stay at the school.

I had long striven for acceptance as an equal, in accordance with my technical expertise, along with the professionals dominating the Institute. The majority would recognize the extent of my experiences which were constantly being called upon to alleviate problems in conjunction with their professions. My help was asked for and accepted, the material significance of my assistance taking precedence. I was able to assist with knowledge not offered in the academic curriculum leading to their degree, fulfilling requirements for finalizing projects. I was never asked to attend staff meetings, notwithstanding the fact that these meetings frequently included discussions of projects that were ultimately channeled to me for execution. I was told it would be a waste of my time. Requirements of my position were difficult to fulfill in the absence of total briefing necessary for successful culmination of a project. The entire situation could be laid to lack of communication.

There existed a member of the research group, a senior electrical engineer, who became my friend and offered technical assistance in electrical matters which I was not familiar with. I enjoyed the times we worked together. His name is Arnold Heidbreder. We still see each other occasionally and I enjoy his company.

Many evenings were spent in doing odd jobs for the administrative staff – Dr. Calvert, Dr. Silverman, Dr. Lane, Irvin Shore and Dennis. They all lived within a short radius of my home in Richmond Heights and I enjoyed the evenings when I could work with them. I would never accept any money except to cover the cost of materials.

Dr. Calvert, the director, had mentioned several times the condition of the old steel water pipes in his two-room basement with nine-foot ceilings. On one very cold day I told him that I would be able to come over to replace about fifty feet of pipes that night. They had asked me to come for dinner and we started to work about six in the evening. Some of the old pipe had to be cut out, being too badly rusted to unscrew. We had two eight-foot ladders and his part was mostly to hold the old pipes as I got them loose, and then to hold the new copper pipes as I soldered them. They were mostly in ten-foot lengths. He also cut them to length and prepared them for soldering. He was a very good helper. We were both becoming tired and the job had to be finished so we could turn the water back on. It was close to the end and about two in the morning when I was joining three pipes on a tee. I was holding them together and they were getting hot from the torch. A short piece of pipe fell from a fitting and I couldn't get it since I was holding two pipes together and the lighted torch in the other hand. I told him to pick up the piece and was nodding towards it. He couldn't see it for a while and the pipe was getting hotter all the time and I forgot who I was working with. I suddenly exclaimed rather angrily, "You stupid bastard, pick up that pipe!" He suddenly saw it and got it to me. In a few minutes we were finished and cleaned up the waste parts. I was tired and forgot what I had said and went home. The next morning I saw him as he came in the lobby and I said, "Good morning, Dr. Calvert." He said, "Good morning, Arthur." Later in his office I apologized for what I had said the night before. He said, "No problem. I would have said the same thing. Just don't call me that around the school. I don't want anyone to get the wrong idea," and laughed.

Apparently Calvert was well versed in appropriate language when called for. One Saturday during vacation time while his wife Rae was out of town and before my marriage, he and I were invited to the home of Mr. and Mrs. Burgess, the business manager, for a barbecue at their home in Bel Nor, a rather long distance from school. My car was in the shop, so Don came to the house to pick me up. We were going along with fairly heavy traffic when a woman came up to pass and cut us off to make a right turn. Don braked sharply and seemed to automatically flip a finger and exclaimed a fitting expletive.

Dr. Silverman had chosen to remain at the school for a number of years after his retirement as director. One time upon meeting him in the hall, he half jokingly and half seriously asked me if I thought he should move to Florida. I answered that I was not the one to say, but his daughter, Becky and her family lived in Gainesville and her husband, Dr. Richard Howard, was a transplant surgeon in the University hospital. Because of that he would probably be happier there, but that everyone at the school would miss him. One time I went to his office and told him of the problems that had arisen since the change in administration. He said that he could see the difference and had seen how it was affecting me. When I asked his advice, he said he was no longer in position to interfere and hoped that in time the problem would abate. He and Dr. Calvert were writing a book on deafness for college use, and when it was completed, they gave me a copy signed by both of them. Two years before Dr. Silverman's death, Dr. Nielsen and his wife went to visit him and Mrs. Silverman in Florida. They had an hour-long conversation and Mrs. Nielsen videotaped it. It was loaned to Laura and me and at the beginning he made mention that he wanted to greet his friends at CID and especially said he remembered Laura and Arthur. Dr. Nielsen told of something at CID and Mrs. Silverman remarked that "it looked like something Arthur McCann would do." I wrote to them later and thanked them for the things they had said. He had been very frail in the videotape and he passed away before he could write again. They were both friends and ones that I loved. They were both about 88 or 89.

Over a period of time, the deaf have formed organizations of their own in quest of recognition. In the early years of struggle, when it was discovered that insurers would not accept them because of their deafness, they formed their own insuring medium. Numerous social groups have come into being, making it easier for the deaf to seek entertainment. Dissatisfied with progress being made vocationally by so-called experts in rehabilitation, the deaf instituted their own groups and were finally able to gain acceptance through constitutional channels. Communication systems ignored their pleas for help, and it was through the inventive skills of a deaf engineer that the teletypewriter came into existence. Television presented a new challenge, and it was because of combined efforts of the deaf themselves and interested hearing supporters, that the networks were finally compelled to furnish captions to selected prime-time and news programs. Use of an adapter made closed-captions visible on television sets equipped to receive them. It wasn't long before a federal law went into effect that compelled television manufacturers to include captioning equipment on any television sets to be sold in the United States. Any older deaf person who succeeded in obtaining an education in normal hearing schools and colleges using only lipreading for whatever it was worth, will show support and encouragement for proponents of the interpreter system which has only recently become universally accepted and which enables deaf students to acquire a more comprehensive education comparable, or in some instances, superior to that gained by their normal contemporaries who all too often take education for granted. Interpreters, using sign language or the total system, are acclaimed by the oral deaf who acquired the signs after learning to speak well, as profusely as those who are unable to talk. The system has afforded a release from dependence upon others in the classroom, and instills a sense of freedom which, in turn, releases the deaf from their limited confines. It is this that caused me to regret not having learned the sign language.

  In their anxiety to participate in activities alien to their abilities, many pseudo leaders have emerged, themselves lacking in available information for successful culmination of an undertaking made in behalf of their lot. From the beginning, the deaf have had an uphill struggle. Inroads have been made in education for the deaf and many battles have been fought for recognition of advances made in teaching deaf children. Many hotly contested debates have been waged in relation to acceptable methods. Proponents of the oral, as well as those supporting the total system, are equally adamant in their views. Each feels they have the only method worthy of consideration. In the final analysis, it is the child who sheds the brightest light. Even when the light grows dim, some educators will stubbornly hold to their convictions when it becomes apparent the child is not making progress, and will give little thought to the effects of their teachings upon the future life of the child when it is no longer in the protective confines of the school and develops into adulthood. It is when the school no longer has an interest in their individual welfare that the deaf attempt to assert themselves with group meetings, organizations which they hope will dispel some of their frustrations, and attempts at invading the domain controlled by a society dependent upon hearing. It is here that deaf leaders of the deaf can either display ability sufficient to promote their convictions, or step aside for others.

Generally, the deaf will instinctively follow a leader who has shown ability and who displays initiative. They are receptive to almost anything that will alleviate an existence in which loneliness predominates. All too often, hearing contemporaries display misgivings in accepting the deaf and their help is usually spasmodic and inconsistent. They are unsure of their ability in reaching the inner sanctums that comprise the insecure world of the deaf, and hesitate in penetrating the unknown. An exception can be found on the other side of the coin in those who assert leadership and assume control of situations in which they possess little, if any, understanding. They will talk to the deaf in what they believe to be a "deaf" language, abbreviating sentences and chopping words. They applaud the mediocre, and express astonishment and surprise at halting performance, leading the gullible into believing their efforts have been exemplary. This type of person is illusionary. Their proffered help will usually result in instilling a false sense of excellence, and will sometimes lead to embarrassing situations, resulting in still further feelings of frustration and inferiority. Fortunately, there are individuals in between the two types who have no difficulty in forming a good rapport with the deaf. Referring to applause, whenever the deaf feel there is a reason to give applause, clapping of hands is useless. Instead, they wave their hands wildly overhead.

As stated previously, those born deaf have an advantage over the deafened. Being deaf from birth, they often grow up and reach adulthood in a world that to them is normal and they have few misgivings about the ways in which they are accepted. Their deafness is not something to be overcome, but is a state of learning. Their learning process is more complicated and becomes compounded when well-meaning educators decide what is the best way to educate them, which usually is well and good but, unfortunately, is not always the best thing for each individual involved. The deafened have a totally different approach, finding it necessary to adjust to an altogether alien lifestyle than they had become accustomed to in the hearing world. They cannot be completely sure of their acceptance, resulting in a continuous feeling of insecurity. They find it difficult to realize that they must continue to live in a world of silence. They must acquire a philosophy of conjectural understanding in dealing with more fortunate members of society who are unable to grasp the significance of life in a soundless world. Many of those born deaf show pride in their deafness and are happy. Some will seek out and marry one that they hope will carry the gene that will assure deaf offspring. They use such terms as deaf power and there are some oral deaf who prefer to use the manual system in communicating, it being less time consuming.

Disillusionment would be an apt description of my first years after returning to the school. I expected a general acceptance and a genuinely profound understanding instead of the rejection and toleration with which I had been confronted. I had become friends with a teacher, Norman Pava who was interested in the work I was doing and wanted to help and learn all he could in his off hours without pay. He did so for a while until one day Dr. Calvert told me it was interfering with Norman's teaching duties and asked that I have a sixty-year-old African American utility worker who could neither speak or read lips help me. He thought, as I have mentioned before, that anyone could learn skilled work if shown how. I was able to work around that contention alone until a regular helper became available. Before he stopped helping, I asked Norman to go into the crawl space under the lobby and help bolt down the pedestal I had made for Hillis Arnold's sculpture. The concrete floor was a foot thick and the space was cramped. Norman said he had to "slither" to get to the right space. Norman left the school after a year and moved to Berrien Springs, Michigan. He and his wife Purita have recently retired after over twenty-five years of teaching deaf students in the public schools there. We are friends and visit occasionally, and often by email. There never seemed to be time or an inclination to explain the things necessary for a smooth implementation of the tasks at hand. I was unable to initiate projects which would ordinarily fall under my jurisdiction since I was unsure of the need and was never briefed on the amount of money budgeted for the operations of the department. There appeared to be an attitude of distrust involving finances. A superior air of arrogance appeared to prevail. I never felt free to inquire about the availability of funds for a project and was unable to offer constructive suggestions. It was difficult to accept these adverse situations in any way other than to regard them as direct outgrowths of my handicap. Being unable to understand or to comprehend a reason, frustration and depression followed. Deeper involvement in my work resulted in the aforementioned administration fiasco. Dennis had always striven to keep my work as uncomplicated as possible, considering the circumstances. I was always free to stop by his office to confer without an appointment since I was unable to use the phone.

      Following a series of window-breaking burglaries at the research building, the police department was called and asked to help in apprehending the ones responsible. Repeated entries had been made in one of the laboratories. The police suggested an alarm connected directly with headquarters, becoming activated with interruption of an electric beam. Shortly after installation of the system, I was awakened late one night by the flashing lights of my teletypewriter and answered a call from the guard. Another window had been broken, although no entries were made, and the alarm had not been set off. Arriving at the Institute and meeting the guard, we went directly to the research building and entered the laboratory that was located in the basement. Throwing a switch that I thought would deactivate the alarm, we entered an adjoining room through a side door which I further thought to be neutral. Mounting a ladder to the broken window, I commenced measuring the opening prior to closing it with plywood. Suddenly, the area outside was swarming with police officers who had seen me silhouetted in the window. They were running toward me with drawn revolvers and searchlights. Becoming terrified, I froze on the ladder knowing that if I attempted to move, I could not hear a command from the officers to stop and, being mistaken for a burglar, would probably be shot. I called for the guard who had gone into another room. He appeared in the doorway, saw what was transpiring and immediately recognizing the impending danger, he began yelling and waving his arms, assuring the police that I was there to repair the window.

Unknown to me, a research associate, Dr. Miller, working late on another floor, had entered the laboratory and had thrown the alarm switch to the "off" position and had gone off and left the switch in the "off" position before the attempted break in before the guard and I had arrived at the building. This resulted in my belief that I had turned the system off when I had in fact turned it on, showing how my life had been endangered through the irresponsibility of a scientist. Although the guard had been notified of the attempted break-in, he was not told of the manipulation of the switch, and I was not informed of the proceedings. This illustrates graphically how a totally deaf person's life can be endangered when vital information is withheld and also illustrates the irresponsibility of those in charge. Trauma from the incident was difficult to shake off.

Gradually, I came to realize the scope of the situation as it existed. Having exhausted every avenue in an attempt to bring about a more harmonious relationship, I decided that it would be necessary to accept things as they were, or offer my resignation. Considering that my services had been requested and, further, that they were needed by the Institute, I resolved to ignore my personal feelings and continue with the task of restoring the buildings and equipment to their original condition.

The undiminished hope continued, that with the inception of the research department many years earlier, and further assuming the broad scope of scientific knowledge garnered by research associates, many of whom held doctorates, that a method would be formulated instituting a beginning of a process benefiting the deaf. Understandable disappointment resulted with the discovery that there appeared to exist a lack of interest in total deafness. Emphasis seemed to be chiefly upon preservation of existing hearing and improved types of hearing aids. While employed in the aircraft industry, I helped as the space program was conceived and was instrumental in helping to create the first space ship that was to evolve into its final stage of landing on the moon. I reasoned, logically, that if scientists could produce a feat of the magnitude of landing a several ton craft on the moon, then it should not be considered impossible to devise a way of bypassing a deadened nerve. Each time the subject was broached, I was met with evasive answers and with the explanation that their work did not involve medical research, but was limited to whatever could be achieved by electrical means. Recent experiments involving the inner ear would probably cover medical research. One day an associate in the electronics department, Joe Sharp, showed me a powerful vibrator which he had succeeded in hooking up with a small transistor television sound receiver. He explained that the receiver would bring in programs being shown on an adjacent television screen, transferring the sound to the vibrator and allowing the beat of music from the television to be felt while seated across the room. Although it was a crude device, I was elated--not only with the unit, but also with the thoughtfulness of the one who built it for me. I suggested we take it to the office of an audiologist on another floor and explain its operation. During the course of conversation, I chidingly mentioned to the audiologist that no one had ever before attempted to help me in this way, and I was very grateful to the one who had developed it. He looked at me condescendingly, saying that I should give up the thought of having my hearing restored since there was no way anyone could help me. He spoke with an authority that rankled. I told him quietly that perhaps no one there could help me, but that we should not forget the possibility that God might be able to intervene. He replied that even God couldn't help, but if it would make me feel any better, he would kneel and pray for me. I have never known whether he was being sarcastic or humorous, or if he believed my mentality was on a level where I would grasp the opportunity as offered. I have purposely omitted the name of the Ph.D. audiologist if only to prove that I harbor more feelings for his ignorance than he does for my more tolerant feelings.

  I was once asked by a teacher in the upper school, Ellen Rajtar, to speak to her graduating class at the school before graduating. Some of the class members seemed to feel that once they were in the outside world, things would be easier than what they were experiencing in school. Among other things, I explained to them was that they would encounter obstacles, disappointments and frustrations and that they must learn to live with them and attempt to understand them. I hoped that I had been able to give them an insight into the world awaiting them as members of a deaf society.

  A few days later, I happened to be in the office of Dr. Calvert and mentioned what I had done. He told me that disappointments and frustrations were common and went on to add how he and his wife, Rae, being avid tennis players, could experience frustrations when awakening the morning of the day of a planned match and finding pouring rain. I tried to argue that they could play later when it stopped raining, while the deaf had no relief, and had to continue with the frustrations. He vehemently insisted that there was no difference, and dismissed the subject. Herein lies a tragedy in the making, whereby a highly educated individual purporting to lead, fails miserably in the very field in which he has been educated.

It is attitudes such as displayed by the foregoing incidents that renew feelings of defeat. It has been established that the authoritative manner displayed by those purporting to help is the prime deterrent in a continuous struggle for acceptance. I have long displayed contempt for holders of degrees in higher education who show total ignorance in matters unrelated to their field, but who often express opinions having repercussions which can reach tenaciously into the lives of the innocent, resulting in renewed struggles. Foremost among the groups which must contend, but who are ineffective in countering with rebuttals, are the deaf. Their communication gap prevents constructive repair to the damage inflicted.

Life with Laura

In spite of the harassment, negative attitudes and repression, I managed to make a number of friends at the Institute. Among them was a very attractive young college student working on her Masters degree in deaf education. Her father was a retired Army Lt. Colonel and she had spent a lot of time living in Europe with her family while going to high school in Heidelberg, Germany. We spent many hours talking, much as I had done many years before with the girl I mentioned previously, and since I was a staff member and she a student, we found it necessary to not appear too friendly.

During her second year, I developed my first hernia and went into the Deaconess hospital, very close to the school. After the surgery, which kept me in the hospital for five days, she came to see me and brought mail from the school and letters and drawings from the deaf students. On her first visit, we had become engrossed in talking until the nurse came and gave her an uncomfortable look. The nurse left and immediately the head nurse came in. Looking at Laura, she said, "Young lady, do you know the visiting hours?" Laura said, "Yes, until eight o'clock." The nurse pointed to the clock, which showed ten o'clock. Laura was embarrassed and started to leave and the nurse escorted her to the elevator. A bit later another nurse came in and I asked if the head nurse was still on duty and asked that she come to see me. She came in, visibly upset, and I told her I wanted to apologize for the girl who had just left. She demanded to know who she was and I was becoming a bit upset myself. I told her that the girl was a Washington University graduate student at the Central Institute down the street and had come to bring me mail and greetings from the deaf students, who all knew me as the building engineer. I went on to say that this was a private room with the door opened, then becoming a bit angry, said, pointing to the telephone, "If I wasn't deaf, I would be on this damn phone till midnight the same as the rest in the place." Her attitude visibly softened and she said, "All right. I see your point. So from now on she can stay until nine thirty but please see that she goes by then." I thanked her and said I would. Then she said, "Good night, Mr. McCann."

Our Marriage

Laura's father had contracted cancer several months before. Laura had gone to her home on Jekyll Island, Georgia, for Christmas and had told her parents about me and of our desire to marry. I had told her beforehand that if there were any objections to our marriage, such as my deafness or the age difference, that I would not marry her. On her return she was elated that they were both in agreement and her dad expressed a wish to meet me. We drove down to the Island at Easter and found him back in the hospital. A short talk with him showed that there were no objections. We hoped that he would be well enough to attend our wedding and he had expressed a desire to do so, but he died a few weeks later.

Shortly after announcing our intention to marry, Dr. and Mrs. Calvert and Dennis and his wife had a beautiful dinner party for us at the Calverts' spacious home. They had invited some family and friends of ours who were not associated with the school. Warren and Mary Sexson of Blue Mound, Illinois, and my brother Raymond and his wife, Louise from Jefferson City, Missouri, came. Ruth and Elmer Meyer and Frank Petelik of Kirkwood, Missouri, were also there. Frank's wife Carolyn was out of town and couldn't attend. Frank was our insurance broker and long time friend. He pretended to be miffed that I hadn't told him before of our planned marriage. Later he sent a note in the mail that said, "Art, just a brief note to tell you that I believe you have a very lovely girl in Laura. I wish the best to you both. Sorry Carolyn wasn't in town. Sincerely, Frank."

It was after she graduated that we married at her parents' home on Jekyll Island. Her mother had decorated the house beautifully and the minister from their local church, Father Wright, presided. My brother, Raymond, was my best man and Laura's sister, Elaine, was her matron of honor. My brother, Howard, and his wife, Kathy, came down with their children, Amy and Robert. We left for a honeymoon trip to Charleston, South Carolina. We had a reservation in the Mills Hyatt Hotel, where we found real southern hospitality. A wedding was in progress and there were several horse drawn carriages bringing guests in full antebellum regalia. We felt a bit out of place until we got in line and a uniformed attendant came and took our car and brought our luggage up.

It was in Charleston that we saw the twenty-foot high marble spire memorial with all the names of the sailors who went down on the SS Hobson. We found the name of one of my classmates, Buell Breuer. From there we went on to Charlotte, North Carolina, and spent the night with Laura's classmate from CID, Melinda Richardson and her husband, and later visited the Biltmore Estates in Asheville. On the way home, we stayed in Gatlinburg, Tennessee, for a night. We later left for home.

Laura is a wonderful wife, and has brought solace into my life. She has made each day a time to look forward to. The lost music has been found in her heart and the sounds I once heard have been resurrected through her compassionate understanding and love. After teaching the deaf for many years, she has become a teacher coordinator and Washington University lecturer to student teachers.

We had planned to be married in St. Louis where all our friends were. Laura's father's death brought about a change in plans as described above but we still wanted to share our marriage with our St. Louis friends. I mentioned to Irvin Shore, the principal at CID and a friend of long standing, that we were going to rent a hall for a belated reception party. He said, "No. You can use this school for the party." I protested that it was for private use and that wasn't ordinarily allowed. He said, "I am the principal here and I say it's allowed."

In the end, we had a five-piece orchestra, the same ones that Granvil Bates used when he formerly had parties for friends on his return trips from California. The head of the kitchen had a chicken dinner in the dining hall for 60 guests, including most of the teachers and administrators. Dr. Silverman gave the toast. The auditorium was beautifully decorated with the help of Laura's mother who had come into town for the party and Fanya Worth and ourselves. Granvil and Ara Bates had come in from California for the party. Ken Nicolai did the photography during the evening. Later, Maxine and Bill Chambers had a lovely party for us and our St. James friends at their home, an estate outside of St. James.

Trials encountered during the later years at the Institute fade into insignificance with the realization that prayer led me to return. Our marriage was an indirect outcome of that decision and our resulting happiness has made otherwise insurmountable difficulties endurable.

Total deafness, coming after the joys and

experiences of a normal world have become established, is akin to being cast adrift and struggling to reach shore, but like in a nightmare, the current keeps pulling you away.

From the time I entered a world of silence, and became rather proficient in lipreading, there has been a continual exasperation in being unable to understand what has been going on around me.

As a child, my family was unable to understand or cope with my tantrums and questions. They made no effort to explain situations that came up in group discussions. While I could understand very well where only one was involved, I was at a total loss in groups. My marriage brought out amazement in family and friends, who had previously been convinced that I was understanding everything said, when they saw how much my wife helped with interpretations. My brother Raymond has often helped when the need arose and is still the sole assist at functions when my wife isn't present. There have been others, but I am usually forced to ask for help.

Sixty-two years later, Laura and I journeyed to Detroit in hopes of seeing again the places where I spent my last days in the hearing world. Our first stop was on Montclair Avenue where it all began. The house had been razed, along with several others on the block, which was now in an area of general deterioration, and St. Clair School was also gone. In its place was an industrial parking lot. I remembered how I had first become ill on that school playground and asked to be taken home. Both houses in Highland Park were also gone. The area where they had been was developed into high rise apartments. The McKay's home is still there and is in excellent repair although they had long since moved away.

I imagined that although the buildings were gone,

my hearing was still there and remembered the fleeting time I was able to hear the sounds of the city. We found a friend from my years in Detroit, Raleigh Bodenbach, in Troy, Michigan, and spent a night and the next day with him and his family. An older brother, George, who drove me to the faith healers many years before was visiting from Florida. He had been the Postmaster in nearby Clawson, Michigan, before retiring. Later, back home, we returned to the farm where I had grown up and spent so many lonely and frustrating times. The barn still stands in its splendor although in need of paint, with the vanes atop the steel cupolas turning in the wind. The house has burned, and the outbuildings, including the large garden and orchards, are obscured with undergrowth and large oaks. Like many farms, it was abandoned just after my parents sold it and moved into town. Benton Creek School had burned many years before. My parents passed away a few years later. Dad was 93 and Mom 84.

My fiftieth high school reunion in 1990 brought back many memories. Classmates who had assisted me were still supportive. Our class had not been large, only 44, and the war, accidents and disease had taken 19. Mr. Donati, after many years as superintendent, serves as the city engineer. Mrs. Bohon has been busy restoring the old grade school into a museum, and Mr. Potter and Mr. Cahill have died. Mr. Donati told us at the banquet that our class had produced more successful members than any class in the history of the school. In my own opinion as far as successful graduates, I would nominate Bill Cowan who started with a service station and became the vice president of one of the state's largest hospitals, the Missouri Baptist Hospital in St. Louis. Ira Wilson became mayor of St. James, Missouri, and he and his wife, Margaret, have a family owned lumber company and home improvement store headed by their son, Dennis, who was formerly the high school principal for several years. Tony and Muriel Mingo have about twenty-five acres of vineyards outside of Rosati, a few miles east of St. James, Missouri. They are about ready to turn some of it over to a son. I consider all of these and several others as friends.

Years of oppression, disappointment, frustration and denial have taken their toll, but there have been times where the end result has evolved into a feeling of contentment found only in a world where sound had been totally absent. Looking about me, seeing only moving objects, mouths shaped in talking and laughter, cars rolling by silently and rain falling in a soundless staccato, has gradually forced me into a realization that, while life has generally been good considering the obstacles I have been forced to surmount along the way, I have finally accepted as fact that for the remainder of my life I must resort to continue as a prisoner in the Glass Cage.

Our Travels
Alaska

The glass cage has not been so lonely since our marriage. We both have enjoyed long vacations and have traveled extensively.

We drove through the western states to Vancouver, British Columbia, and had a reservation on a cruise ship, which accepted our van and took us to Haines, Alaska. From there we set out to drive the remaining eight hundred miles into Anchorage for a visit with my sister and her family. We spent two weeks there. They took us to several large glaciers and my nephew Jimmy took us on a day-long tour including an old Russian cemetery where there were small houses built over the graves. It was a very enjoyable trip both ways. There were many wild animals along the narrow road. (I say road because there was only one.) There were wild horses, grizzly bears seven feet high on their hind legs, brown bears, and moose. There are many moose in Anchorage and they are protected by law and must be given the right of way in traffic. Downtown, we went through a wild animal museum and traveled through Elmendorf Air Force Base where my brother-in-law, Jim Roller, was in charge of medical supplies to bases worldwide. The statue of Captain Cook, the founder of Anchorage, is on the bay downtown. Anchorage is ringed by snow capped mountains year round. I awoke one morning at two o'clock and saw a bright light coming through the window. I got up to look and saw the moon thirty inches in diameter rising just above the mountains.

After leaving Anchorage, we went on to Fairbanks. We found both a new and old town. Some of the houses of log were from the early settlers. On one of the days we were there in July it was one hundred degrees. Later in a small town named North Pole we saw teenagers in bikinis. Farther down from Fairbanks, we toured Santa Claus Land. Every imaginable gift could be found in the huge building. Shoppers came from all over the world to shop there.

On the return trip we spent a night in Whitehorse in the Yukon Territory and saw the Alaskan oil pipeline. Halfway between Anchorage and Fairbanks, we stopped at a roadside clearing and visited a souvenir store run by two sisters. We bought about seventy dollars worth of souvenirs and I offered my credit card. They said they didn't take them there and asked if we had cash or a check. I gave them a personal check on a St. Louis bank. She didn't even look at it and put it in a drawer. I asked if she wanted identification and she said no. I asked why and she said she wouldn't know if it would be any good. She asked if the check was good and I said of course. She said that in over fifteen years they had never had a bad check. She added that people coming through there were not there to pass bad checks.

I had a month vacation plus left over time from the last year. Laura had three months and Dr. Calvert gave us a "lucky buck" for the trip from him and his wife Rae and told us to round the trip out to two months.

Our trip to Alaska was made in a new ¾ ton GMC conversion van with a V8 engine. In addition to the front driver's and passenger's seats, it had a lounge, which opened into a bed, and two captains chairs. The first thing we did was to take out and discard the two captains chairs to make room for a built-in floor to ceiling cabinet along the left wall. The cabinet housed an electric mini refrigerator, small storage cabinets for food and dishes and a sink with a five-gallon water tank underneath accessed by a hand pump. We also took with us a portable chemical toilet. Being novice and therefore naive campers, we thought we had a nice set up, but the long daily travel became tiring in the cramped spaces. On our return, we decided to sell it and get a regular camper van but couldn't find anything we liked. Then we decided to further convert the van. First, I cut the top of the van off with an electric hacksaw and had a raised ten-inch top with front windows installed. Later I cut a 30 by 30-inch hole in the floor and welded a six-inch deep metal pan in the space. This gave us all the headroom we needed for standing up to dress, cook and move around. Next came a new refrigerator and a microwave oven, both built in. A new flush-type toilet with a fifteen-gallon holding tank under the floor was added. A seven by eleven-foot awning, which rolls into a cylinder at the top of the side of the van, was attached. The dropped floor was ideal for a shower. A drain was placed in the center and rings for the curtain were placed in the ceiling. A new electric water heater was added with hot and cold faucets at the sink. The drain in the floor pan was hooked to fittings for draining into the sewer lines at campgrounds, as was the sink. The toilet was enclosed in a built-in lounge chair in front of the side wall and a full size bed with a six-inch rubber mattress was placed in the rear. A 5000 BTU air conditioner controlled by a wall thermostat was added in back under the bed with the vent going through the rear door with a mesh covering the hole. A second battery, which a friend Ken Nicolai hooked up with the first battery since I wasn't familiar with this, for extra lights and the refrigerator, and a propane tank, added for a new two-burner stove built into the "kitchen" counter, were added in built-in alcoves under the floor. A 13-inch TV was added in the corner over the bed at the ceiling with a closed caption decoder for my use while relaxing in campgrounds.

  Another trip took us through Canada. An interesting, comical incident happened in Quebec, which is French speaking. Driving through a small town, we came upon a large white sign, which said in English "camping." Then below that it said "free douches." This left us mystified until a bit later on we found out that "douches" means "showers" in French.

  There is always something on each trip that serves as a highlight or a special part of the trip. In Lunenberg, Nova Scotia, we were setting up camp in a campground on a cliff overlooking the bay. We had only been there a short time when we saw a man walking toward our van. He came up and said he had noticed our Missouri license plates and was curious since they were from Missouri, too. He asked what part of the state we were from and we said St. Louis. He further asked what part of St. Louis and we said Richmond Heights. They were from Webster Groves very nearby. We had a nice long visit with him and his wife. A few weeks after we arrived home, we received a call from them. They wanted to come to further inspect our van, and we asked them to come for dinner. That was the beginning of a beautiful friendship. We visit each other for dinner several times during the year. They are Bill and Jacquie Tretinik

  After looking over our van, they went out the next week and bought a new van just like ours was before we converted it. He cut the top off and put on a raised one and did beautiful cabinetwork on the inside almost identical to ours. They enjoy traveling in it throughout the country. That was twelve years ago. They said they will be taking a final trip soon and will give the van to one of their daughters. It is still in new condition.

  Over a period of fifteen years we traveled through every state in the country, including the first Alaska trip, and into the Canadian Rockies, Lake Louise and Banff. Later we went through northeast Canada into Nova Scotia and back into Maine. We finally tired of traveling in the van and now use the car and motels. Charlie, my nephew, an Army Lt. Colonel who teaches military science at Johns Hopkins University in Baltimore, had long wanted it and we finally sold it to him last year. It is in 90% perfect condition, considering its age and mileage, and rust free.

Caribbean Cruises

  Two cruises have taken us to different parts of the Caribbean and one to Alaska. The first cruise took us to the western Caribbean and was to celebrate my Uncle Harry's and Aunt Inez's fiftieth anniversary. Wilma and Jim flew down from Anchorage to Miami and other family members from both sides as well as friends went along. The last seven-day cruise was won with a fifty-dollar donation to the St. Louis Hearing and Speech Center during a special fundraiser. Shortly after making the donation, Rita Tintera, the Director, called me on my teletype to tell me we had won. I didn't believe her at first, but she insisted we had, and wanted us to come to the office for a picture in their publication. At the end of this cruise that took us to the southern Caribbean we docked at San Juan, Puerto Rico. We were met with open arms by our good friends, Dr. and Mrs. Tono Giannoni, parents of Josefina, their deaf daughter, who had lived with us for two years of high school after attending CID. Her older sister Rosa lived in an apartment nearby while attending St. Louis University and would spend numerous hours at our home. We enjoyed having them. They are both very beautiful Puerto Rican girls. We were sorry when they left St. Louis but we have seen them at various family functions, weddings and graduations where their parents came to attend. Josefina has married a deaf graduate of Central Institute, a computer expert and they have four children. They live in Illinois. We had a nice three-day visit with Rosa and her husband, a handsome and witty Cuban, Alfredo Soccoro, and their two children in Miami three years ago. We spent an additional four days at the Fountainbleu Hilton Hotel on Miami Beach. While in San Juan, the parents drove us all around the old and new city and to the Old Fort. At noon they took us to the San Juan Hilton for Easter dinner. The dining room was full and we were told there would be a forty-five minute wait. We

The author and his wife, Laura
aboard a Carribbean cruise in 1988.

The author and his wife, Laura
London, England in 1997.
Queen Victoria's Monument in front of
Buckingham Palace.

didn't have that much time before flying back to Atlanta. The doctor's wife asked to speak to the manager. This resulted in us being taken to the terrace of the hotel facing the ocean. When we arrived at the airport, we discovered that there had been a mix-up in tickets and we were put in First Class to Atlanta. At the airport, we were going through security when it was found that I had to go through again. They frisked me all over three times, then found it was my metal belt buckle causing the beeping. I had dropped my key ring into the cup three times and was becoming upset. When they finally passed me, I went on hurriedly and forgot the keys. The ring had both car keys, three house keys and another one. When I remembered on the plane that I had left them, I really became upset. Now, on some more about keys, we left for a month in Europe three months after returning home from San Juan and decided to leave the keys at home this time. We hid them so well that when we returned home a month later, we couldn't find them. We had to make another set of keys. We finally found them in the bottom of a drawer two years later when we were packing to move into our Clayton home. We plan on another trip to Europe, which would include Rome and Greece.

Europe

Laura and I had planned a trip to Germany to visit my nephew, Charlie and his wife in Heidelberg. We flew nonstop from St. Louis to Paris in nine hours in 1996. We then took a train to Heidelberg where Charlie and his wife met us at the train station. Laura's dad was also a Lt. Colonel and she had lived in Heidelberg with the family when she was in high school. We spent four days with them looking the place over and went to see the house Laura lived in while there. They took us on a day-long cruise down the Rhine River and saw many castles, thousands of years old. We saw several beautiful parks and small towns within a 50-mile radius of Heidelberg, and antique shops and restaurants. I had my first taste of German beer, which I thought tasted like dish water.

After four days we took a train to Lucerne, Switzerland, where we spent two days exploring and enjoying the old and new city. We then took a train back to Paris. The first thing we saw at the train station was two Paris policemen walking together with two French soldiers behind them staring straight ahead with their fingers on the triggers of assault rifles. There must have been some sort of trouble before this and they weren't taking any chances. Another thing that surprised us in Paris was how public the public restrooms were. The women were lined up as usual waiting their turn, but the men were using urinals, twelve of them, on the open wall opposite the line of women. I went inside, thank you. We saw Mona Lisa in the Louvre and although a sign said no flash photo taking, everyone else did so I did, too. We sat for about an hour opposite the Arch de Triumph. Laura said her dad marched through the Arch at war's end. Then we went for a walk down the famous Champs-Elysees.

We went to the top of the Eiffel Tower where a couple from our home in Chesterfield took our picture. After coming down, we were walking around in the Place de la Concorde, near where Princess Diana was killed later that summer, and came upon two lovely French girls selling souvenirs. We bought a few things and I told one of the girls that we were from America. She spoke English nearly perfectly and said excitedly, "Oh, I have always dreamed of going to America!" I said, "Why don't you come over? You can stay with us. If you give us your name and address, we will send you information about St. Louis." She did and we did. She was a student at the time in the University of Paris. She was 21 years old. We sent her some things that we thought she would like and sent her some Christmas gifts. She sent us two large bottles of French wine for Christmas. The next year in July, she came over and spent two weeks with us. We asked her what her parents said about coming over alone and staying with strangers. She said her dad told her that we weren't strangers. We had exchanged several letters and she translated them to her parents who couldn't speak or read English. He told her to go and enjoy herself. While talking to her, I sometimes felt as though I was talking to a deaf person since I wasn't too sure she could understand me. We took her to all the high spots in the city, which she enjoyed immensely. She was one of the best houseguests we ever had. When it was time to leave, she hugged and kissed both of us and cried. Upon leaving St. Louis, her plane had an unexpectedly long layover in Detroit. The airline gave her flying coupons worth four hundred dollars for that inconvenience and she sent them to us. We had a letter from her recently saying she was getting married this fall. She wanted us to come over but of course we couldn't. We really love that girl. Her name is Nouara Bouzeraa. She always started her letters with "My dear Arthur and my dear Laura" and would write up to six pages and sign them with lipstick prints.

From Paris we went by train again through the tunnel under the Channel to London at 125 miles per hour. We saw lots of London and enjoyed it. The first thing I saw was Big Ben. They were repairing Windsor Castle where fire had damaged it and went through all that we were allowed to. One of the Queen's sons, Prince Edward, had taken a movie of the fire. The Queen and Philip were in a bucket brigade wearing overalls. After leaving the castle we went through the chapel close by where all the kings and queens for thousands of years are buried – some under marble slabs in the floor and some in crypts above the floor.

      Upon leaving the chapel, I saw one of the Queen's guards, a lady of perhaps forty in a beautiful blue and red uniform. I approached her and told her we were from America. She smiled and said, "That's nice." I asked her if it was true that when the flag flies on top of the castle that it means the Queen is home. She said, "Yes," and looking up said, "She is home now." Trying to be funny, I told her I had written to the Queen before coming to England. She asked what I had written. I said I had written, "Since Diana and Charles no longer lived there, could we stay for a few days?" The guard laughed and asked, "Did she answer?" and I said, "No." She said, "That was rude of her, wasn't it?" I said, "It sure was and you should talk to her about it." We both laughed and I said that we had been enjoying our visit in London. She smiled and said, "Come back again." We were there four days. I might add that a cup of coffee anywhere in Europe is five dollars and there are no free refills. Also, in London, we were standing near the entrance of St. Paul's Cathedral. The Queen's mother, Queen Mum, alighted from a long black Rolls Royce and walked about waving and smiling before going into the church along with several robed dignitaries that had come out to meet her. I got several close up pictures of her. She was 98 at the time.

      Because of my imbalance, it was necessary during our travels in Europe, more especially in London and Paris, that I use a cane. A number of times on the subway, people would offer their seats to me, which I refused. At one time a Japanese couple in their twenties rose and offered their seats. When I thanked them and refused, the young woman left no indecision when she pointed to the seat and vehemently ordered me to sit down, which I did.

From London we went on to Ireland. We were met by Gerry McCarthy, on of Laura's college friends. He is in charge of deaf education in that part of Ireland. He lives in Galway. He took us on a tour of the Aran Islands and all around the city. Downtown we saw the church where Columbus prayed before setting sail for the new world. Many of his seamen came from Galway, an important seaport at the time. Gerry lives in a very old concrete two-story house with a slate tile roof. While we were there, they were having some sort of celebration in the large park across from Gerry' home. An interesting note, we saw four F15 Eagles fly over in formation. We were told that the four Eagles comprised the entire Air Force of Ireland. We were also told that Ireland was the size of one-third of the state of Missouri. Of interest concerning time lapse – We left Ireland at 9:00 A.M. and arrived in St. Louis at 5:00 P.M. the same day.

These trips we have made, whether within the borders of the United States or to Canada or Europe, have been enjoyable up to a certain extent. While in Paris we toured the grounds of the Notre Dame Cathedral, but the chapel was roped off that day due to the funeral of Jacques Cousteau, the ocean explorer. I was told that beautiful funeral music was wafting out, but it was not for me to hear. On the Caribbean cruises, at night we would be up on the decks enjoying the moonlight over the ocean, while in the background, music and dancing were going on. My enjoyment came in the knowledge that Laura was there at my side, enjoying what we could together.

Our Homes

I had purchased a nice little two-bedroom brick bungalow from Wayne's real estate company before Laura and I were married. It was in very nice shape but the first thing I did was to tear out the kitchen and replace it with a new one that I made. Before going to McDonnell Douglas, McCann and Company had built several kitchens around town, including as I have mentioned before, one for August Busch at Grants Farm. Not satisfied with just the new kitchen, I tore out and enlarged the bathroom, and later removed a wall to enlarge the living room. Later came a sixteen by thirty-foot family room addition on the back of the house and a sixteen by thirty-foot deck behind the room. Not long after our marriage, we decided we needed more room. My nephew, Jimmy, who at the time was in the Air Force at Scott Field in Illinois, agreed to take off two weeks and along with his brother-in-law, both about twenty-six, we made plans to add a second story on the house. I made a basic drawing of what I had in mind, a gambrel roof and with all new copper plumbing throughout to replace aged steel pipes, and a new electric system. These boys were not carpenters but were hard workers and unlike regular carpenters, never questioned me.

I went to the Richmond Heights City Hall and talked to the Building Commissioner, Don Dill, telling him what I wanted to do and asked if I needed a blue print of the plan. He knew me from other work I had done and said, "No. You go ahead and build your house. If I don't like it, I will make you tear it down." He laughed and gave me the permit and said it was good for six months. I told

The custom-made camper van we traveled in for 15 years and sold to the author's nephew, Lt. Col. Charles E. Roller, shown here with our pet and fellow traveler, Sammi.

The original house in Richmond Heights, Missouri before adding a second story

1980: Two weeks after construction began, the framework and roof were on. The author's nephew, James Roller, Jr., helped with the construction.

The finished house three months after beginning construction.

him I would have the new roof on in two weeks. He asked if I had already started it and I said, "No, but I have arranged for all lumber to be delivered as I need it and we will start tomorrow." Dennis Gjerdingen came over one day to help. It was like our earlier days at Central Institute.

Being an experienced builder and using knowledge that I had acquired while working in engineering at McDonnell Douglas, I was able to cut all the gambrel roof rafters on a radial saw using the same angle for all cuts. The rafters were all 2x6 pine and 16 inch centers. I made a jig out on the large blacktop driveway and assembled all the rafters in three sections. We had the old roof off in two days and since the 2x6 ceiling joists were not strong enough for the new upstairs floor, we laid 2x10s between them and put down ¾ inch fir plywood subflooring before starting to assemble the rafters. Five-eighths inch sheeting was put on the rafters and a friend who was a roofing contractor had agreed to put on the shingles. Two weeks to the day after we began, the shingles were going on and Laura called Mr. Dill and told him to come take a look. He came right over, and climbed the ladder up to the new second floor. Looking it over, he exclaimed, "Who in hell built this thing?" I said, "I did." He asked, "Who helped you?" I pointed to the boys and said, "They did." Then I added, "Are you going to make me tear it down?" He said, "Hell no. I'm buying it. I have never seen a house put together like this. It's like a strong barn." Later when I had permits from the County for the electric and plumbing work and was finished, I asked him to come back and inspect the entire house. He wrote a letter to my insurance company saying, among other things, that what had been a regular one-story house had been transformed into a two-story house which had amenities found in finer homes. He also wrote that construction throughout met and exceeded all the then current Richmond Heights and St. Louis County building codes and safety requirements.

Work such as this, where I have the details in my head as work progresses, makes it easier to forget the sounds in my head, which can amount to torture if allowed to run rampant.

We were happy in this house for ten years when undesirable neighbors started to move in and we had wanted more land and trees, so we decided to sell it and moved twenty miles west to Chesterfield. Claymont Estates was a beautiful subdivision and we made a number of friends there. The house was a story and a half with five bedrooms, four bathrooms, living room, family room, dining room, kitchen, a half-finished basement, and a large fishpond in the huge backyard. I set to work making it over with a new kitchen and two first floor bathrooms were torn out and new modern ones put in. We had the entire interior painted and papered where needed and carpeting throughout. I also added a laundry room off the kitchen. After eight years we found the two-thirds of an acre to be too big for us and the drive to school each day, twenty miles in dense highway traffic, to be too much for Laura so we put it up for sale and found the pond to be a problem. When it was sold we found a much smaller place in Clayton much closer to school. We commenced the usual with a totally new kitchen and one of the bathrooms, and all-new floors and carpeting. New thermal pane windows were installed. We again had a professional painter and paperhanger. I added a new eleven by twenty-four-foot deck and a first-floor laundry although we have a full basement. At this point, we wrote "finis" to house buying and moving.

My Last Years at CID

This chapter deals with the later years at Central Institute and my difficulties with new administrative personnel.

Disillusionment would be an apt description of the ten years following the change in administration after Dennis became the principal and the new man took over. I had hoped for a smooth implementation with the new man who incidentally, made no move to introduce himself during the first two days and it was Dr. Calvert's secretary, Helen Roberts, who asked me if I knew who the new man was, and when I answered in the negative she introduced us. His face was expressionless and he showed no indication in accepting me as a co-worker as Dennis had done. He later showed no interest in discussing projects with me but instead would make plans with whoever happened to be head of the department where the project was to be included. I thought he might be interested in some suggestions regarding the housekeepers and thought I would comment on how they were using too much supplies and told him how Dennis and I had been handling it. His attitude rankled and I was taken by surprise since I was under the impression that we would assume a good working relationship. He sarcastically asked if I wanted to be in charge of the housekeepers. I replied that considering my other duties I wouldn't have time to do it all but that since the duties had been shared in the past, I felt that we could continue on that basis. He made it clear that he had no interest in sharing, and said that supervising the workers was his job and that he did not need any help. That ended the discussion.

The Institute was comprised of four interrelated

departments: the school, the research department, the clinics and the teacher training college. There was also a preschool for very small children and their mothers. Since my position was "at large" and my duties involved a good rapport with personnel in all four buildings comprising the Institute, I was usually occupied in more than one project at a time. An inter-office mailbox had been assigned to me by Dennis since my first day back from McDonnell Douglas, and I would check it each morning after arrival. It was located near the door of the school office and I would sometimes stop to have a few words with the secretary before starting the day's duties. I would check it for jobs periodically when in the area, and would also check with Dennis in his office for work that had come to him to be relayed to me. This had always worked well and it kept things going smoothly and I had no reason to think that it would change.

One morning, as I stopped by the office to check the box, I found it gone. I asked the secretary if it had been moved to a different location in the office and she said that the new man had removed it and told her that he had issued a memo that in the future all requests for work were to be forwarded to him. He had not told me about the change and when I asked him about it, he pointed to a space on the bulletin board in his office that he had reserved for me. Any personal mail or work orders that came for me after that would be thumb tacked to the board. On another occasion an envelope with a valuable picture was found with a thumbtack hole in the middle. Since I was often engaged in building a special piece of equipment besides the daily requests for work from personnel, fewer and fewer requests reached me. He had been giving them out to utility workers whom he thought were qualified to do the work. He would never follow up to see if the work had actually been done correctly, if at all. The restrooms had turned into a deplorable state.

Dennis and I, often along with Dr. Calvert, would go back to the school in the evenings and on week ends to do odd jobs and to catch up on more important projects. Dennis and I had torn out three classrooms on the third floor in the school and remodeled them into two larger ones with amenities not found in ordinary classrooms. Circular desks were provided so that the deaf students could more easily follow the teacher who sat in front with the chalkboard behind her. Dennis had designed the desks and I had built them. The rest of the casework in the rooms was left for me to design and build. For all practical purposes the rooms were finished at the opening of the school year except for a few finishing touches that we decided to leave until later. It was after the change in administration that I decided to finish them. An upcoming meeting of the board of managers was to be held the next week and I was anxious to have the rooms complete since I knew the board members usually toured the classrooms after a meeting. It was after nine at night before I was satisfied that the rooms would stand muster and went down to the lobby and talked to the guard for a while. The next morning this fellow called me into his office and very brusquely informed me that the guard had made a report that I was working in the building until after nine as he was required to do in his reports and asked if that was true. I told him it was and he wanted to know what I had been doing there so late in the evening. I told him that I was putting the finishing touches on the upstairs desks so that the rooms would be presentable when the board members went through them. With a stern look on his face, he told me that he would over look it that time but in the future he would have to know in advance if I wanted to come to the buildings after hours. I protested that I had been doing this for many years and always with the approval of Dennis and Dr. Calvert, and that most of the time it was spontaneous and that it would be difficult to plan in advance. With that, he jumped up from his chair and going over to close the door behind me, took me by the arm and pushing me into a chair said that I was working for him and that I would do as he asked me to do. I told him he was taking a chance by pushing me in the chair and to keep his damn hands off of me. This all happened about nine years before I finally decided that I had had enough and was going to leave. But I decided to stay on, partly because Dr. Calvert had asked me to return and help him with the buildings, and further because my wife, Laura was a teacher there. Naturally, I never again went down in the evenings or on weekends and I have wondered if he ever calculated the amount of free work the Institute had lost through his arrogance. I am lucky that I am not a man of violence or I might have knocked him over.

One day while making rounds through the buildings I came upon a very disagreeable situation. Since it was part of the utility workers' responsibility, and remembering how this fellow had reminded me several years before that it was his responsibility, I decided to ignore what I had seen and hoped it would be taken care of eventually. It was about a month later that I was called into his office and asked about the situation that I had come across earlier. I told him I had known about it for a long time, and he asked why something hadn't been done about it. I reminded him of how he had told me several years before that he did not need any help in taking care of what he had made it very clear was his job. And that I had decided to see if he would remember to do what he had insisted was his job. He became angry and said things that were beginning to make me angry as well, a few more exchanges led me to a point that I had hoped during the years of associating with him would never erupt. Losing my temper I said several things which would not be printable. I reminded him that Dr. Calvert had come to me and asked if I would be willing to give up a lucrative position with McDonnell Douglas Engineering Department and return to the school to help him restore the buildings and equipment to near original condition. And when I agreed to his proposition I surely did not expect anything like what I had been putting up with since he came into the picture. I had been assigned several responsibilities that he had taken upon himself and a lot of what had been going on was bringing the place back to the conditions I had been trying to eliminate. He was not the sort of person that should be in a position such as he enjoyed. He was nothing but a damn dictator and would be better off as a sub-foreman at the Ford Motor Co. but he wouldn't last a month before the union kicked him out for his bullying methods. Regaining my composure, I told him that what I had said was not the way to talk to the boss and that I would apologize and leave at the end of the day. His countenance changed, and he asked that I not apologize since most of what I had said was probably true, and that he did not want me to leave because he said they needed me. In retrospect I believe that if I had told Dr. Calvert that I was leaving, he would have investigated the problems and taken the fellow to task for his behavior.

  Not long afterwards he told me that he would send out a memo that all requests for work were to be sent to me. I told him it was too late in the day for the change to make much difference as the personnel no longer knew who I was or what my position was supposed to be, and for him to just leave it as it had been for the past several years.

One day my nephew, Jimmy Roller, had just returned from Germany and was wearing his Air Force uniform. He and his wife and two small daughters came by to see me. It was close to lunchtime and I asked if they would join me for lunch. In the beginning, I was given free lunch and told that if occasionally a friend or relative came by, to ask them to have lunch with me. I had helped them fill their trays at the counter and we were at a table. The head of the kitchen had probably called this fellow, as he came into the room and she was pointing to us. He came over and asked who those people were. I told him it was my nephew and his family from Germany and that I had asked them to eat there. Haughtily, he said, "Alright, but they have to pay for the dinner." I told him I would pay for it. I don't know why I hadn't reported this to Dr. Calvert.

From shortly after returning to the school, I had donated fifty dollars to the school each month. Dr. Calvert had commended me for that and said that it was unusual for a staff member to do that. I told him I was happy to do it and hoped it could be used. From the day of the fiasco in the dining room, I stopped those regular monthly donations.

One year, after a number of complaints from teachers, it was decided to replace the chalkboards in two second-floor rooms. There were two boards on opposite sides of the room in each room each being slate and four by twelve feet. The day after school had closed for the year, I told him that I would start getting the heavy boards down and prepare the walls for the new ones, of a much lighter material. He said to wait a while. A week later on Thursday, he told me that the new ones would be delivered and installed on the following Wednesday. I immediately had two men help remove the boards. The following week, I found that the men who were to help prepare the walls had been told to take their vacations that week starting Monday. That left me with no help but I decided to go ahead with the job. It was the hottest part of the summer and there was no air conditioning. The old plaster holding the boards had to be removed and new wood frames made and put in. I worked steadily against time. If Dennis had been there, he would have taken it upon himself to help. We would help each other on projects at our homes and enjoyed it. As it was, I was able to finish the work late Tuesday.

One day Dr. Calvert took me over to the college library and told me he wanted a new bookcase made. It was to be eight feet long by two feet wide by thirty inches high and divided to make eight units. It was to be made of walnut. Since work was a bit slack at the time, I decided to make it along the lines of the fine furniture I used to make in my company. The result was that it was pegged together without screws, nails or glue. Years earlier I had made a glass front case eighteen feet long and seven feet high of oak for displaying antique hearing aids. I had made this case while operating McCann and Company and donated it to the Institute. It was displayed in the auditorium of the research building. I was and am very proud of both pieces. When the bookcase was completed, Dr. Calvert was so proud of it that he had it temporarily displayed in the school lobby with a sign on it that said I had made it and how. Dr. Calvert went away for a few days and the fellow in charge had been on vacation. When he returned, he angrily asked what that thing was doing in the lobby. I told him it was Dr. Calvert's order. He found some utility workers and had it taken to the library across the street, but not before the sign that was on top of it had disappeared. By this time I had become used to these happenings and just let them roll off.

      The school lobby had no air conditioning and once, during the hottest part of the summer, Katie, the receptionist asked that a ceiling fan be installed over her desk. The usual way was to run electrical conduits over the ceiling and down the wall to a wall receptacle, a very unsightly procedure. I decided to go through the ceiling into a junction box in a second floor closet. With some opposition, I measured the second floor and the lobby and decided the best way to proceed. The ceiling was ten inches thick and after drilling the hole, found it within four inches of the junction box in the closet on the second floor as I had planned. I could see this fellow was miffed since I hadn't done the job as he suggested. Later I was ready to install the fan and needed to put a half-inch pipe through the hole for the wires and to support the heavy fan. I had the ladder and the necessary equipment and was waiting for my helper to come. The fellow was walking by and I asked if he would go up the ladder and hold the pipe in place while I went up to the second floor to secure the top end of the pipe. He just looked at me and walked off. In a few minutes Dr. Calvert came by and asked what the trouble was and I explained the pipe. Without a word, he took the pipe and went up the ladder and pushed the pipe through the hole. I went to the second floor and finished the operation. I thanked him and he smiled and said, "I enjoyed it. Call me when you need some help." Later this fellow came by and asked what I had wanted. When I told him that Dr. Calvert had helped me, he became angry and said that I couldn't ask the Director to help. I told him that he had volunteered and wanted to help. He told me to get a helper before starting a job. I told him I had asked him to help and he had walked off. He said he wasn't a helper.

Instances of this nature were common and the aggravation and harassment continued almost daily in various ways.

Although Dr. Calvert had been upfront with me generally, I felt that there were things that he had done which threw a cloud on the overall picture. I recalled the promised promotion and thought back over other incidents that had occurred during the ten years since Dennis had left, including the controversial issue of one of his and Dr. Eldredge's published books, which unceremoniously included me but which I had decided to ignore, and I also decided that he had never told the new man what my duties were when he hired him. And he had further never made a move to investigate conditions after I had repeatedly gone to him about irregularities. But that probably wouldn't have made any difference as to whether or not he had told the fellow what my duties were since the fellow was so nasty and, recalling Marshal Roy Kirgan's words, a damn son of a bitch.

It was apparent that this fellow had never been in contact with a deaf person before and had a feeling of insecurity that a deaf craftsman had invaded his domain. He fought back in the only way he knew, showing his ignorance. I had long suspected that he thought I was being paid too much and that his harassment would give me cause to leave or do something that would prompt my dismissal, although my contract protected me. I have no way of knowing how he explained my position to others, however, in the four years with Dennis, I had found a rapport with the entire Institute staff which surfaced when I went in the hospital for my first hernia operation. I had a private room and kept a list of my visitors. Most of the teachers came with letters from the deaf children, as well as all the top administrators and most of the research personnel. In my six days there, a total of sixty-eight visitors came to see me. Dennis was having a problem with his car and I gave him mine to use while I was there. He came every evening with news of happenings around the school, often bringing Laura. Another frequent visitor was June West, a retired nurse and close family friend. About six years later, I had another hernia operation in the same hospital with the same doctor. Outside of Laura who came every afternoon after school, I had only one visitor, a teacher, Paula King. Apparently I had lost my identity because of that fellow.

      In spite of the happenings coming up every day, there was a comical side to the first hospital fiasco. I had developed a sever pain in my lower abdomen and went to my regular doctor. He said it was a kidney stone, which would pass in time, and referred me to a doctor at the Jewish Hospital. This doctor agreed that it was a kidney stone, but the pain persisted and I decided to see Dr. Green. He was the head doctor at McDonnell Douglas Medical Services and his father worked in my department. He also headed a clinic near where I lived, so I went to see him. After examining me he said I had a hernia. I questioned that since two other doctors had said it was a kidney stone. He had just returned from a month-long hunting trip to the north woods and had a heavy beard. He asked me if the other two doctors had a beard and I said no. He said that was the reason. Then he said he wanted to have his surgeon examine me. He didn't tell the surgeon what he thought the problem was. The surgeon, Dr. Battacharia, examined me and immediately said, "You have a very serious hernia and it needs immediate surgery." Fanya Worth, who had worked in my office a few years before, would still do phone work for me. She made arrangements for my admission to Deaconess Hospital and drove me down. After the surgery, she would stop by my house and bring my mail to me.

The surgery was on Tuesday. On Friday morning, Dr. Green came in and said, "You can go home tomorrow." I said, "Now wait a minute. I have had hospital insurance for thirty-five years and this is the first time I have ever used it. I live alone and I am enjoying it here." He said, "Alright, alright, but you are going home Monday."

As I have mentioned before, Dr. Calvert gave me two months leave after each surgery. After the first surgery, about twice a week, one or two teachers together would bring me dinner. In between, Laura would come over and fix it. Some of the administrators and teachers would come to keep me company, but only an occasional visitor came by after the second surgery.

Dennis, who was earlier the assistant to the director and later became the principal, was appointed president of the Clarke School for the Deaf in Massachusetts. We are friends and visit occasionally. It was a great disappointment when we could no longer work together. He came to me one day after the lunch hour. He had made an announcement to the faculty and wanted to tell me before someone else did. He told me he would be leaving as principal. He said he had enjoyed our time working together and considered me a friend. I said I felt the same way and was sorry he was leaving and that I would miss him. It didn't take long to find out how sorry I was. The school had been buying residential homes down Clayton Avenue east of the school, which would eventually be razed for the new campus. They were in terrible condition but Dennis and I convinced Dr. Calvert that we could rehab them into condition to be rented. There were five of them and we did the work over a period of about two years in our own time. Dr. Calvert would give us what we estimated it would cost to do the work. After the materials were out we would split the difference. In the beginning, Dennis wanted a 40-60 split because he felt he didn't know enough about the work, but I insisted on a 50-50 deal and it wasn't long before I had trouble keeping up with him. Since he left and took over the position of President of Clarke School, I have seen him whenever opportunity presented. Once not long ago, he and his wife Karen were in town and came to the house for breakfast and a visit. He came again alone recently for breakfast and a short visit. We once spent a weekend with them in their beautiful president's mansion at the edge of the school campus on Round Hill Road overlooking Northampton, Massachusetts. They took us on a tour of the beautiful huge campus. He travels extensively to oral schools for the deaf around the country and to the four satellite schools he has established in the east from Boston to Jacksonville, Florida. A key reason for his success is in never having lost sight of his beginnings and the common touch. On his most recent visit we asked him if he had any plans for retirement. He is close to the age but he said that would come when the work is no longer fun.

It is ironic that in my entire career from the time I first came to Central Institute until I returned at Dr. Calvert's invitation many years later, I never came across a situation such as I encountered and lived with for the remaining ten years of my time there. Dr. Lane had written a three hundred page history of Central Institute. She had mentioned me repeatedly telling of my past history and projects for the school. The alumni had given me an honorary membership and a plaque recognizing my outstanding and dedicated services and contributions to the Institute. Upon my retirement, Dr. Calvert had written what he called "a CID Profile" titled "Works of Art" in the quarterly CID newsletter which I have decided to enter here. Either he had been unaware of the previous happenings, or had decided to let me fend for myself and ignored them.

CID PROFILE
Works of Art

One can look in few rooms at Central Institute without seeing examples of the art and craft of Arthur E. McCann. Yet, most will be unaware of their origin.

Mr. McCann has been CID's Building Engineer since 1973 but his association with Central Institute actually goes back to 1941 when he came here for speech help and stayed on to teach shop skills to boys in the school. In time he took a position with the Curtiss-Wright aircraft company but maintained his interest in the Institute and its students. McCann founded his own company for the design and construction of kitchens, cabinetry and fine furniture. Later he joined the McDonnell-Douglas Corporation Engineering Department where he contributed to the design of America's first spaceship and the F-15 Eagle fighter jet.

Arthur McCann's joining Central Institute in 1973 coincided with a concerted effort to improve the physical plant. An avowed perfectionist, he sets high standards for all work in which he is involved. When something has to be replaced, it is replaced with modern materials and installed to endure. When improvements are to be made, he designs them to serve their intended purpose and to fit in well with the persons who will use them. Then he often personally fabricates and assembles whatever is needed, be it cabinetry, plumbing, electrical wiring, hardware or any combination.

McCann's urge for perfection has paralleled the Institute's striving for excellence in its services, its research, and its preparation of scientists, teachers and clinical professionals, and it has contributed markedly to that overall effort. When a teacher at the end of a day sits at her built-in classroom desk to review each child's progress and to plan for the next day's instruction, she sits at an efficient desk and book shelves remodeled by McCann from an old closet that was previously little used. In many offices his tailor-made formica tops cover battered old desks that have been rejuvenated through his vision and skill. His sense of "form-following function" is unerring. Shelves and cabinets and counter tops and radiator covers have been built in so that they look like they have always been part of the building itself.

Miniature sinks and toilets now service our youngest children where old plumbing has been sealed up and unused for years. The fountain in the school courtyard runs today after so many years of "not working" that no one at CID could remember seeing it flow before. In the school library the stage modules of the Goldstein Little Theater were created by McCann from plywood and carpet, and similar lifesize blocks provide play objects for children in our hearing, language and speech clinics. Through his efforts, partitions and windows have been added here and there to permit old research laboratories to be the site of new investigations, and special housings for computers have replaced counters where hand computation had been required.

Our "Learners" sculpture in the school entryway rests upon a brass and walnut base crafted by McCann so that it complements the marble figure and secures Hillis Arnold's sculpture to the terrazzo floor. The base is a beautiful piece of craftsmanship in its own right, but it is largely unrecognized because its function is to serve as foundation for the more apparent art resting upon it.

In a very real sense, this symbolizes the nature of Arthur E. McCann's contribution to Central Institute for the Deaf. His designs and fabrications that grace our buildings both upgrade our working environment and make it possible for scientists, teachers, professors, clinicians and others of us to pursue our work with high standards. To those unfamiliar with what existed before, his best efforts will be invisible but the quality of work is always there to inspire the best efforts we have to give.

However, Art McCann has not just been an invisible hand working his wonders in wood and metal and plastic. He has been an incarnate conscience to our research staff who recognize the urgency of their quest to benefit significantly those who are deaf. He has been our not-always-gentle goad to "do it right the first time," sometimes elevating curmudgeonry to an Art form. He has been friend to many of our staff and children, and in 1977 married teacher Laura Williams. Most significant of all, he has been a constant reminder of the importance of our efforts to maintain the opportunity for oral communication.

Arthur McCann retired from CID in 1988 after 15 years of active service and nearly 50 years of affiliation.

Reflections

The carefree days which Mom and Dad experienced during the earlier years of their marriage came to an abrupt end with their decision to move to Detroit. There had no doubt been financial and other difficulties, but nothing of the magnitude or illusion shattering which came with their arrival in the city. The death of their only daughter, followed closely by the inception of my deafness; coupled with the beginnings of the Great Depression and Dad's inability to find gainful employment left them in a regressive state of shock. Finding themselves in a situation compounded by obstacles of which they had never dreamed, their ability to rationalize became clouded by an antagonistic frustration. Each had been forced to leave school at the elementary level, but their achievements in practical experience had more than made up for their lack of higher formal education. They were able to adjust to Frieda's death, but harbored guilt feelings that they had not done all they could in denying her hospital care from the outset. They had no difficulty in coping with the economic situation since they could see similar problems of survival all around them. Their past experiences had familiarized them with death and money shortages. Deafness was something totally alien to anything they had ever known, and they were helpless. They developed a fear of the unknown and groped aimlessly for a solution. The onset of my deafness must have had an effect on their subconscious. They seemed to show no remorse. Their actions toward me were basically cruel – pointing me out as being deaf, which happened more times than I could count; tearing up the rose; selling my lamb; telling Aunt Minnie and the hay man they were wasting their time talking to me; giving me only five dollars for a month in California after I had spent the entire summer rehabbing the farmhouse which put Wayne and Arthur Howald in the position of making up the difference; selling the car which I needed in my work but which they failed to recognize since their knowledge of deafness consisted of the fact that the deaf were not on a plane with those they called normal. They refused to see me for what I was. In spite of all their transgressions towards me, I continued to do things for them until their deaths. I added a guest room onto the house, and put in a new kitchen and full bathroom with a plumbing system. All I ever asked of them was the cost of materials. All this work was done on weekends while I lived in the city and made hundred-mile trips out to the farm. Many other cruel things surfaced that I would rather not elaborate on here out of respect for them as my parents. I forgave them but could never forget. I appeared to feel guilty for changing their lives. Counselors had suggested at the beginning that I should be sent to the Institute in St. Louis, but this had been out of the question considering the cost and distance. They put their faith in healers and quack doctors who preyed upon victims of circumstance. They felt trapped and feared a future that included a deafened child. They became bitter and felt it necessary to apologize for my shortcomings. I knew that something had transpired which had made my life different, but not knowing what it was, thought that I should be afforded special treatment. I became rebellious, which led to general family difficulties. I was punished repeatedly with severe whippings that served only to heighten the rebellion. Life was fraught with disillusionment, disappointment, lack of understanding, and an unexplained fear. I attended the Detroit Day School for the Deaf for several months before I realized what deafness meant and that the rest of the students were also deaf. Believing it to be something temporary, I disregarded the incentive to accomplish in the classroom and waited for the condition to abate.

My oldest brother, Wayne, was able to accept my deafness with understanding and compassion. While I did not know what was being said, he would intervene when Mom became upset and would talk to me in a way that offset tantrums brought on by frustration. He took me for rides through Palmer Park in Detroit on the crossbars of his bicycle, and would take me to the library in the evenings. It was his compassionate treatment that taught me tolerance of others. My other brothers were helpful, but were easily upset by my antagonistic behavior, and would retaliate in ways which earned me another whipping; sometimes, but not often, undeserved. It was at this early age that I became familiar with the communication gap.

It is the deaf child's inability to express himself, coupled with the hearing parents' or teacher's inability to understand the frustrations inherent with total deafness that widens the gap between the two worlds, and which had made the counseling and therapeutic professions so lucrative. Their services are often brought to the fore at the crucial stage in a child's development when it would be ready to find its way if left to its own initiative. There are untold numbers of older deaf who were capable of organizing their lives long before the professionals were ever heard of. On the other end of the stick are to be found underdeveloped older deaf who would have benefited from counseling. There is no disputing the issue that the deaf have found improvement in their living standards, brought on by an increased awareness of their needs. However, much of the credit for this must go to the efforts of a number of the deaf themselves who have become disillusioned with the caliber of assistance offered through professional channels.

Although my parents were hopelessly inadequate in their knowledge of deafness, their lack was to my advantage. Their ignorance of ways to alleviate my problems left no alternate than for me to formulate my own through trial and error. It was their lack of knowledge that often led to flare-ups of misunderstanding, and which were instrumental in my developing a comprehensive philosophy which had served as a buffer in softening the blows of misconceptions.

Difficulties encountered during the early years of deafness have continued in various ways to the present. The handicap itself is endurable, with the contingent problems being surmountable. Feelings of helplessness prevail when situations arise with which we cannot cope, being unable to understand the reasons behind them. Incidents such as Dad telling an aunt that she was wasting her time talking to me because I was deaf, and when he reminded me that I would be out of place at a church singing revival, while being singularly factual in themselves, were responsible for a continuous withdrawal socially and emotionally. They also revealed an inner feeling of animosity and resentment toward the unknown on his part.

A change came over both parents as they grew older. Never having known how to express themselves in ways commensurate with their feelings, their actions revealed emotions they had been unable to express. After working hard all their lives, a rather large accumulation of money and property was realized. In their usual frugal way, they refused to enjoy it themselves but left it, at their deaths, for distribution among their family, the sum of twenty-five thousand dollars for each child. They had made a tour by bus of the United States from California to New York and into Mexico. They had especially wanted to see President Kennedy's grave in Arlington, Virginia. Later, after Mom's death, Dad spent some time in Europe.

I feel a sad injustice has been done to the memory of our Uncle Henry McCann and although he passed away many years ago, I would like to set the record straight. The history was written by a family member too young to know the facts and he relied on others also too young and who gave haphazard information, which had been given to them over the years. The history states that Uncle Henry went to his parents, my grandparents, and asked that they mortgage the farm so he could start a business in California. This is all grossly incorrect.

In reality, his parents sold the farm in the early twenties after their children had grown and moved away from home and they moved into Owensville, Missouri. It was about 1932 or so that Henry went to his parents and asked them for fifteen hundred dollars so he and his brother-in-law, Ezra Crider, his sister Ruth's husband, could open a dry cleaning company in Sullivan, Missouri, close to Owensville. His brother Tom had a very successful dry cleaning business in Union, Missouri, also close by, and Henry hoped to be as successful.

This was at the bottom of the great depression and within a year, the business failed. I remember the following from when I was fourteen. Late one afternoon during the summer a well-dressed gentleman drove up to the farm and was asked to stay for supper. During the meal, I could see that some rather forceful conversation was going on between this gentleman and Mom and Dad, although I could not understand it. After the meal, the man left after what looked like some curt exchanges. Later I asked Mom about it and this time she gave me the complete story. I had not known about the loan, and this visitor was the president of the Owensville bank. He had come to tell them that the note was overdue and that he had been going to all the siblings in turn and asking them to help Henry with paying the amount. At that time fifteen hundred was equivalent to today's fifteen thousand. The banker, a family friend, begged each of the siblings in turn to help Henry and save the home, but no one would or could. He had said he would pay the interest on it for the year and renew the note. A year later he came out again and told them of how disappointed he was in the siblings since they were all friends. He said he would pay the interest one more time, but could not renew the note again, and in the end he was forced to foreclose, and my grandparents had to move into what was once a college building. They were very disappointed but did not blame Henry.

Henry had moved to Los Angeles and after a while, organized an insurance agency. Over time he became fabulously wealthy, but too late to help his parents. He was a very religious man and the grief he caused his parents stayed with him and aged him beyond his years. He died in 1977 at the age of 77. Laura and I visited his widow, Aunt Gwen, in her beautiful home in Uplands, a suburb of Los Angeles. We exchange greetings each year at Christmas. She is the last of the family. This was another tragedy brought on by the great depression.

Miscellaneous

Traffic Incidents

About a week after getting my first car, I was stopped for going too fast and was taken to the police station. I asked them to call Granvil Bates, the man I had bought the car from. He was the manager of Hoehn Chevrolet Company and a personal friend. The police knew him and after calling him, he told them my car had a defective speedometer and that it was his fault. He asked them to let me go, which they did.

One time while hurrying to keep an appointment, I came to a traffic light that had turned yellow and I sped up to get through before it turned red. It turned red before I was through it and a motorcycle policeman was on the corner and came after me. I stopped and his first words were, "What color was that light?" I replied, "Yellow when I went into it." He said, "What does yellow mean?" I said, "It means to stop if you can before it turns red." He said, "Yes, it means to stop, not hit the gas and go through a red." He gave me a ticket to appear in city court a week later.

Never having been in a court before, I had no idea what to do. The room was full and I noticed the officer across the room waiting to testify against me when called. There was a ten o'clock recess and I got up and walked over and sat down beside him. I got his attention and asked if he was the officer that stopped me for the red light at Vandeventer. He looked startled and sort of pulled away and said, "Yes." I told him that I was deaf and didn't know what to do and wouldn't know when my name was called and asked him if he would help me. He looked relieved and asked me how I was going to plead. I said, "Guilty, of course. I ran a red light." He got up and said he would be right back. He went up to talk to the clerk and after a short time, she pulled a file, no doubt mine, and went back to the judge's chambers.

When she returned to the officer, he was smiling and motioned for me to come up. He said that the judge had decided that the fine was fifteen dollars and court costs another ten. I paid it and we both left the room. Outside on the courthouse steps, I turned to thank him. With a broad smile, he said, "No. I thank you. If you hadn't come to me, we could have been there all day and again tomorrow and this is my day off." We shook hands and I told him he wouldn't catch me going through lights again. I often saw him on his bike in the area and sounded my horn. He would flash a broad smile and wave.

Outside the time I went halfway through a red light and asked the officer to help me in court, I have only received two other tickets. One was on South Kingshighway on a Sunday morning when four cars including mine were stopped for going 38 in a 30-mile zone. It was on the downgrade of a viaduct and all the cars naturally picked up speed. I received a ticket to appear in city court, but since I knew it was a speed trap, I gave it to a friend who knew his way around City Hall. The ticket eventually wound up in the hands of my Mom's cousin, Joe Weissenberg, head of titles department, who mailed the proceedings to me and sent a note that said, "Arthur, take care of these papers. The fellows here at City Hall have a habit of forgetting. Joe"

There was another ticket for speeding right after I got my first car. It was only a couple miles over the limit and I thought I would take it downtown to headquarters where another one of Mom's cousins was a captain in the police department. I didn't really know him so I introduced myself. He said, "Oh yes. You are Mamie's boy." After some family information was exchanged, I brought out the ticket and asked him what he thought I should do with it, hoping he would void it. He laughed and said, "Well, if I were you, I would take it downstairs and pay it." He added, "Tell your mom hello for me." His name was Oliver Kortjohn. I once read a piece in a police department chronicle before Ollie became a captain. His captain was telling him to go on a case where some woman was wearing swimsuits out of the Famous Barr store under her dress. Ollie said, "Yes, sir, Captain. I will start to unravel that tomorrow."

  I got off the night shift at McDonnell Douglas at one in the morning and liked to buy a morning newspaper. The only place to find one was downtown near City Hall. Once after buying a paper, I started home and stopped at a traffic light across from City Hall. It was cold and the motor was running and I stayed for several changes of the light while reading the paper. I was parked at the curb. A city police car stopped behind me with its red light on. Two policemen, a younger one and an older one, came up to my car and I got out. The older one asked what I was doing there. I showed him my badge and told him I often came down there to get a paper. The younger one had been shining a light around inside the car and then asked me for the key to the trunk. The older one put his hand on the trunk and said, "He's alright. Leave him alone."

  I have stated previously how working the night shift at McDonnell Douglas left me free to do work on the side. I had built a kitchen cabinet for a neighbor a few blocks from my home in Richmond Heights. My nephew, 16 year old Charlie Roller, was helping me. We had the cabinet in a trailer. It looked like rain and I was hurrying to get the cabinet inside. About two blocks from my neighbor's house, a police car came up beside me and motioned for me to pull over. He was a local policeman and I had seen him before. He said that the speed limit was 30 and that I was doing 35, too fast for the trailer. I explained that I was trying to beat the rain. Looking my license over, he asked if I was deaf. I said I was and that I worked full time at McDonnell Douglas. He said he had heard of me and my cabinet work around town. He added that I wasn't going fast enough for him to give me a ticket but that he wanted to warn me about going too fast with a trailer. It started to rain lightly, and he hurriedly gave my license back and, waving me on said, "Better get those cabinets out of the rain but take it easy." I thanked him and left. Charlie had stayed in the car and when I got back in, he exhaled sharply, and slapping his hand to his forehead said, "Oh boy. That was close."

Once in 1963 in Columbus, Ohio, the home of the state school for the deaf, at close to midnight, I was looking for a friend, Bill Hartwig's home and turned around in the middle of the street. A policeman saw the turn and stopped me and asked where I was going. I mentioned Hartwig's name. Bill was the head of audiology at the school. The policeman knew him and asked me to follow him to Bill's house.

One sunny afternoon in October I was going out to my parents' new home since they had sold the farm. Going down a long hill, I suddenly saw at the left of the highway an old car behind some bushes. I paid no attention to it until I saw a state patrolman up ahead flagging me down. The old car was a radar connection to the patrolman. Coming up to the patrolman, I got out and had my license handy. His first words were, "Do you know the state speed limit?" I said, "Yes, it's seventy miles an hour." He then asked me how fast I was coming down the hill. I said that I really didn't know. Since I was driving a new car and there was no traffic, I guess I just let it roll. He said that I was doing 83 miles an hour. Then looking my license over, he asked if I were deaf and I said I was. Then he asked, with a slight smile, where I was going. I told him that since my parents had sold their farm, I was making repeated trips to Cuba to help them straighten out the new place. He nodded slightly and still smiling asked if I knew who he was. I said that I did and added that I supposed he knew who I was. We both laughed and shook hands and I told him I was sorry to have to meet him this way. I knew from his badge that he was a son of one of my mother's good friends, and he knew that my mother had a deaf son. He handed my license back and I asked if he wasn't going to give me a ticket for speeding. He said, "No, but if I ever catch you doing 83 again, you can be sure I will." I said, "You won't!" He told me to greet my folks when I got to Cuba. Still smiling he told me to go on and to watch my speed."

  Before our marriage Laura and I had been invited to Thanksgiving dinner in Joplin, Missouri, at my Uncle Bill and Aunt Jessie's home. It was two hundred and fifty miles away and we were to be there at three thirty. Having made the trip many times before, I didn't anticipate any problems. There was no traffic and I wasn't paying much attention to the speed. Suddenly, I saw a state patrol car off to the right behind some trees. I looked at my speedometer which showed about 75 and slowed down. The speed limit was 70. With its red lights on, the patrol car came after me, so I pulled over and stopped. There were two very nice looking patrolmen of maybe 45. I got out and before they could say anything, I said, "I know I was going too fast." I gave him my license and he looked it over and noticed I was from St. Louis. He asked where we were going and I told him of the invitation for dinner at my uncle's and aunt's in Joplin. He said, "You were doing 78." I told him that I wouldn't argue that. He didn't say anything for a short time then turned his back and said something to his partner. I saw his partner smile and nod his head. He turned back to me and they were both smiling and he gave my license back. I asked if they weren't going to give me a ticket and the first one said, "No. It's Thanksgiving Day. Go on and enjoy your dinner with your uncle and aunt. But watch your speed." I thanked them and told them I would be more careful. They waved and returned to their car.

Once I was looking for a welding shop that could weld aluminum. I was told to go down Gravois and turn left at Jefferson Avenue. Nearing Jefferson, where Gravois was eight lanes, I had the green light and since no one was coming, I started to turn left. Halfway through, I saw a sign that said no left turn. I hit my brakes but was too far into the turn so I went on. A motorcycle policeman was on the corner and saw it all and came after me. He was a very nice African American and in giving him my license I told him of the directions I had been given and said I saw the sign too late to stop. Looking my license over, he said, "You're from Richmond Heights?" I said, "Yes. I am not familiar with this part of the city." Handing my license back, he said, "It's all right. The place you are looking for is three blocks ahead on the right." I thanked him and apologized for the bad turn. He patted me on the arm and said to go on and be careful. I could tell by the way he talked to me that he knew I was deaf.

Another time my wife and I were on our way to

work through Forest Park. The school was at the end of the park and as we neared the zoo, there was a slow moving truck ahead loaded with debris. I speeded up a bit to pass it and as soon as I got back into the lane, there was a city police car parked at the end of a curve. He turned his red lights on and I stopped. The policeman was a friendly middle-aged man and told me I was speeding. I told him I had just speeded up to pass the truck and that I didn't think I was going that fast. Looking in the car, he asked me who was with me and I said it was my wife and that we both worked at the Central Institute down the road, she as a teacher and I with the buildings. He asked if he could talk to her and I said, of course. He walked around and after talking with her for a while I saw him laugh and show his badge to my wife. He gave my license to her and started walking away. He waved to me and went back to his patrol car. My wife laughed and told me that he had said I was speeding and I passed the truck. There was no passing allowed at that point. He told her he should be giving me two tickets but would let me go if I would promise to take her out to dinner that night. He added, when showing his badge, that if I didn't, for her to call him. He smiled and waved to me as he went back to his car. We went out the next night. I saw him a few times afterwards and would wave to him.

  Stacy Gates, a lovely deaf girl of 16, whose parents weren't happy with the school's dormitory situation, lived with us for one year, her last year at the school. She was one of Laura's students. A few years after her graduation, she sent us an invitation to her wedding, which was to be near her home in Illinois. It was about a hundred and fifty miles away and on a Saturday. We had stopped in Mount Vernon for lunch and lost some time. Back on the road, we hoped to be able to reach the wedding in time. We had turned off the Interstate and the road was nearly new and there was no traffic. I suddenly looked in the rear view mirror and told Laura, "I hope those flashing blue lights are an ambulance." She looked back and said, "No way. That's a state cop." I pulled over when he got close and waited for him to come to the door. It was a very nice and polite African American of about 35. After looking my license and registration papers over, he said, "You were doing 68." I said, "But isn't the speed limit 65?" He said, "No. This is a state road and the limit is 55." Laura had the wedding invitation and directions in her lap and we were both dressed for a wedding and driving a new car. I handed them to him so that he could see the reason for a bit of speed. The wedding was in DuQuoin, Illinois, about another 20 miles and time was short. Turning to return to his car, he said, "I'll be right back." I told Laura that I wondered what the cost would be in Illinois, which is very strict. Returning, he handed me a paper and said to sign it. I asked, "Aren't you giving me a ticket?" He said, "No. This is a warning. Go on and watch your speed." I apologized and thanked him.

  Since none of these infractions were serious, I feel that except for the ones that asked if I were deaf, the rest assumed I was by the tone of my voice. These eleven traffic stops started in 1944 and continued off and on for forty years. I haven't been stopped again for any reason for twenty years or more. I was never stopped while driving our camper van throughout the United States and into Alaska and Canada, mainly because I always stayed within the speed limit.

  One afternoon I was driving down the main street in Steelville, Missouri, my home town, and was turning and driving back down a few times, looking over the changes I had noticed since my last time of paying attention to the town. I was doing what is frowned upon, "cruising," and was stopped by the lone city policeman on foot, the town marshal, James Decker. Before he could say anything, I asked him if he knew who I was. He didn't seem to for a moment, then I told him I was the brother of his new son-in-law. I had met him at the recent wedding and he didn't recognize me. He laughed and said, "I remember you now," and after a few words, he said, "Tell Howard and Kathy hi for me," and motioned me on.

Once while on a cruise ship in the Caribbean, we were eating dinner with a group, all strangers, at the midnight buffet and I was talking to Laura. After a while, I noticed a lady across from us looking at me intently. She looked a bit confused and finally spoke to me. She asked if I would mind if she asked me a question, and I said, "Of course not." She asked what country I came from and I told her the United States. Then she asked if I was born there and I said, "Yes, in the state of Missouri." She looked even more mystified and continued, asking if my parents were American. I was beginning to enjoy it and finally told her I was deaf. She became embarrassed and I told her there was no reason to feel that way since I was used to it. She was a cruise director and said she had contacts with many foreigners but couldn't figure out where I was from. We both laughed. On our first night on the ship on the second cruise, we were told at dinner that we and our table mates, all teachers except me and a nurse, were invited to have dinner with the Captain the next night. I had no difficulty in talking to him since he talked slowly. He was a Norwegian. I asked him how high the ship was and he said five stories. I asked what kept it from turning over and he said the bottom was flat which kept it on an even keel.

All the above incidents had given me confidence in my ability to understand strangers and are not intended to show that I had been able to "beat" traffic tickets but rather led me to be more careful and to respect the laws and those who uphold them.

Although this deals with a traffic mishap, no police were involved. It was about mid-February and it was sleeting. Streets were slick. I was driving west on Clayton Road and was nearing the intersection of Big Bend Boulevard. When the light turned yellow, the car ahead skidded to a stop and I ran into it. There was little damage to either car and the driver of the other car said he was a doctor and for me to send my agent to his office at the hospital and he would sign off any claim. He did. About a week later I had a letter from my insurance company, Michigan Mutual, telling me my insurance was cancelled. This had been my first accident. Once you have been cancelled, it is impossible to find a carrier.

Frank Petelik, an insurance broker I had just met through a mutual friend, Elmer Meyer, put me in a high risk pool but would not let me pay for it. I had written a long letter to the president of Michigan Mutual and shortly afterwards received a very nice letter from him. He explained that the company advertised that they were a company with a conscience, and said that it wasn't just a slogan, but they practiced it, and reinstated my insurance with full coverage and apologized. Frank had written to the Travelers Insurance Company, the company covering me in high risk and told them of the developments. He said he had a great deal of respect for Michigan Mutual and added that it appeared that an over eager underwriter had classified me as a bad risk which he said was certainly not the case. Later on, when the rates increased, I transferred my coverage to Frank's company. That all happened 45 years ago and Frank and his wife Carolyn, Elmer and his wife Ruth, and Laura and I have become good friends.

Hospital Incidents

Bill Cowan received the Medal for Citizenship, the highest award, when we graduated from high school. I had received the medal for Scholarship, the second highest. After returning from military duty, he and his future brother-in-law, Walter Earls, opened a service station in St. James, Missouri. This led to various other endeavors and finally he became the administrator of the Phelps County Memorial Hospital in Rolla, Missouri. While there, he built it into one of the finest medical centers in the state. Eventually he became administrator of the Missouri Baptist Hospital in St. Louis County, and went on to become the Vice President of the hospital.

An amusing incident happened while I was a patient in that hospital for what is commonly called "roto rooter" surgery. An infection set in and my stay developed into almost two weeks. Bill would stop by my private room each morning before going to his office. Now, there are devices available which enable the deaf to use the telephone and to watch television programming with captions. Before I entered the hospital, my wife had called them and they assured us that the devices were available to patients who requested them. We asked again the day I entered as a patient and were told they would be brought up and installed right away. Almost the first week went by and nothing happened. One afternoon a nurse was in the room and I asked her if she would please call down to administration and ask Mr. Cowan to come see me. She said, "Oh, I can't do that. Mr. Cowan is the Vice President of the hospital." I said, "I know that and he is also a personal friend of mine. Now, will you please call him?" She hurriedly said, "Yes, sir, I will." I suppose that being his friend rated me a "sir." He came running in the room within three minutes and asked, "What's the trouble, Art?" I told him the story and he said, "And they aren't here yet?" When I said no, he grabbed the phone by my bed. I have no idea what he said, but the expression on his face said it all and could not be printed. I told him I didn't want to take advantage of our friendship. He said, "Art, what are friends for?" The devices were there in ten minutes. I am sorry to say that Bill died a little over a year after our last high school reunion. It was a shock to everyone. Bill had been the class president all through school and he had been the leader at every reunion.

An incident came up at the Deaconess Hospital during my second hernia surgery. In making preparation, the anesthetist said that she heard something unusual in my heart beat and ordered a twenty-four hour monitor on my heart before an operation could be done. My regular doctor had examined me thoroughly only a month before and recommended that I have the operation. He said my heart was fine. After the monitoring was complete, the heart specialist came into my room on succeeding days and merely said that everything was fine both times and left the room. Shortly after arriving home following the surgery, a bill came from the heart specialist, listing two consultations totaling seventy dollars. I turned the bill over and wrote on the back referring him to Websters' Dictionary, where he would see that the word *consultation* means a thing talked about by two people and added that his short visits did not fit into that category and that I did not feel that I should pay seventy dollars towards his bill. I added that I felt he could recoup that from the seven hundred dollars for the monitor and added further that I hoped that this would be the end of the issue. It was. The surgeon performing this operation was the same doctor who had performed the first one, Dr. Battacharia. This operation had resulted in some infection and while being discharged, he handed me a prescription for some antibiotics. I asked him how many pills there were and he said twenty. I asked how much they would cost and he said a hundred dollars. I exclaimed, "What the hell? I had no infection when I came in here and your operation brought this on and now you want me to pay a hundred dollars for some pills that you hope will do some good." He said, "Ok. Ok. Tell your wife to come to my office this evening and I will give them to her." I said, "This makes it worse. If you have them to give away, why are you asking me to pay a hundred dollars for them?" A bit sheepishly he said he was sorry and to have my wife come before six.

      Although it is contrary to Central Institute policy, Dr. Calvert insisted that I take a two-month leave after each surgery, at full pay. When I asked him about it, he said I was a valuable employee and he didn't want anything to happen from the surgeries. The first surgery was work related.

My Family

Charles Wayne McCann

Wayne was born in 1913 in St. Louis. He had spent his early years on the home farm except for the three years with the family in Detroit. He had built up an egg business while still in high school. He was in his last year at St. James High School in St. James, Missouri, and graduated in three years by carrying six subjects each year. He played saxophone in the school band and was one of the school bus drivers, as well as holding the record for the mile for several years. After school on Fridays he would buy eggs from local farmers and along with our own, he had a full load. Every Saturday he would leave the farm at four in the morning and drive the hundred miles into St. Louis to, as he called it in the beginning, "peddle the eggs." After graduating in 1935 he made it a full time business.

He was drafted into the Army in 1941 and was sent to Camp Polk, Louisiana, and was assigned to the 23rd Armored Engineers. Shortly after that he was sent to Officers Candidate School in Virginia. He told me later that his entire platoon from Camp Polk except him was sent to California and then overseas, and that they had all been killed. As a lieutenant, he was sent to England four days into his marriage to Eleanor Bax in 1943. He was stationed just outside of London for his entire stay there and was made a Captain. He sent me a check from London and asked me to buy two silver captain's bars for his wife and sister. I did. He served in the Provost Marshal's Office and had to sign death warrants, which were executed in Ft. Leavenworth, Kansas. He left the Army in 1947.

He and Eleanor had four daughters, Kathy, Charlene, Patricia and Peggy. On his return home in 1947, he had a few different jobs. He and Eleanor opened a grocery store in South St. Louis for a while and then he entered real estate. He became the sales manager for one of the largest real estate and development companies in St. Louis County, Fischer and Frichtel, for ten years until he died of cancer in 1967 at the age of 52. He was on his way to fulfilling his dream of owning a real estate corporation and owned many rental units at his death. He was buried with full military honors.

My brother, Wayne, a 1st Lieutenant in theArmy, later promoted to Captain.

Earl Clark McCann

Earl was born in 1915 in St. Louis. His early years were spent on the home farm near Steelville, Missouri, except for three years with the family in Detroit, Michigan. He moved to St. Louis and went to work for the Chevrolet Motor Company in the parts department as soon as he graduated from St. James High School in 1934. He was drafted into the Army in the spring of 1942 and was sent to North Africa. He was ordered to cut the wires on top of a thirty-foot pole, carrying thirty-three thousand volts, in a rainstorm at night. He became tangled in the cut wires and fell to the ground badly injured. He was missing for three months and finally turned up at the Fitzsimmon Hospital in Denver. He was a Technical Sergeant in the Army Air Corps. After returning home, he worked at odd jobs before forming an automobile agency with Leonard. He married Dorene Neet in 1945 and they had two daughters, Connie and Mary. After a few years in the automobile agency, he left to operate his own long distance refrigerated trucking business. After fifteen years, he joined the transportation department at McDonnell Douglas Aircraft Corporation. He retired at seventy and died of fibrosis of the lungs at the age of 85.

He had been having lung problems for several months, which necessitated a trip to the hospital for treatment, and after only a short time at home, had to go back to the hospital. On one of the trips home, Laura and I took him and his wife and daughter Connie to his favorite restaurant in St. Peters, Missouri, where they lived. Arriving back at home, he and I sat away from the rest and talked for a couple of hours. Among other things, he told me he could never have lived through life as I had without hearing and said he had always admired me for that. On his last trip to the hospital, the doctor told him they couldn't do any more for him. The next day he told the doctor to remove all life support except the oxygen and let him go home to die. When the support had been removed, he wasn't able to go home and died two days later. The St. Luke's hospital had moved him into a large private room so the family could all be there. A few hours before he died, he was still lucid and I went to the side of the bed, and took his hand and told him I was going to do something I had never done before. He very weakly asked, "What?" I said, "I am going to kiss my brother." He turned his cheek and I kissed him and he said, "Thanks. I love you." I said I loved him, too. He died shortly after. He was buried with full military honors.

My brother, Earl, as a Technical Sergeant in the Army Air Corps.

My brother, Leonard, as a Seaman First Class in the U.S. Navy.

Leonard Henry McCann

Leonard was born in 1917 near Cuba, Missouri. Like his brothers before him, he spent his early years on the home farm except for the three years with the family in Detroit. He graduated from St. James High School in 1936. He spent a month and a half in Rolla, Missouri, training to become a teacher and taught the 1936-37 school year at Benton Creek School. He worked for a while with the Inter County Electric Company, installing power lines to farm homes. He married Marie Wilson in 1940 and they had one daughter, Lois. During World War II he was a machinist with the Alco Valve Company and later joined the Navy and served most of his time at Great Lakes in Illinois. He was a Seaman First Class. After the war he was in the automobile business with Earl and later became the sales manager for the Vincel Pontiac Company, the largest in the state, for fifteen years until the company was sold to Mr. Vincel's nephew. He then became the sales manager for the Anheuser Ford Company. He earned a diamond ring from the Ford Motor Company for being the best sales manager two years in a row. He was there until he retired. I bought two great cars from him over the years – a silver blue 1959 Chevrolet Impala sport coupe and a 1969 Ford LTD Country Squire station wagon. They were both nearly new and had been repossessed. These were both favorites of mine that I kept for many years. He died of cancer at the age of 80. His wife had died nine years before in 1989.

Frieda Marie McCann

Frieda was born in 1925 near Steelville, Missouri, and was a welcome addition to a family of four boys. Many of the neighbors brought gifts for her, usually a beautiful handmade dress or a toy. When she was two years old, the leg of the heating stove broke, spilling a pot of hot water into her playpen. The accident brought several of the neighbors in to see her and she was always happy to see them. She suffered burns, which left many scars on her lower body. She was four years old when she died of pneumonia in 1929 shortly after our arrival in Detroit.

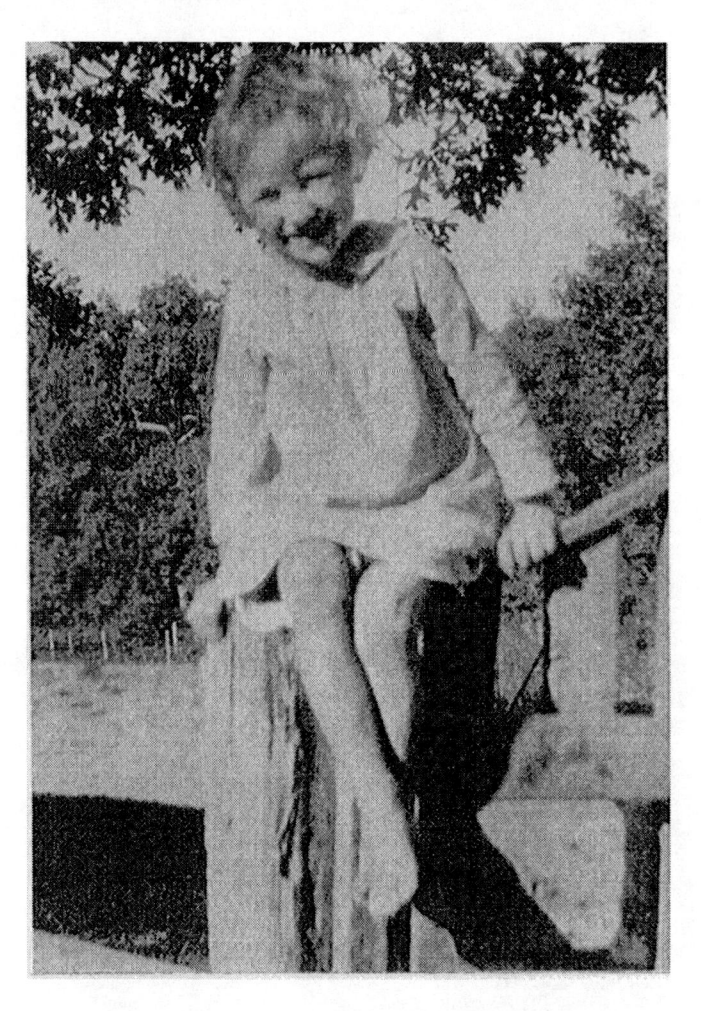

My sister, Frieda, taken at the farm
before moving to Detroit.

My brother Raymond, as a Petty Officer
Third Class in the U.S. Navy

Raymond William McCann

Raymond was born near Steelville, Missouri, in 1927. As a very young child, he spent three years with the family in Detroit. He graduated from Steelville High School in 1945 and enlisted in the Navy. After Boot Camp at Great Lakes, he was assigned to the Atlantic Reserve Fleet, and served on the USS Snowden and the USS Frost. He attained the rank of Petty Officer Third Class, and received the American Theater and World War II Victory Medals. After release from active duty in 1946, he affiliated with the naval Reserve, and after graduating from college, he was commissioned as a Lieutenant (junior grade) and served in the Naval Intelligence program until retiring in 1971 with the rank of Senior Lieutenant.

He graduated from Washington University in St. Louis in 1955 with a B.S. Degree in Business Administration. Before finishing college, he had worked for Western Electric Company, McCann's Market, and Cotton Belt Railroad. After graduating, he worked for Alton Box Board Company as a Production Planner, for Rawlings Manufacturing Company as a Personnel Assistant, and for Katz Drug Company as a District Personnel Manager. Then in 1961, he went to work for the Missouri Division of Employment Security in the St. Louis area office as a Personnel Research Analyst, and then served as Administrative Assistant to the Area Manager. He was then promoted and transferred to the Central Office in Jefferson City, where he served as the Division Personnel Officer from 1965 until he retired in 1993.

He married Louise Stibick in 1948 and they had two children, Phyllis and David. Louise passed away in 1980. He then married Katie Schnieders, a widow with five children, in 1981.

Wilma Joan McCann Roller

Wilma was born in 1933 near Steelville, Missouri. She graduated from Steelville High School in 1952. For a while, she worked as a maid in a private home in Ladue, Missouri. After that she worked at various jobs until soldier James "Jim" Roller came home from Germany and they were married in 1953. They first lived in Leavenworth, Kansas, where Jim was stationed in the Army and worked as a military guard in the military prison and Wilma worked for the Hallmark Card Company. Jim was discharged in 1954 and they moved to St. Louis where he worked for a grain company and then to Illinois where he worked for Granite City Steel Company. Here they had four children, Jimmy, Debbie, Charlie and John. They bought a lot and I helped them finish a shell house in Granite City in 1957. During this time, my nephews Jimmy and Charlie spent many Saturdays working with me on my house in Richmond Heights and we became and remain very close. My brother-in-law Jim worked with me on many projects at McCann and Company in his off hours, and later as a machine operator at my Arcy Manufacturing Company plant. Wilma worked for the tax assessor's office for two years and then for the Missouri State Employment Service. When Jim decided to make the Air Force a career, he was sent on a year's tour to Thailand and the family stayed in Granite City. On Jim's return, they moved to Cannon Air Force Base at Clovis, New Mexico. After three years, Jim volunteered for a tour at Elmendorf Air Force Base in Anchorage, Alaska, which lasted fifteen years. While in Anchorage, Wilma worked in different positions in the school district offices and finally became the head of Accounts Payable. Jim retired from the Air Force in 1984 as a Senior Master Sergeant and began working for Civil Service. They both retired in 1991 and returned to Clovis, New Mexico, where they are enjoying their retirement. They spend a lot of time traveling in their large motorhome and visiting with their kids, grandkids, and great grandkids. Wilma joined Mary Kay Cosmetics and they both do product demonstrations at grocery stores in town. They do a lot of canning, freezing and dehydrating of foods in summer. She enjoys making quilts, sewing, and working on her embroidery machine.

My sister, Wilma, and her husband, Jim Roller, on their wedding day in 1953.

Howard Kampman McCann

Howard was born in 1936 near Steelville, Missouri. He stayed on the farm after graduating from Steelville High School in 1955 and operated the home farm along with several other farms in the area. He married Kathleen Decker in 1964 and they had two children, Amy and Robert. For thirty-five years, he owned a successful livestock brokerage business in Steelville. In November of 2000 he was supervising the loading of 600 cattle when one bolted and rammed him in the midsection, knocking him off his feet. He went on for a time, not realizing the extent of his injuries. Subsequent surgery revealed extensive internal injuries and following surgery, he went into a coma for a month and died at the age of 64. I had seen him briefly in the hospital the night before the surgery. He appeared to be in good spirits. I told him he would be out of there in a few days. He shook his head and holding up two fingers, said, "No. It will be about two weeks."

One Sunday when he was on the home farm, some fellows from St. Louis came out to fish in the Meramec River. They had a pickup truck with a boat behind it and had backed too far into the river. It was up to and over the axles. They came up and asked Howard if he would come down and pull it out with his tractor. He decided his small one would do, but upon trying, all it would do is spin the tractor wheels in the loose gravel. He had to go back to the house and get his big Farmall tractor. This time it came out easily and when the truck was on the road, one of the fellows said, "Oh boy, thanks a lot." Howard said, "Thanks, hell, you owe me fifty dollars." The fellow said he didn't have any money, so Howard told him to leave his spare wheel and come back next week and pay it.

My youngest brother, Howard, a livestock broker in Steelville, Missouri for 35 years.

The McCann family together for our father's 80th birthday in 1966 — the last family picture before Wayne's death six months later. Standing: Howard, Leonard, Earl, Wilma, Raymond, Wayne, Arthur
Seated: Charles and Mamie.

The author's mother and her brother, Bill Kampman, in 1966.

Harry and Inez Riefenstahl
the author's uncle and aunt.

The McCann Family

Grandpa and Grandma McCann (*seated in center*)
on their 50th wedding anniversary in 1933
at their home in Owensville, Missouri.
Standing: Uncle Jim, Uncle Tom, Dad, Aunt Ella,
Aunt Alice; *Seated:* Uncle Henry, Uncle Walter,
Aunt Maude, Aunt Ruth.

Grandma and Grandpa Gus Riefenstahl *(seated)* on their 60th wedding anniversary in 1962 at Charles and Mamie McCann's farm.
Standing: Aunt Annie, Aunt Emma, Grandpa Gus' sister, Grandma's sister-in-law (Albert Jaide's wife), Aunt Bertha, Aunt Kate.